Catalysing Development? A Debate on Aid

T0355673

***Development and Change* Book** Series

As a journal, *Development and Change* distinguishes itself by its multi-disciplinary approach and its breadth of coverage, publishing articles on a wide spectrum of development issues. Accommodating a deeper analysis and a more concentrated focus, it also publishes regular special issues on selected themes. *Development and Change* and Blackwell Publishing collaborate to produce these theme issues as a series of books, with the aim of bringing these pertinent resources to a wider audience.

Titles in the series include:

Catalysing Development? A Debate on Aid
Jan Pronk et al.

State Failure, Collapse and Reconstruction
Edited by Jennifer Milliken

Forests: Nature, People, Power
Edited by Martin Doornbos, Ashwani Saith and Ben White

Gendered Poverty and Well-being
Edited by Shahra Razavi

Globalization and Identity
Edited by Bergit Meyer and Peter Geschiere

Social Futures, Global Visions
Edited by Cynthia Hewitt de Alcantara

Catalysing Development?

A Debate on Aid

Jan P. Pronk et al.

Blackwell
Publishing

First published in *Development and Change* 32.4, 33.2, 33.3, 34.3 and 35.2

BLACKWELL PUBLISHING
350 Main Street, Malden, MA 02148-5020, USA
108 Cowley Road, Oxford OX4 1JF, UK
550 Swanston Street, Carlton, Victoria 3053, Australia

First published 2004 by Blackwell Publishing Ltd

Library of Congress Cataloguing-in-Publication Data has been applied for

ISBN 1-4051-2119-X
A catalogue record for this title is available from the British Library.

Set by Jane Foster-Jones

For further information on
Blackwell Publishing, visit our website:
http://www.blackwellpublishing.com

Contents

Notes on Contributors

Morag Bell is Professor of Cultural Geography at Loughborough University. She has research interests in cultural geographies of British imperialism and its legacies: her recent work draws on postcolonial critiques to examine the role of international philanthropy in the exercise of western cultural power. She has published widely on these themes.

James K. Boyce teaches economics at the University of Massachusetts, Amherst. He is the author of *Investing in Peace: Aid and Conditionality after Civil Wars* (Oxford University Press, 2002), *The Political Economy of the Environment* (Edward Elgar, 2002) and editor of *Economic Policy for Building Peace: The Lessons of El Salvador* (Lynne Rienner, 1996).

At the time of writing his contribution to this volume, **John Degnbol-Martinussen** was Professor of Development Economics and Political Science, Dean of the Graduate School of International Development Studies, Roskilde University, and Chairman of the Danish Council for Development Co-operation. Sadly, Dr Degnbol-Martinussen passed away in 2002.

A. Geske Dijkstra is Associate Professor in Economics in the Faculty of Social Sciences of Erasmus University, The Netherlands. Her research interests focus on the effectiveness of aid and debt relief, including both macroeconomic and political economy effects of the aid system, and on the impact of economic liberalization and reforms. Her most recent books are *Programme Aid and Development: Beyond Conditionality* (Routledge, 2003, co-authored with Howard White) and *Towards Sustainable Development in Central America and the Caribbean* (Palgrave, 2001, with Anders Danielson).

Gus Edgren is a Swedish development economist and development aid administrator, who has worked with the Swedish Government, the trade union movement, and various United Nations organizations. He has been a part of the ILO's World Employment Programme, has headed the Asian Employment Programme (ARTEP), served as State Secretary for Development Co-operation in the Swedish Government, Assistant Administrator of UNDP, Assistant Director-General of Sida, and as Sweden's Ambassador to Vietnam. He has written on wage and employment policy, labour standards and foreign trade, aid and development and on the political economy of development co-operation.

Louis Emmerij was Rector of the Institute of Social Studies, The Hague, President of the OECD Development Centre in Paris, and Special Advisor to the President, Inter-American Development Bank, Washington. Since 1999 he has been Co-Director of the United Nations Intellectual History Project and Senior Research Fellow at the Graduate Center, City University of New York.

Joseph Hanlon is a Senior Lecturer in the Development Policy and Practice group of the Open University, Milton Keynes, UK. He is the author of five books on Mozambique including *Mozambique: Who Calls the Shots* (James Currey, 1991), *Peace Without Profit: How the IMF Blocks Rebuilding in Mozambique* (James Currey, 1996), and *Mozambique and the Great Flood of 2000* with Frances Christie (James Currey, 2001). He is also the editor of the *Mozambique Political Process Bulletin*.

Wil Hout is Associate Professor of World Development at the Institute of Social Studies, The Hague, The Netherlands. He has written many journal articles on issues of international political economy; he is the author of *Capitalism and the Third World* (Edward Elgar, 1993), co-editor of *Regionalism across the North–South Divide* (with Jean Grugel; Routledge, 1999) and co-editor of three Dutch-language volumes on issues of international relations and political science.

Santosh Mehrotra is currently Senior Economic Adviser, The Human Development Report at the UNDP, New York; from October 2004, he will be Lead Economist for Asia, based in the UNDP Regional Centre, Bangkok. He previously led Unicef's research programme on economic and social policy for developing countries at the Innocenti Research Centre, Florence, Italy. His published works include: *India and the Soviet Union: Trade and Technology Transfer* (Cambridge University Press, 1990); and *Development with a Human Face: Experiences in Social Achievement and Economic Growth* (Oxford University Press, 1997). Three co-authored books are forthcoming: *Financing Elementary Education: Uncaging the Tiger Economy in India* and *Public Spending for the Poor: Getting the Fundamentals Right in Macroeconomic and Social Policy* (both from Oxford University Press); and *Informal Work in the Value Chain: Protecting Workers Locally against Capital Investing Globally*.

James Petras is Professor Emeritus of Sociology, Binghamton University, New York and Adjunct Professor, St. Mary's University, Halifax, Canada. He is author and co-author of numerous studies on Latin America and world development, including *Unmasking Globalization* (Zed Books, 2001) and *Brasil de Cardoso: Expropriação de un pais* (Petrópolis: VOZES, 2001).

Jan P. Pronk has served in several governments of the Netherlands as Minister of Development Co-operation (1973–77 and 1989–98) and as Minister for Environment (1998–2002). Presently he holds a Chair in the Theory and Practice of International Development at the Institute of Social

Studies, The Hague, The Netherlands. In June 2004, the Secretary-General of the UN, Kofi Annan, appointed Jan Pronk as his Special Representative for Sudan.

Ajit Singh is currently Professor of Economics at the University of Cambridge, UK, and Senior Fellow at Queens' College. He has been a senior economic advisor to the governments of Mexico and Tanzania and a consultant to various UN development organizations. His most recent publications include a co-edited volume with C. Howes, *Competitiveness Matters: Industry and Economic Performance in the US* (University of Michigan Press, 2000) and the policy monographs, *The Global Labour Standards Controversy: Critical Issues for Developing Countries* (South Centre, 2000, co-authored with A. Zammit), and *Global Economic Trends and Social Development* (United Nations Research Institute for Social Development, Geneva, 2000).

David Slater is Professor of Social and Political Geography at Loughborough University, UK. He is author of *Territory and State Power in Latin America* (Macmillan, 1989), co-editor of *The American Century* (Blackwell, 1999) and an Editor of *Political Geography*. His research focuses on geopolitics, development and social movements.

Rehman Sobhan is currently Chairman, Centre for Policy Dialogue, Dhaka, Bangladesh, and Executive Director of the South Asia Centre for Policy Studies. He was Chairman of the Board of Directors of Grameen Bank for six years. He has published extensively on issues of aid policy, economic reforms, poverty eradication, governance and regional economic co-operation. His recent publications include *Bangladesh: Problems of Governance, Agrarian Reform and Social Transformation*; *Aid Dependence and Donor Policy: The Case of Tanzania, Transforming Eastern South Asia*; and *Rediscovering the Southern Silk Route*. He is currently working on the theme of 'Correcting Structural Injustice: Refocusing the Agenda for Poverty Eradication'.

Henry Veltmeyer is Professor of International Development, St Mary's University, Halifax, Canada, and Adjunct Professor, Unidad Posgraduado, Ciencia Politica, Universidad Autónoma de Zacatecas, México. He is co-author of, amongst others, *Dynamics of Social Change in Latin America* (Macmillan, 2000) and *Community Economic Development* (Kumarian Press, 2001).

Preface from the Editors of
Development and Change

International development assistance — 'aid' — has long occupied a prominent place in debates on development. However, perceptions of its role and significance have changed dramatically over the years. As thoughts and theories about development itself have shifted, so too the role assigned to aid. Whereas for several decades after the end of World War II, the need to provide aid to low income countries in order to stimulate and promote their economic and social development was widely accepted, in recent years both the provision of aid itself, and the question of its role in development, have come under closer scrutiny and have become matters of controversy. The geopolitics of aid, the increasing prominence of aid conditionality, and the reality of aid programmes on the ground, all play a part in this discussion.

In an article entitled 'Aid as a Catalyst', published in the September 2001 issue of *Development and Change*, Jan Pronk argued that:

> Aid is not the prime mover of development; it has sometimes even been an impediment, but this need not be the case. To use aid as a reward for good development governance may indeed be justified under certain conditions, but often such conditions can only be met with some outside help. Aid should, therefore, be used primarily as a catalyst, sometimes to help generate other resources or gain access to them, sometimes to help create domestic capacity or manage conflicts resulting from various forms of unsustainable development. At this juncture, what is required is a special focus in aid policy on social harmony, political stability and peace, as preconditions for economic growth and development — not the other way around. (Pronk, 2001: 627–8)

As Editors of *Development and Change*, we thought that this article, contributed by a prominent exponent who served for thirteen years as the Netherlands' Minister of Development Co-operation in various cabinets between 1974 and 1998, would be a good point of departure for a revisit to several key issues in the aid debate. We therefore approached a number of commentators, representing different analytical perspectives, with an invitation to reflect upon and respond to Jan Pronk's article. The reaction was invariably one of keen interest. In the meantime, we also received two independent contributions on the topic, whose authors were also invited to participate in the debate. Finally, Jan Pronk was given the opportunity to respond to the commentators in a rejoinder.

The resulting essays reflect a wide spectrum of theoretical and policy perspectives; in our view, they make an important contribution to a debate which has taken on added salience in the light of developments since

September 2001. Evidently, there is a wide range of opinions and interpretations as to the efficacy of development aid, highlighting the complexity
of the issues. While most agree that aid in its present form is not achieving
the desired results, this leads to different conclusions and recommendations,
from refining the instruments, through reforming the institutions and re-
negotiating the relationships, to revisiting the whole rationale for development aid.

Demonstrating as they do the relevance and sensitivity of the topic, we felt
that the various contributions to this debate — previously scattered across
several issues of the journal — deserved to be brought together into a single
volume. As one of the contributors to this volume notes, 'development aid is
the repository of accumulated ideas and priorities of development theory of
the last sixty years' (Emmerij, p. 36). We hope that this book will prove a
valuable addition to this repository and the debate on this important topic.

The Editors, *Development and Change*

REFERENCE

Jan P. Pronk (2001) 'Aid as a Catalyst', *Development and Change* 32(4): 611–29.

Chapter 1

Aid as a Catalyst

Jan P. Pronk

INTRODUCTION

More than fifty years ago, in 1949, President Truman launched his Point Four Programme. This made it 'the policy of the United States to aid the efforts of economically underdeveloped areas to develop their resources and improve their living conditions'. The launching of the programme is often considered the beginning of international development assistance. After World War II several other countries had already introduced funds to finance development and welfare programmes in their colonies. Immediately after its establishment in 1946, the United Nations too had placed development assistance on its agenda, but funds were limited and the recipient countries were not yet independent. In the early years, priority was given to financing the reconstruction of countries after the war, rather than to investment programmes in developing countries. Reconstruction was also the main aim of the Marshall Plan and the World Bank, both of which were launched in the same period.

After 1949, international technical assistance grew and funds for foreign aid increased. Co-operation between donor countries and aid agencies began to take shape. An aid doctrine developed, reflected in official documents and frequently discussed in the literature. Both economic and political aspects of international assistance were discussed, along with motives, aims and means. As early as August 1945, Jan Tinbergen had written an article in *Economisch-Statistische Berichten* pleading for worldwide economic co-operation to assist countries with a low standard of living (Tinbergen, 1945). In the Netherlands, Willem Brand and Egbert de Vries followed his lead, while in the United States Walt Rostow, Max Millikan and Edward Mason were amongst the first to take up the topic of aid, not only as researchers, but also as policy advisors. In the 1950s and 1960s,

---

This is a revised version of a paper presented as the Tinbergen Lecture, at the Annual Meeting of the Vereniging voor Staathuishoudkunde (Amsterdam, 15 October 1999). The author wishes to express his appreciation to two anonymous readers for their helpful comments.

authors such as P. T. Bauer and Milton Friedman argued against aid, because in their view it could not be effective: while the original objective of aid had been to help countries to develop their own resources, the critics argued that aid would only substitute domestic resources. The debate which followed has resulted in a rich literature on what became known as 'the economics of aid', discussing not only motives and objectives, but also effectiveness and impact.

Aid itself has of course changed during this half century. The technical assistance of the early years was followed by community development support in the 1950s, aid to fill trade and investment gaps in the 1960s, aid to provide for basic human needs in the 1970s, assistance to structural adjustment and debt relief in the 1980s, humanitarian assistance in combination with support for rehabilitation of countries after the civil wars of the 1990s and, at the turn of the century, aid for human development, and aid to prevent violent conflicts and to foster democratic governance. To a certain extent these shifts were in answer to altering international relations. Decolonization, the Cold War, the wars in Vietnam, the Middle East and Southern Africa (three areas where the North–South conflict and the East–West conflict coincided), the oil crisis and the world economic recession of the 1970s and 1980s, the end of the Cold War, new internal conflicts, and last but not least, economic and cultural globalization — all these have challenged the motives, aims and character of international development aid.

Changes in aid policy were not only the result of changing circumstances, however. Foreign assistance in the framework of international co-operation was in itself a new phenomenon. The economic and welfare programmes of the colonial period were not a good basis for a development assistance policy aiming at the self-reliance of young nations. Different lessons had to be learned. Solving specific development problems could give rise to new bottlenecks (such as access to markets in order to sustain production increases that had resulted from technical and financial assistance); and these bottlenecks, once recognized, called in turn for new and different approaches. Rendering development assistance was often a matter of learning-by-doing, on the basis of trial and error. In a few cases it involved the breakthrough of a new vision of the concept and process of development itself.

Originally development was seen as a more or less linear process. It was understood that this process would not occur by itself, which led to such theories as the 'big push' (Rosenstein-Rodan), the different stages in economic growth (Rostow), the inherently dualistic structure of a developing economy (Arthur Lewis), and the centre–periphery structure of the world economy within which a developing nation had to find its place (Prebisch). There were many different and often conflicting views concerning the importance of domestic versus external factors in national development. Different theories emerged concerning the relationship between economic growth and the distribution of assets and income, reflecting the different weights being attached to economic and social factors. Even greater divergences arose between theories concerning the relationship between economic and cultural factors.

Thus, development assistance was a process of learning-by-doing, and one which was played out against the background of major changes in international relations. The divergence of views about the process of development itself made the situation even more difficult. Add to this a fundamental lack of knowledge amongst aid agencies about the developing societies concerned, and one should perhaps be surprised to read that aid has achieved any successes at all. And yet this is the message of a recent World Bank report (1998) — that aid has at times been 'a spectacular success'. The report does issue one important warning, however: aid only works in a good policy environment; it does not work when policies are wrong. If this is true, the success of aid is no less than a miracle, which would surely justify augmenting the current aid effort substantially, and continuing to follow the current policy direction. But is this a legitimate conclusion? Let us first look at this 'miracle', and then examine the recipe for its continuation.

A MIRACLE?

That aid could have been a spectacular success despite the four potential pitfalls mentioned above — lack of knowledge about the countries, incomplete understanding of the process, inadequate experience with the instrument, and an ever-changing setting — is quite a miracle, given the different aims pursued by different donors in different periods. There has never been a simple consensus that the sole objective of aid was to sustain the economic development of recipient countries. From the start, aid programmes have been based on three different categories of considerations: charitable, economic and political. Charitable objectives were described in terms of action against hunger, misery and despair. Economic objectives were defined in terms of sustaining the efforts of the populations of the economically underdeveloped countries to develop their resources and to create conditions for self-sustained economic growth. Political objectives were seen in terms of political stability, reducing the potential for conflicts, supporting peace, the promotion of democracy, the preservation of political independence of former colonies and the maintenance of a sphere of influence for Western donor countries.

Not only were there multiple objectives, however: there were also many and varied political motives, all of which played a role in decisions concerning the level of aid, the allocation to countries, the distribution amongst economic and social sectors, the channelling through various public and private agencies (commercial as well as non-governmental) and the choice of partners (governments, the military, international organizations, grassroots movements and others). Moreover, there were many different categories of aid (grants and loans; financial and technical assistance; project and programme aid; debt creating and debt reducing transfers). Even if it were possible to add these up and relate the total to one overall indicator of progress in a recipient country — such as economic growth — the question remains whether this would have any meaning. Could the resulting ratio be considered an indicator of the effectiveness of aid? Effectiveness of what aid? Measured against which objective? Nor would it make much sense to compare such ratios with each other, either for one country in different periods, or between countries in the same period. The impact of aid would always be time and country-specific, dependent on history, stage of development and international relations.

Despite the differences and possible incompatibilities between their objectives and motives, the overriding view of donors, at least initially, was that aid could help in meeting them all. In 1957 this was characterized in a position paper of the United States House Committee on Foreign Affairs, which justified assistance as follows: 'The most important reason is that nations are determined to develop. Only by participation in that process will we have an opportunity to direct their development along lines that serve our interests' (quoted in Ohlin, 1966: 25). This position illustrates three donor motives: to be present in the development process; to steer the development process; to subordinate the development process to the donor's objectives — or at least, to avoid a clash between donor's and recipient's objectives.

There is, however, a difference between believing, on the one hand, that aid in one form or another can help meet different objectives and motives; and, on the other, that there is a direct causal relation between aid and the specific objective of economic growth, whatever the motive of the donor and whatever the background of the recipient. Whilst it might be desirable to be able to measure the effectiveness of aid with a yardstick reflecting a one-to-one relationship between aid and economic growth — or any other overall indicator of development, such as an increase in investment or a decrease in poverty — the methodological difficulties of such a statistical analysis are well known. To measure the effectiveness of aid requires an analysis of the difference between the actual (macro-) economic performance, including aid, and the hypothetical performance in its absence. This is a purely theoretical exercise. Moreover, the outcome of such an analysis does not provide insight into the reasons behind change, or explain why the situation differs before or after aid. Such an analysis cannot attribute changes to aid per se, but can only show that aid has been accompanied by economic growth, a decrease in poverty, or whatever.

Moreover, both the variables involved here — aid and development — are notoriously difficult to define. For instance, the many different forms of aid (such as project and programme aid, commodity aid and import support, debt relief and technical assistance) all have different effects and different time lags. The real value of aid when comparing grants and loans differs and changes over time. There are different ways to define net and gross aid. Should aid commitments or aid disbursements be chosen as target variables? What constitutes development and who should determine this?

These difficulties can be partially overcome by relating specific forms of aid to specific target variables, such as economic growth or imports or investments in the recipient country. But this does not solve the causality question. Are there other factors which might explain differences in the target variables and which should be incorporated? How are they related to aid? In many developing countries, data are scarce and not reliable. Historical data are often completely absent. This problem can be addressed by using cross-section approaches, but with so much variation between countries, the models used can hardly be expected to reflect all relevant factors in the relations assumed. This applies particularly to differences in the history, culture, geography, size and natural resource endowment between countries. Although a statistical time series analysis of the development process in a specific country is preferable, this too has shortcomings. The development history of the countries concerned is too short, and is character- ized by so many shocks — decolonization, revolution, regime changes, wars, droughts and other natural disasters — which cannot be taken into account in a plausible model, that much caution is required in using the results of such a quantitative analysis.

Thus, in-depth qualitative studies of the longer-term development process per country, of all relevant factors playing a role in that process, and their mutual relationships, would provide much better insight than any attempt to find a measurable effect of an isolated factor such as aid. Yet there have been numerous efforts to justify aid by seeking a rational basis for aid decisions with the help of measurable effectiveness criteria. Aid evaluations have been carried out by researchers and by aid agencies in an effort to lay a rational basis under future aid policy decisions. In a survey of evaluation studies, White (1994) concluded that direct regressions between aid and economic growth do not yield meaningful results. A more fruitful approach is to examine the channels through which aid is intended to increase growth, namely by increasing imports and investments and by raising the efficiency of investments.

THE IMPACT OF AID

In fact, this had been the approach of the first overall evaluation study of development assistance given by the Netherlands, which was carried out at the request of the Government of the Netherlands, and in which I was in- volved (see Jansen et al., 1969). The original aim was ambitious: to determine the optimal allocation of a marginal guilder of development aid. A number of different Dutch aid programmes (such as granting fellowships) were evaluated against related objectives (such as strengthening the skill levels in a country). In addition, a correlation was sought between the economic growth of a country and the total aid received from different sources, including the Netherlands. This was done using a very simple cross-country analysis: there were no time lags assumed; calculations were made with the help of five year averages for the period 1960–64 only.

One of our findings was that, during the period concerned, per capita economic growth had been higher in countries that had received more aid. In about 75 per cent of the recipient countries, between 0.2 per cent and 1.4 per cent of economic growth was ascribed to the aid received. The analysis also led to the conclusion that aid enabled a recipient country not only to finance a higher level of investment but also to improve the productivity of its capital. The latter result was considered of greater importance than the former and led to several policy conclusions, such as giving priority to technical and other assistance in order to increase the capacity of a country to use its capital. The quality of assistance was found to be just as important as the quantity. Aid that would, in one way or another, result in a distortion of the allocation of economic resources of a developing country was to be avoided.

One example of such a distortion is that aid which is intended to finance a specific investment project indirectly binds other investments in the country, for instance in infrastructure and in complementary sectors. The relative merits of project aid versus plan or programme aid have been discussed by a number of authors, including Singer, Little, Clifford, and Chenery, who all come to different conclusions regarding the so-called fungibility of aid. Singer has suggested that 'the project actually financed by aid may be quite different from the one to which the aid is ostensibly tied' (Singer, 1967: 539) — the aid would in fact finance the marginal project. Little and Clifford have argued that this would only apply in 'countries whose governments include development amongst their objectives and have a reasonably clear understanding of development priorities' (Little and Clifford, 1965: 301). Nowadays we would describe these countries in terms of 'good governance'. In such countries the high priority project would be financed anyway, plus a new one: together they would be financed out of the sum total of domestic resources and aid. In countries with good governance, fungibility — whether it occurs or not — does not represent a problem. However, Little and Clifford considered these cases to be rare. In countries with bad governance there is only a faint notion of development priorities. Here, the question of fungibility would not even arise, indicating that project aid would be the wiser choice. Chenery, however, argued that well-engineered projects in countries with poorly-run economies would make a low net contribution to development. The necessary redirection of resources towards sectors complementary to the project would either not take place at all or would occur to the detriment of development elsewhere (Chenery, 1967: 9–18). This was an argument against project aid and in favour of general balance of payments assistance. Chenery made clear, however, that he advocated such assistance only to countries with a good macro-economic policy: the aid had to be provided on the basis of performance of the country concerned.

In the Dutch aid evaluation report (Jansen et al., 1969), it was argued that in case of project assistance, irrespective of the assessment of a country's overall development policy, finance would not only have to cover the costs of the project itself but also all necessary complementary investments, if distortions of any kind were to be avoided. With the help of the so-called 'semi-input–output method' for development programming — which had been developed by Tinbergen (1967) — Pronk and Schreuel (1969) calculated that in the case of India, about 40–60 per cent of total necessary investment (and necessary imports) would be neglected if a project were considered in isolation. This finding could be interpreted as an argument against project assistance to countries with good governance, which should be given balance of payments or programme assistance instead. If project aid was preferred for some reason — such as bad governance in the recipient country — the finding could be seen to support either assistance to bunches of related activities (nowadays known as sectoral assistance), or the combining of project finance with substantial general finance, of about the same order of magnitude as the costs of the project itself. Only by employing one of these strategies could misallocation or distortion of domestic resources ('indirect fungibility') be avoided.

CATALYST OR IMPEDIMENT?

Since the mid-1960s numerous, much more sophisticated, evaluation studies have been presented, to provide a rational basis for aid allocation decisions. Towards the end of the decade, Rosenstein-Rodan introduced the concept of aid as a catalyst. In his view 'aid should be allocated where it will have the maximum catalytic effect in mobilising additional national effort' (Rosenstein-Rodan, 1969: 1). An evaluation should assess a country's development effort as a whole, on the basis of three general criteria: 'the country's capacity to restructure, its absorptive capacity, defined as its capacity to organise investment in a productive manner and its capacity to mobilise savings, and its capacity to repay' (ibid.: 9). Chenery and Carter (1973: 459) elaborated on this, describing the analytical and philosophical basis for aid and development programmes as follows:

- external resources can be used by developing countries as a basis for a significant acceleration of investment and growth;
- the maintenance of higher growth rates requires substantial changes in the structure of production and trade;
- external capital can perform a critical role in both resource mobilisation and structural transformation; and
- the need for concessionary aid declines once these structural changes are well under way, although further capital inflow may be productive.

In this analysis, based on the so-called two-gap approach (the savings gap and the trade gap), aid enables a country to increase investment beyond the limit set by the domestic savings rate. According to Chenery and MacEwan (1966: 177): 'the main function of aid is ... to permit an economy to grow at a rate determined by its ability to invest rather than by its initial ability to increase savings'. Higher economic growth than would have been possible given the domestic savings rate will lead to higher income and production and increase future savings and exports, making aid less necessary to reach a given target in later years — in other words, aid as a catalyst *pur sang*.

Keith Griffin has criticized the two-gap models developed by Chenery, Strout and others because of their assumption that all aid will result in higher investment. Aid may simply substitute domestic savings, resulting in increased consumption. In that case, aid will not result in higher investment and growth, nor in higher savings. Aid may, according to Griffin, also retard long-run economic growth in many other ways, for instance by altering the composition of investment with a bias towards activities that are not directly productive or have a long gestation period. Aid may have a bias towards capital-intensive technology and a tendency to increase the receiving country's subsequent need for capital. Aid may frustrate the emergence of an indigenous entrepreneurial class or delay institutional reform, and thus slow down rather than accelerate growth (Griffin and Evans, 1970). Aid then does not function as a catalyst, but, on the contrary, as an impediment.

This is not very different from earlier criticisms by Friedman, who had argued against aid because it would substitute domestic resources. In this view, there is no necessity for aid. If other conditions for economic development are ripe, capital will be readily available through the market; if not, for instance because of inadequate policies of the government concerned, capital made available would be likely to be wasted. A lack of domestic savings reflects a lack of opportunities, not of income (Friedman, 1958).

In response to this, Chenery has argued that in only a minority of cases studied by him, could a parallel reduction in domestic savings be ascribed to inefficiency in transforming aid into increased investment. Only in those cases can one speak of substitution. In a majority of cases there were other constraints, such as a trade constraint. Lack of access to foreign markets, for instance, would render domestic investments less profitable. Moreover, Chenery and Carter (1973) were able to demonstrate that, in general, countries that had raised their savings rate as a result of an aid-supported growth process outnumbered the cases in which an unnecessary diversion to consumption took place. The substitution effect should not be overestimated. If the marginal propensity to save is greater than the average, higher income will lead to higher savings and aid will result in both higher savings levels and rates. Aid will function as a catalyst, even allowing for a displacement effect.

One may even go a step further and assume that a crowding-in effect takes place rather than a substitution or crowding-out effect. Aid-induced growth may open up new investment opportunities in order to meet an increasing demand for domestically produced goods, in industry as well as in agriculture. An aid-financed infrastructure may enhance the efficiency of production. For large and complex investment schemes private capital is often not available. That is not so much due to inadequate policies of recipient governments, but to a specific risk assessment by the market. Contrary to the assumptions of Friedman and others, markets do not function properly; this applies especially to developing countries, and certainly to international markets when these are not fully accessible for those countries. Capital markets are far from willing to provide capital to a number of priority sectors, such as feeder roads, rural water supply, health and education. Investment in these sectors is necessary not only to increase welfare, but also to accelerate growth. For all these activities aid finance can be seen as vital, as a possible multiplier in order to accelerate development. This is particularly true when financial and technical assistance go together, bringing skills which would not otherwise have been available.

It should not come as a surprise that three decades after Chenery published his findings, Hansen and Tarp came to a similar conclusion (Hansen and Tarp, 2000). They surveyed existing studies on the relation between aid and savings and found that, using a Harrod–Domar framework, only one showed a substitution elasticity of below -1. In all other studies, aid had a positive effect on investment and income.

Two conclusions can be drawn so far. First, the substitution effect of aid may exist, and often does, but it can be dealt with. On balance and in the long run, catalytic crowding-in effects will outweigh fungibility or crowding-out effects. Second, however, this does not imply that if and when such a substitution has been avoided or its effects have been counteracted by good policy-making, a direct causal relationship between aid and economic growth can be considered as proven. It is not possible to argue an unequivocal relationship between aid and a net increment to overall economic growth in developing countries. Results vary per country; there is no general pattern; and for each individual country the correlation varies over time, because of frequent changes in exogenous variables.

It has been argued that the inability of development aid over decades to provide a net increment to overall growth in developing countries provides a case against aid altogether. In my view this is not true. It may be impossible to prove such a causal relation, but — more importantly — this does not mean that aid does not have a positive effect on development, or that it has never had such an impact, or worst of all, that it never could have such an effect, as seems to be the current wisdom of aid-watchers looking back at fifty years of development aid so far. On the contrary, if aid were conceived not as a direct cause of development, nor as its origin, its source or its prime mover, but only as a catalyst, many studies of the impact of aid could have been left undone or replaced by less abstract analyses. Expectations concerning the results of aid could have been toned down and made more realistic. It is surely preferable to look at specific forms of aid, in specific circumstances, to specific countries, in order to reach specific objectives. These are the only aid evaluations that make sense. For it is only in the light of lessons learned from concrete experiences, studied with the help of an analytical framework and taking all relevant factors into account, that a rational basis can be found for future aid allocation decisions in more or less similar situations.

GOOD POLICY

In fact, quality is the only thing that matters, whether we are talking about the quality of aid or the quality of a recipient's policy. Much aid has failed, but country- and sector-specific studies show that where quality conditions are met by both the donor and the recipient, 'good aid' does result in a decrease in poverty, reflected for instance in improved rural development, reduced infant mortality or greater access to primary education (see, for instance, Cassen, 1994).

In trying to attain this quality, good donor governance is essential. Aid itself should not create distortions, nor should it result in a foreign debt that might never be financed out of the increased income attributable to aid. With this in mind, we can begin to assemble a set of criteria for 'good aid'. Aid should mainly consist of grants. It should be adapted to the technical and institutional capacity of the recipient. It should be compatible with the culture of the country concerned. It should be demand-driven rather than supply-driven. It should cover additional, current and complementary costs as long as these cannot be financed from increased domestic income. It should not replace domestic skills or entrepreneurship by introducing a bias in favour of foreign expertise or networks. It should not result in a distortion of salary scales and consumption patterns, or a brain drain, which the recipient country could not afford — bad aid can decrease rather than increase the productivity of the domestic resources already available within the country itself. Last but not least, aid should be accompanied by policies within donor countries to open their markets for the goods and services produced as a result of aid.

All this is good governance on the side of donors. It should accompany good governance on the side of recipients in order to render aid effective. One might even say that good donor governance should set an example, without which good governance in developing countries has even less chance of sustainability. Good foreign governance may have to precede good domestic governance. Aid could thus become a catalyst not only for economic growth, but also in terms of furthering good policy-making, with future aid being made conditional on the implementation of good policies in the developing country itself. While this approach seems attractive, however, it has limitations. The questions arise: what is a good policy and who is to be the judge of that? The donor agency, the recipient government, or the people of the country concerned, the intended ultimate beneficiaries of aid? And, even more difficult, what happens when the donor decides that the recipient's policy or governance is not good enough?

This last question drew much attention during the debate on structural adjustment in developing countries in the 1980s. Policy reforms were considered necessary in order to stabilize the economy as a precondition for economic growth. Aid agencies, led by the International Monetary Fund and the World Bank, made aid conditional on the implementation of such reforms, and many bilateral donors followed the same course. This prompted an interest in analysing the effect not only of policy adjustment on stability and growth, but also of external finance for such adjustment programmes on these policies. The impacts of adjustment policies, and thus indirectly of adjustment assistance, have been analysed in terms of stability indicators (such as budgetary deficits or inflation) as well as indicators of subsequent economic growth and poverty reduction, both during and after a period of adjustment.

The debate on structural adjustment and its impact has been quite sharp. The findings have diverged widely, depending on the country or sector studied. However, some common features of the findings have gradually emerged, and can be summarized as follows (see for instance, World Bank, 1994):

- policy stance is a vital factor in economic reform;
- there is a positive impact of economic reform (structural adjustment) on growth, but reform plus aid is superior to either one of them alone — there is an increased combined effect;
- there is no clear relationship between change in aid and policy change; increases in aid do not necessarily forestall or retard reform, while decreases may lead some countries to improve their policies.

In other words: aid cannot buy policies; policies have a greater impact than aid, but together they have a greater impact than either one alone; and this combined effect is greater than the sum of the two isolated effects. Analytically this is a little puzzling, but in terms of aid policy-making it is helpful, because it highlights once again the functioning of aid as a catalyst.

Some light has been thrown on this by Lensink (1993), in a study on the impact of aid to sub-Saharan countries in the 1980s. Lensink concluded that the positive impact of aid on economic growth was counteracted by government behaviour, since in response to aid, governments relaxed their efforts or increased their unproductive consumption expenditure. This could explain the so-called micro–macro paradox: that even where aid projects are successful, positive effects on the economy as a whole might be eliminated by government policy, so that the macro-economic impact of aid falls short of the micro-economic results. Lensink made a distinction between country groups. From his analysis, the tentative conclusion can be drawn that in poorer developing countries aid may substitute domestic savings (plus taxes), while in relatively less poor developing countries aid does not have a negative impact on private savings. In all developing countries, aid has a positive impact on government consumption, but the influence of government consumption on economic growth is more negative in richer than in poorer developing countries (ibid.).

Two studies in the 1990s stirred up the public debate on the relationship between aid and the policies of the recipient countries. Boone (1994) presented a model which predicts that all aid will be consumed. His empirical evidence, using data from about a hundred countries, supported this view. For countries receiving less than 15 per cent of GDP in aid, Boone found that the marginal propensity to invest from aid was not significantly different from zero. The marginal propensity to consume was not significantly different from one. In contrast to Lensink, he found no evidence that the latter varied with the income level of the country. Nor did Boone find a significant correlation between aid and growth. He therefore concluded that virtually all aid goes to consumption. This might be seen as desirable in very poor countries if the increased consumption resulting from aid benefits poor people, not the elite. However, Boone found no significant correlation between aid and indicators representing infant mortality, primary schooling or life expectancy. Aid programmes did not change governments' incentives to carry out programmes to the benefit of the poor. On the contrary, Boone concluded that governments consist of rent-seeking politicians maximizing the welfare of the elite (ibid.).

Following Boone's analysis, Burnside and Dollar (1997) found that during the period 1973–93 aid had, on average, had little impact on economic growth. However, they introduced a number of policy variables concerning the budget, inflation and trade openness, and defined good policy in terms of sound macro-economics — a small budget deficit, low inflation and openness to international trade. They investigated two questions, namely, whether aid has a positive impact on growth in the presence of good policies, and whether aid affects policies, for good or for ill. The answer to the first question turned out to be positive: there was robust evidence that aid has a positive effect on growth in an environment of good fiscal, monetary and trade policies. The answer to the second question was less robust: aid has not systematically affected the policies concerned. Burnside and Dollar found that, when good policy and aid happened to coincide, the outcome has been good. In the presence of poor policies, however, aid had no positive effect on growth. This, together with their separate finding that aid is positively correlated with government consumption, might help explain why the impact of foreign aid on growth is not more broadly positive.

THE RECIPE?

Burnside and Dollar also found that although on the margin good policies had been rewarded with aid, donor interests were much more important in explaining aid allocations. This is no surprise to those who are familiar with the justification of aid laid down in policy papers such as those of the US House Committee forty years earlier. Burnside and Dollar calculated, however, that if aid were to be allocated on the basis of policy rather than on the basis of donor interest, while leaving the total quantity of aid and the policies of the recipients unchanged, this would raise the mean growth rate in the sample of poor countries from 1.1 per cent to 1.4 per cent. On this basis they made a plea for aid to be linked to policy improvement. If donors want to have a large impact on growth and poverty reduction, then they should place greater weight on economic policies of recipients. This is in line with the conclusion of the World Bank (1998) report 'Assessing Aid': an increase of US\$ 10 billion in aid, favouring countries with sound management, would lift 25 million people per year out of poverty. By contrast, an across-the-board increase would lift only 7 million out of poverty (World Bank, 1998: 16).

The importance of good policy now seems to be generally accepted. Sachs (1996) has argued that aid should go only to countries which take strong measures to promote market-based, export-led growth. Gwin and Nelson (1997) propose that aid should be much more selective: it should be used as a reward for good policy performance, while bad performers and reluctant reformers should be punished by withholding aid. Following this line of reasoning, Collier (1997) argues that policy conditionality is not sufficient in a system of punishment and reward: conditionality undermines a recipient's own choices in favour of reform, or, in the development jargon of the 1990s, the 'ownership' of the reform process. Aid should instead be allocated selectively to committed reformers only. Aid allocation on the basis of selectivity would focus aid on already reformed policy environments instead of attempting to buy reform in a bad policy environment. Selectivity would have no opportunity cost in terms of policy impact because the best research estimate is that the elasticity of policy with respect to aid is zero. Collier therefore argues that the incentives objective should be abandoned altogether, and aid should simply flow into those low-income countries with existing good policy environments. Collier sees many advantages for aid policy in this approach: good performers, rewarded with aid, would become both a 'role model' and a 'competitive threat' to other countries, thus inducing reform there too. It would send positive signals to the capital market, whereas old-style conditionality merely pointed out a government's inadequacies and thus provided little encouragement to private investors. At the same time, taxpayers and the electorate within the donor countries could be certain that aid was being used effectively rather than being wasted on bad policies.

Is this a convincing analysis and a good recipe for effective aid? It has become the conventional wisdom of today and many donors and aid agencies now seem to base their policies on these findings and prescriptions. However, a number of caveats need to be mentioned. Firstly, there are questions concerning the underlying statistics. Of course, criticisms of regression analyses of aid, economic growth and certain other variables also apply to the findings of Boone, Burnside and Dollar, and the 1998 World Bank report. In addition to general critiques on these regressions a number of authors have shown that the Burnside–Dollar findings are very sensitive to data and model specification (see, for example, Hansen and Tarp, 2000; Lensink and White, 2000). For instance, the results excluding middle-income countries are different from those for all developing countries in their sample. The main conclusion of Burnside and Dollar is based on a significant interaction term between 'good policies' and aid. However, others found a far less significant interaction term between these variables, in particular in middle-income countries (see Lensink and White, 2000). The evidence that aid is only effective when associated with good policies is therefore far from robust. If it were, the interaction could also be interpreted as saying that policies work better if assisted from outside, especially in low-income countries. This would support the idea of aid functioning not as a prime mover of development, but as a catalyst.

In addition to these statistical caveats there is an analytical one. This concerns the assumption, implicit in the analyses by Burnside and Dollar and Collier, that aid only reduces poverty via growth. Of course, economic growth is crucial — but it is not enough. Benefits of growth may occur to the poor through trickle-down effects, but often only if additional parallel or subsequent action is taken. Such action will be dependent both on the resources available — likely to be few in poor countries — and on whether the policy environment is conducive to growth only, or also to poverty reduction. Policies and resources for health care and for land redistribution are obvious examples. International aid can play a crucial role in fostering such policies and supplementing the necessary resources. Statistically such activities are often measured in terms of government consumption rather than investment. However, particularly in low-income countries, such government consumption may have a positive indirect effect — for instance on growth, through an increase in labour productivity. Aid can thus affect poverty through channels other than investment and growth.

This brings me to a third caveat concerning the findings in the World Bank (1998) and related studies — the choice of policy variables. Should a budget deficit always be considered an indicator of bad policy? Is inflation always bad policy, irrespective of the level? Is trade openness a good policy under all circumstances and for all developing countries? Why have other possible indicators of good policy not been included? The variables chosen are related to macro-economic adjustment and stability rather than growth, development or the provision for basic human needs. Even if the inclusion of other policy variables would not have changed the overall finding that 'aid only works in a good policy environment', to omit them from the analysis implies a policy bias against them. These elements will now not easily be included in a package of good policy measures used by donor agencies as criteria for selecting possible aid recipients, as has been advocated by the authors of these reports.

In this respect, what of the policy instruments recommended by the World Bank itself in other reports, such as in its 1997 *World Development Report*? In this report a plea was made for a greater role for the state — not too big, but greater, better defined and more focused on development than is presently the case in many developing countries, and greater than had been advocated by the IMF during the 1980s. There is also a case made for specific policy instruments regarding poverty reduction, which do not always go hand in hand with a policy to reduce the budgetary surplus or to further trade openness. The relationship between poverty reduction and growth policies is too complex for the simple assumption that 'good policy' consists of a focus on growth and on the tripartite policy package mentioned above. Many sectoral and programme evaluation studies have shown that aid focused on specific poverty reduction targets, such as the reduction of infant mortality or the improvement of primary education, can bring about good results, provided that such aid programmes are carried out in a good policy environment with regard to health and education (see, for example, Cox and Healey, 2000). Such a good policy environment is not necessarily positively associated with the stabilization and liberalization policies implied in the Burnside and Dollar package.

BETTER POLICY

Once again, then, we are confronted with the question: what constitutes a good policy or good governance and who determines this? As Mosley (1999) recently argued: 'good policy' and 'bad policy' should be seen as relative to a country's resources and state of development, and not as absolutes. Aid policy, like development policy more generally, needs to avoid reliance on the idea of one standard, inflexible package of 'good' economic policies that will ensure success wherever implemented. Donor conditionality, if applied, should be sensitive to differences in initial conditions between recipient countries and should incorporate so-called 'heterodox' policies, such as less inequality, some agricultural subsidies and social policy measures. Such policies are not part of the 'Washington Consensus', which tends to facilitate adjustment to economic globalization. But they have proved to be effective in a number of countries aiming at poverty reduction as well as economic growth.

This is not an argument against the importance of good policies. However, good policies have to be seen in the context of the development process itself, not as something exogenous. In deciding whether and how to support the process from outside, four considerations are important when assessing the policy of the aid recipient. First, the definition of a good policy: a good policy is oriented towards broad-based sustainable economic growth, including — from the outset — poverty reduction. Second, the country specificity of a good policy: what is a good policy in one country may not (yet) be appropriate in another situation. Third, flexibility: a relatively good policy in, say, health or education or water management might be considered worthy of support, even if the macro-economic policy of the country raises questions. Fourth, what really matters is not 'good policies', but 'better policies', better than before, to achieve a greater impact. Policy improvement and better governance should not be seen as pre-conditions for development and for development aid, but also as development objectives themselves.

For these reasons, well-focused aid conditionality is preferable to rigid selectivity. The difference between conditionality and selectivity is not about the need to make choices: selectivity is a special kind of conditionality, and both imply the need to meet specific criteria. Whether these are many or few, and whether or not they are equal for all countries does not constitute the overriding difference between selectivity and conditionality. The real difference between the two is between ex-post and ex-ante. Selectivity means that a country has to perform first and only thereafter will qualify for aid. Conditionality means helping countries which are themselves trying to meet certain criteria. It means helping to meet the conditions for good governance and good policy-making. It means assessing good intentions, the capacity to fulfil them and the degree of sincerity of the policy efforts so far. If the intentions are bad or if past performance gives any reason for distrust, such a country should not be selected. Aid should then be withheld until there is a new basis for confidence. When donor and recipient views diverge fundamentally, conditionality will not be effective. There are some clear examples of such a divergence (such as Zaire under Mobutu, Haiti under Duvalier and — until recently — North Korea). However, contrary to what is often suggested, this is the exception rather than the rule (see for instance, White and Morrisey, 1997).

Often policy intentions are not bad, they are simply not good enough. A lack of capacity to implement good policy intentions is more often to blame than sheer bad will. It is the conditions for policy-making that matter, and more than ever before the nation state in developing countries is being eroded by forces from outside and within — an imperfect polity, the institutional weakness of a government, inadequate policy experience and skill level of the administration, economic interest groups which resist reforms, cultural traditions, conflicts between different ethnic or religious groups, the pitfalls of democratic decision-making, clientelism, disputes within the political elite, cross-border economic and political pressures. Under such circumstances it is extremely difficult for policy-makers in developing countries to fulfil the conditions for good governance entirely by themselves. Development is by nature a dualistic process with much potential for conflict. Structural change within developing countries can hardly be expected to take place in a situation of harmony and stability. On the contrary, development means turning around well-established power structures which are not conducive to development. Development means shocking traditional cultures, uprooting existing social networks and economic structures. Development implies by definition a change in the status quo, and this is often accompanied by violence — not constantly, but in specific stages of the process, and not by exception, but inherently, as a logical and barely avoidable consequence of the development process itself. This is even more true at the present stage of world development than it was in previous decades, when nation states were not yet strongly influenced by cultural and economic forces from outside. The process of globalization has made nearly all developing countries more vulnerable to external influence than they were in the first two decades after decolonization.

In view of this, the recipe outlined above seems ill-advised. Countries should be *helped* to stabilize, to adjust, to perform and to develop, rather than being expected to achieve all this under their own steam. This brings us back to the concept of aid as a catalyst. This may mean catalysing stability or adjustment, or it may mean catalysing self-reliance or growth, but it will always imply catalysing change, by helping to get access to other resources necessary for sustainable development: domestic savings, international private capital, foreign markets, skills and capacities, institutional as well as human. Aid can help establish the conditions under which development might eventually sustain itself. Economic analysis has indicated that this is particularly valid for low-income economies. The poorer a country and the fewer its own resources, the smaller the risk of fungibility between foreign assistance and domestic efforts, and the greater the potential of aid to supplement resources and to enhance policy effectiveness. Political analysis indicates that it is even more true for failing states, crumbling nations, and societies in disarray. Such countries are not easily selected as aid recipients since their macro-economic policies are usually unstable, flawed or even non-existent. Yet in these countries, in particular, aid can help to establish or re-establish the conditions under which a turn-around can be achieved (see Pronk, 2000). Aid does not create development, but it does help in seeking, finding, choosing and following the right development path. That is the purpose of aid — no more, but also no less.

Aid is not the prime mover of development; it has sometimes even been an impediment, but this need not be the case. To use aid as a reward for good development governance may indeed be justified under certain conditions, but often such conditions can only be met with some outside help. Aid should, therefore, be used primarily as a catalyst, sometimes to help generate other resources or gain access to them, sometimes to help create domestic capacity or manage conflicts resulting from various forms of unsustainable development. At this juncture, what is required is a special focus in aid policy on social harmony, political stability and peace, as preconditions for economic growth and development — not the other way around.

REFERENCES

Boone, Peter (1994) 'The Impact of Foreign Aid on Savings and Growth'. London: London School of Economics (mimeo).

Burnside, Craig and David Dollar (1997) *Aid, Policies and Growth*. Washington, DC: The World Bank.

Cassen, Robert (1994) *Does Aid Work?* Oxford: Clarendon Press.

Chenery, Hollis. B. (1967) 'The Effectiveness of Foreign Assistance', in H. B. Chenery et al. *Towards a Strategy for Development Co-operation*, pp. 9–18. Rotterdam: Universitaire Pers Rotterdam.

Chenery, Hollis B. and A. MacEwan (1966) 'Optimal Patterns of Growth: The Case of Pakistan', in Irma Adelman and Erik Thorbecke (eds) *The Theory and Design of Economic Development*, pp. 149–78. Baltimore, MD: The Johns Hopkins University Press.

Chenery, Hollis B. and Nicholas G. Carter (1973) 'Foreign Assistance and Development Performance, 1960–1970', *American Economic Review* LXIII(2): 459–68.

Collier, Paul (1997) 'The Failure of Conditionality', in Catherine Gwin and Joan Nelson (eds) *Perspectives on Aid and Development*, pp. 31–77. Washington, DC: ODI; Baltimore, MD: Johns Hopkins University Press.

Cox, Aidan and John Healey (2000) *European Development Cooperation and the Poor*. London: Macmillan; New York: St Martin's Press, in assoc with the Overseas Development Institute.

Friedman, Milton (1958) 'Foreign Economic Aid: Means and Objectives', *The Yale Review* (summer). Reprinted in G. Ranis (ed.) (1969) *The United States and the Developing Countries*, pp. 24–38. New York: W. W. Norton and Co.

Griffin, K. B. and J. L. Evans (1970) 'Foreign Assistance: Objectives and Consequences', *Economic Development and Cultural Change* 18(3): 313–27.

Gwin, Catherine and Joan Nelson (eds) (1997) *Perspectives on Aid and Development*. Washington, DC: ODI; Baltimore, MD: Johns Hopkins University Press.

Hansen, Henrik and Finn Tarp (2000) 'Aid Effectiveness Disputed', *Journal of International Development* 12(3): 375–98.

Jansen, Leo et al. (1969) 'Evaluatie van de Nederlandse ontwikkelingshulp'. Tilburg: Tilburg Universiteit.

Lensink, Robert (1993) *External Finance and Development*. Groningen: Wolters-Noordhoff.

Lensink, Robert and Howard White (2000) 'Assessing Aid: A Manifesto for Aid in the 21st Century?', *Oxford Development Studies*, 28(1): 5–17.

Little, I. M. D. and J. M Clifford (1965) *International Aid*. London: Allen and Unwin.

Mosley, Paul (1999) 'Globalization, Economic Policy and Growth Performance', in *International Monetary and Financial Issues for the 1990s Vol X*, pp. 157–74. New York and Geneva: United Nations.

Ohlin, Goran (1966) *Foreign Aid Policies Reconsidered*. Paris: OECD Development Centre.

Pronk, J.P. and E. J. Schreuel (1969) 'Some Reflections on the Effectiveness of Project versus Plan Aid', in H. C. Bos (ed.) *Towards Balanced International Growth: Essays Presented to J. Tinbergen*, pp. 283–307. Amsterdam and London: North-Holland Publishing Company.

Pronk, Jan (2000) 'Development for Peace', in Kamalesh Sharma (ed.) *Imagining Tomorrow. Rethinking the Global Challenge*, pp. 74–82. New York.

Rosenstein-Rodan, P.N. (1969) 'Criteria for Evaluation of National Development Effort', *UN Journal for Development Planning* 1(1): 1–13.

Sachs, Jeffrey (1996) 'Growth in Africa: It Can Be Done', *The Economist* (29 June): 19–21.

Singer, H.W. (1967) 'External Aid: For Plans or Projects?', *The Economic Journal* 308: 539–45.

Tinbergen, J. (1945) 'Internationale economische samenwerking', *Economisch-Statistische Berichten* 30(1476): 50–6 (1 August).

Tinbergen, J. (1967) *Development Planning*. London: Weidenfeld and Nicolson.

White, Howard (1994) 'The Countrywide Effects of Aid'. World Bank Policy Research Working Paper no 1334. Washington, DC: The World Bank.

White, Howard and W. Morrisey (1997) 'Conditionality when Donor and Recipient Preferences Vary', *Journal of International Development* 9(4): 497–505.

World Bank (1994) 'Adjustment in Africa: Reforms, Results, and the Road Ahead'. Washington, DC: The World Bank.

World Bank (1997) *World Development Report*. New York: Oxford University Press for the World Bank.

World Bank (1998) *Assessing Aid. What Works, What Doesn't, and Why*. New York: Oxford University Press for the World Bank.

Chapter 2

Unpacking Aid

James K. Boyce

INTRODUCTION

Aid is often described as flowing from donor countries to recipient countries. This is an oversimplification for two reasons. First, there is often a counterflow of resources in the reverse direction by virtue of both 'tied aid' and capital flight. Second, 'countries' do not send and receive aid. On the donor side, the quantity and quality of aid are shaped by the contending economic, political, and institutional objectives of government agencies and their domestic constituents. On the recipient side, aid flows not to countries as a whole but rather to specific individuals, groups, and classes within them. An analysis of how aid is deployed to serve diverse donor-country interests, and how its distribution affects balances of power among competing recipient-country interests, is particularly crucial in understanding the dynamics of conflict and the current globalization of violence.

In this note, I first unpack the terms 'recipient countries' and 'donor countries'. I then consider the relative merits of selectivity and conditionality in aid policy. Finally, turning to aid provided in the form of loans, I discuss the need for 'credit forgiveness'.

UNPACKING THE RECIPIENTS

'Development', Jan Pronk (this volume, p. 17) writes, 'means turning around well-established power structures which are not conducive to development'. Aid can be particularly important, he observes, in 'failing states, crumbling nations, and societies in disarray', where it 'can help to establish or re-establish the conditions under which a turn-around can be achieved'.

Such explicit reference to power structures, and to aid's potential impact on them, is rare in development discourse. Donor agencies not only consider it indelicate to refer to these matters, but often deny that their aid has any such effects. At the World Bank, for example, many officials are quick to invoke their mandate to make loans 'with due attention to considerations of economy and efficiency and without regard to political or other non-economic influences or considerations'.[1] Yet it is seldom possible to draw a neat line between the two.

Aid is not like rain that falls on whoever happens to be present in a given time and place. Instead it is more like a set of weights placed on the scales of power at the local, regional, and national levels. Whether by design or by default, aid tilts power balances, strengthening some individuals, groups, and classes relative to others. Two examples will illustrate this point. In the mid-1970s, the World Bank and the Swedish International Development Authority installed 3000 deep tubewells for irrigation in northwestern Bangladesh. On paper, these tubewells were supposed to go to co-operatives of small farmers; in practice, they were systematically monopolized by the most powerful members of the rural elite. Much as radioactive dyes injected into a patient serve as a diagnostic tool to identify cancerous tumours, so the tubewell project served to illuminate the rural power structure. This distributional outcome reinforced existing inequalities of wealth and power, and at the same time sapped the project's productivity as the monopoliza-tion of the tubewells led to their chronic underutilization (Hartmann and Boyce, 1983: 256–67).

As a second example, consider Rwanda in the five years prior to the 1994 genocide. During this period, annual aid to the Hutu-dominated govern-ment rose by roughly 50 per cent, sending the message that 'the aid system did not care unduly about political and social trends in the country, not even if they involved government-sponsored racist attacks against Tutsi' (Uvin, 1998: 237). A British parliamentary inquiry singles out the World Bank and International Monetary Fund (IMF) for criticism, noting that 'neither organisation recognised the direct link between growing social tension, human rights abuses, and the subsequent destruction of the entire economic infrastructure' (House of Commons, 1999: para 59).

While donors may ignore the impact of aid on power structures in the recipient country, this does not mean that their aid is or can be neutral. On the contrary, the default setting is for aid to flow to those who wield power. If donors wish to alter this outcome, let alone 'turn around' established power structures, this requires careful attention to questions of who gets what, including the impact of their aid on 'vertical inequality' across income classes and 'horizontal inequality' across racial, ethnic, linguistic, and religious divides (Stewart, 2000).

UNPACKING THE DONORS

We need to unpack the donor side of the aid relationship, too. As Pronk remarks (this volume, p. 3), aid has multiple objectives — charitable,

---

1. International Bank for Reconstruction and Development, *Articles of Agreement*, Article III, Section 5(b).

economic, and political. Different parties within the donor countries have different priorities. Notwithstanding efforts to cloak sectoral concerns in appeals to 'the national interest', there are clearly divergent interests within donor countries. For example, a prime concern of the private business sector is securing contracts for the supply of goods and services. The political muscle of commercial interests is reflected in the fact that about half of bilateral aid is tied to purchases of goods and services from the donor country (de Jonquières, 1996). Other priorities of the business sector include access to raw materials and the favourable treatment of foreign investment. Trade unions may place greater priority on supporting labour standards and workers' rights overseas, not only out of international solidarity but also out of fear of competition from foreign producers taking advantage of exploitative working conditions. Humanitarian organizations call for targeting aid to people in need, regardless of considerations of donor self-interest.

In practice, however, geopolitical concerns often play the most decisive role in donor priorities. As a World Bank (1998: 40) assessment acknowledges, aid allocations by multilateral and bilateral agencies were 'dominated by politics' during the Cold War. The collapse of the Soviet Union increased the space for donor attention to issues of 'good governance' and democracy in recipient countries. Nevertheless, strategic self-interest remained the single strongest influence on the allocation of US aid in the 1990s, with Israel and Egypt the top two recipients (Hook, 1998).

Donor decisions are not simply the weighted product of these competing interests. The aid agencies themselves also exercise a degree of independence, with their internal incentive structures and institutional agendas generating a momentum of their own. For example, in many agencies the 'approval and disbursement culture' (World Bank, 1998: 6), judging staff performance in terms of the quantity rather than the quality of aid flows, militates against careful attention to the impact of aid on the political economies of recipient countries.

CONDITIONALITY VERSUS SELECTIVITY

In recent years, conditionality — whereby donors condition their aid on the adoption of specific policies by recipients — has fallen from favour. As Pronk (this volume, pp. 13–14) observes, a new 'conventional wisdom' is emerging that aid should be allocated instead on the basis of 'selectivity', preferentially channelled to those governments that already have demonstrated their commitment to policies that the donors wish to support. Several rationales are offered for this shift: selectivity is said to be less intrusive on national sovereignty; policies are more likely to prove effective if they have domestic 'ownership'; reallocating aid to 'good performers' will maximize its short-run impact on growth, poverty, and other development indicators; and in the long run, selectivity will inspire other governments to emulate these worthy role models.

A related reappraisal is happening with regard to the mandates and competence of aid agencies. In the past three decades, in response to criticisms and political pressures, aid agencies have broadened their avowed objectives to include not only macroeconomic stability and economic growth, but also such aims as employment generation, poverty reduction, gender equity, environmental protection, good governance, and democratization. The actions of donors in these areas often have failed to live up to their public pronouncements, but their embrace of these new aims was not purely a matter of empty rhetoric. Today, however, a backlash against 'mission creep' is gathering force across the political spectrum, and calls are increasingly heard for the agencies to return to their 'original mandates' and 'core competencies'.[2]

Neither selectivity nor the back-to-basics movement offers a promising recipe for making aid a more effective instrument for the improvement of human well-being. There are two inherent problems with selectivity. First, if donors decide simply to wait until 'bad performers' see the light and mend their errant ways, they may have to wait a very long time. This is particularly true in the case of countries in Pronk's category of 'failing states, crumbling nations, and societies in disarray'. The costs of an indefinite wait-and-see attitude — to innocent people within these societies, and to others if the violence spills beyond national borders — may be very high.

Second, once we unpack recipient countries, and recognize that they are comprised of diverse individuals, groups, and classes who often have divergent interests, it becomes impossible to speak unequivocally of policy 'ownership' by recipients. Instead, we find a variety of policy alternatives supported by contending political forces, both inside and outside the government. The ownership and implementation of any given policy mix requires a political process of domestic coalition building — a process in which aid can serve as a catalyst (Milder, 1996).

The challenge for donors, therefore, is not to select *countries* that should receive aid, but rather to select *who* within the recipient countries should receive aid, and *what* policy objectives the donors should support.

The problem with the back-to-basics approach is not only that it prescribes a simple, axiomatic answer to the relative importance of different policy objectives — embracing the old-time religion of macroeconomic stability

---

2. For example, the majority report of the Meltzer Commission, established by the US Congress to review the role of the international financial institutions, criticizes the IMF's recent decision to extend its mandate to poverty alleviation, and advocates 'placing credible bounds on authority to ensure that the IMF does not continue to experience mission creep' (International Financial Institution Advisory Commission, 2000: 39–40). In response to such criticisms, IMF Managing Director Horst Koehler has recently launched moves to 'streamline' conditionality (*IMF Survey,* 2001).

and economic growth — but also that it assumes that these objectives can be neatly divorced from other issues. Yet issues such as environmental quality, governance, and violent conflict are inextricably related to economic performance: economic failure can exacerbate these problems, but failures in these dimensions of development can undermine the economy, too. Donors cannot simply ignore these linkages by crawling back into a technocratic hole and pulling a lid over their heads.

To be sure, the competence of aid agencies to tackle these issues often leaves much to be desired. But the remedy for such deficiencies is to improve donor competencies, not to retreat from their responsibility to confront the manifold consequences of their actions and inaction. Of course, building competence takes time. In the meantime, however, some issues can be more readily addressed by drawing on existing competencies. For example, the international financial institutions are well-endowed with expertise in matters of fiscal policy. It would not require a gigantic intellectual leap to extend their focus beyond the size of budget deficits to devote more attention to the overall ratio of revenue and expenditure to national income (as opposed to the gap between the two), the composition of public spending (for example, the relative magnitude of military versus social expenditure), and the distributional incidence of taxation and expenditure — all of which are particularly critical issues in war-torn societies (Boyce, 2000).

CREDIT FORGIVENESS

Aid is provided not only in the form of grants, but also as loans. The latter leave behind a residue of debt. Although the terms on these loans are more favourable than those available in private credit markets — which is why they qualify as 'aid' — the obligation to repay them in subsequent years is no less serious.

This is a further reason to 'unpack' aid. As noted above, the benefits of aid typically are distributed unevenly within recipient countries, with some people benefiting more than others. Indeed, some may be adversely affected by aid, as when the prices farmers receive for their crops are depressed by imports of subsidized food aid, or when aid helps to maintain in power a predatory and repressive regime.

In the case of loans, a further cost must be added to the scales: the cost of debt repayment. Just as aid is often described loosely as going to 'recipient countries', without disaggregating their citizenry, so debt is often ascribed to countries. For example, the World Bank uses the phrase 'severely indebted low-income countries' to describe countries on the basis of their per capita income and various indicators of their public external debt burden.

This language ignores the existence of private external assets: financial and other wealth held abroad by private citizens of 'debtor countries'. Data on private external assets are less readily available than data on public external debts, in part because many of the assets were acquired through dubious means and transferred abroad in violation of foreign-exchange controls. Annual capital outflows and their cumulative stock can be estimated, however, using the methodology developed by the World Bank (1985) and others (for example, Lessard and Williamson, 1987) to measure capital flight.

In many cases, the estimated volume of capital flight exceeds the country's total public external debt. In the 'severely indebted low-income countries' of sub-Saharan Africa, for example, cumulative capital flight amounted to US$ 193 billion (in 1996 dollars) in the period 1970–96, a sum 8 per cent greater than the same countries' combined public external debts of US$ 178 billion (Boyce and Ndikumana, 2001). Adding imputed interest earnings on this flight capital, the total stock of private external assets stood at US$ 285 billion, 60 per cent greater than their public external debts. In other words, if we add public liabilities and private assets together to obtain a picture of the net external position of *countries* as opposed to *governments*, we find that sub-Saharan Africa as a whole is a *net creditor vis-à-vis* the rest of the world.

Capital flight and the associated accumulation of private external assets were financed in no small measure by external borrowing. For example, Ndikumana and Boyce (1998) review documentary evidence indicating that creditors knew that a substantial fraction of their loans to the government of Congo (the former Zaire) under the Mobutu regime was being diverted into private hands. Mobutu was not alone in using 'aid' to finance private accumulation while repressing dissent at home. An analysis of sub-Saharan Africa in the 1970–96 period reveals that roughly 70 cents of every dollar that flowed into the region from foreign loans flowed back out as capital flight in the same year (Ndikumana and Boyce, 2002).

This phenomenon underscores the need to unpack aid — to disaggregate 'recipient countries' — so as to distinguish between those who benefited from foreign loans and those who did not. Such an unpacking can help to rectify the stark asymmetry between the current treatment of external debt as the liability of the country as a whole and the treatment of external assets as the private wealth of a narrow stratum of the population. It is often difficult to identify the individuals who diverted the proceeds of loans into their own pockets, let alone to trace exactly where the money went. But the same end can be accomplished indirectly by identifying that subset of the loaned funds that benefited the public, and assuming, in the absence of evidence to the contrary, that the remainder of the loaned funds did not. Invoking the doctrine of 'odious debt' under international law, successor governments could selectively reject liability for that portion of the debt from which their citizens derived no visible benefit (Ndikumana and Boyce, 1998).

This strategy differs from 'debt forgiveness,' in which creditors write off debts, forgive the 'indebted country' for having borrowed unwisely, and urge them to take steps to restore their credit worthiness. Instead it can be termed a strategy for 'credit forgiveness': the citizens of the country 'write off' credits, forgive the creditor institutions for having lent unwisely, and urge them to take steps to restore their 'debt worthiness'.

CONCLUSION

To analyse aid's catalytic role — and to ensure that aid catalyses broad-based improvements in human well-being rather than deepening inequities and indebtedness — we must unpack both sides of the aid relationship. Instead of viewing aid as a flow of resources from 'donor countries' to 'recipient countries', we must reframe the discourse and practice of aid to ask the critical questions: aid from whom, aid to whom, and aid for what ends?

REFERENCES

Boyce, James K. (2000) 'Beyond Good Intentions: External Assistance and Peace Building', in Shepard Forman and Stewart Patrick (eds) *Good Intentions: Pledges of Aid for Postconflict Recovery*, pp. 367–82. Boulder, CO: Lynne Rienner.

Boyce, James K. and Léonce Ndikumana (2001) 'Is Africa a Net Creditor? New Estimates of Capital Flight from Sub-Saharan Africa', *Journal of Development Studies* 38(2): 27–56.

Hartmann, Betsy and James K. Boyce (1983) *A Quiet Violence: View from a Bangladesh Village*. London: Zed Books.

Hook, Steven W. (1998) 'Building Democracy through Foreign Aid: The Limitations of United States Political Conditionalities, 1992–96', *Democratization* 5(3): 156–80.

House of Commons, International Development Committee (1999) *Conflict Prevention and Post-Conflict Reconstruction. Volume I: Report and Proceedings*. London: The Stationery Office.

IMF Survey (2001) 'IMF Seeks to Streamline and Focus Conditions for Lending to Member Countries', *IMF Survey* 30 (September): 10–11.

International Financial Institution Advisory Commission (Meltzer Commission) (2000) *Report*. Washington, DC: US Department of the Treasury [available on the worldwide web at: *http://phantom-x.gsia.cmu.edu/IFIAC/USMRPTDV.html*].

de Jonquières, Guy (1996) 'Tied Aid Dinosaur Defies Extinction', *Financial Times* 17 September.

Lessard, Donald R. and John Williamson (eds) (1987) *Capital Flight and Third World Debt*. Washington, DC: Institute for International Economics.

Milder, Daniel C. (1996) 'Foreign Assistance: Catalyst for Domestic Coalition Building', in J. M. Griesgraber and B. G. Gunter (eds) *The World Bank: Lending on a Global Scale*, pp. 142–91. London: Pluto Press; Washington, DC: Center for Concern.

Ndikumana, Léonce and James K. Boyce (1998) 'Congo's Odious Debt: External Borrowing and Capital Flight in Zaire', *Development and Change* 29(2): 195–217.

Ndikumana, Léonce and James K. Boyce (2002) 'Public Debts and Private Assets: Explaining Capital Flight from Sub-Saharan African Countries'. Working Paper No. 32. Amherst, MA: University of Massachusetts, Political Economy Research Institute.

Stewart, Frances (2000) 'The Root Causes of Humanitarian Emergencies', in E. Wayne Nafziger, Frances Stewart and Raimo Vayrynen (eds) *War, Hunger, and Displacement: The Origins of Humanitarian Emergencies. Volume 1: Analysis*, pp. 1–41. Oxford: Oxford University Press.

Uvin, Peter (1998) *Aiding Violence: The Development Enterprise in Rwanda.* West Hartford, CT: Kumarian Press.
World Bank (1985) *World Development Report.* Washington, DC: World Bank.
World Bank (1998) *Assessing Aid: What Works, What Doesn't, and Why.* Oxford and New York: Oxford University Press.

Chapter 3

Aid as a Flight Forward

Louis Emmerij

This article is in two parts. The first part reviews the evolving development theory of the last sixty years and deduces its implications for development aid. The observed changes in development thinking explain in no small measure the amazing shifts in, and accumulations of, aid priorities. The second part moves from theory to practice by looking into the lessons that can be learned from a concrete development success story and reviewing the present situation of development aid, touching on several points made in the first chapter of this book by Jan Pronk.

DEVELOPMENT THEORY AND DEVELOPMENT AID CONSEQUENCES

When development aid started some fifty years ago, the early writers on the subject of development tried to clarify the delicate balance between income, savings, investment and output required to maintain stable growth and full employment. W. Arthur Lewis stressed in his *Theory of Economic Growth* (Lewis, 1955) that the decisive step in the development process is a 'rise in the rate of productive investment from, say, 5 per cent or less to over 10 per cent of national income'.

A number of theorists focused on the difficult questions of how to start economic growth in backward areas, and how — once started— to nurture it. Igniting a process of industrialization became a central concern to these authors, whose work has been labelled by catchphrases: 'big push' for Rosenstein-Rodan, 'balanced growth' for Nurkse, 'unbalanced growth' for Hirschman, 'growth poles' for Perroux, 'take off' for Rostow and 'great spurt' for Gerschenkron.

Rosenstein-Rodan was probably the first 'modern' development economist. As early as 1943 he argued that investment decisions are interdependent and that — at early stages of development — investment projects are often too risky for individual investors. He came out in favour of the 'big push' development strategy, involving government planning to co-ordinate and provide incentives for simultaneous investment in several complementary industries that would increase both production and the size of the domestic market (Rosenstein-Rodan, 1943). The solution Nurkse proposed was related, namely a synchronized and simultaneous application of capital throughout industry in order to bring about a generalized expansion of the market (Nurkse, 1952). Contrary to Ragnar Nurkse, Albert Hirschman argued that the deliberate creation of disequilibria is the best way to achieve development (Hirschman, 1958). Nurkse's balanced growth approach implied a need for investment in agriculture along with industry; Hirschman's analysis suggested a concentration of investment in key large-scale industrial projects, those that have the largest number of linkages.

Rostow's article (1956) and book (1960) were important for putting forward the notion of the leading sector — a sector that grows considerably faster than the economy as a whole and that gives dynamism to the rest of the economy. Rostow's view of economic take off and the concept of the leading sector were also fed by the early work of Gerschenkron on Europe's growth experience during the nineteenth century. Gerschenkron argued that the more backward a country's economy, the more likely was its industrialization to start discontinuously as a sudden great spurt (Gerschenkron, 1952, 1962).

The emphasis in the 1940s and 1950s was, therefore, on economic growth, how to start it, and how to maintain it. And this focus was reflected in the rationale for development aid. Underdeveloped countries were supposed to have low savings rates (the 5 per cent of W. Arthur Lewis) and a need for high investment rates. This (temporary) gap between national savings and investment needs could only be bridged by an inflow of international savings. The rationale for development aid was, therefore, clear and simple.

During the 1960s, however, empirical studies were undertaken to test the hypothesis that significant increases in national savings were closely correlated with rapid industrial growth. This hypothesis was not confirmed. The correlation was found to be positive in some cases, insignificant in others, and negative in a few (Houthakker, 1965). These results led to the elaboration of the 'two-gap' model. The two-gap model assumes that in the early stages of industrial growth the principal constraint may well be insufficient savings, but once things get underway the principal constraint may also become the availability of foreign exchange required to import capital equipment, intermediate goods, etc. The foreign exchange gap would thus supersede the savings gap as the principal development constraint. The role of aid was further reinforced in that it combined investment resources and foreign exchange (Chenery and Bruno, 1962; Chenery and Strout, 1966).

Much of the mainstream development literature of the early post-war days refrained from looking deeply into the factors that determine income distribution. This initial neglect was due in large measure to a belief in the existence of a 'trickle-down' mechanism. For example, one strand of thought — whose proponents included Walter Galenson and Harvey Leibenstein — held that a highly unequal income distribution was necessary for generating savings that would facilitate investment and hence economic growth (Galenson and Leibenstein, 1955). This contention was based on the assumption that the rich save a high proportion of their income locally and the poor consume most of theirs. Given the relationship between economic growth and savings (investments), it follows — so the reasoning went — that the more a country's income distribution is skewed in favour of the upper income strata, the greater will be the savings and hence growth rates. Moreover, the more growth occurs, the more income will trickle down to lower income strata via the market mechanism.

This line of reasoning was reinforced by Simon Kuznets' analysis of the relationship between per capita income levels and income distribution during the process of economic growth., known as the Kuznets' U-shaped-curve hypothesis (Kuznets, 1955). According to this hypothesis, there is a historical tendency for inequality first to increase, then to level off and eventually to decline during the course of economic growth. During the early period of development there is a large low-income agricultural (traditional) sector. Everybody is poor and poverty is equally distributed. As development proceeds, labour moves from the traditional sector to the industrial (modern) sector. Income inequality becomes greater, but in the longer run it will reduce inequality because wages in the traditional sector will also increase, according to the Lewis model of unlimited supplies of labour (Lewis, 1954; Ranis and Fei, 1961, 1964). Although Kuznets based his theory on evidence from developed nations, it was generally believed to hold also for developing countries. In sum, it was assumed that in the longer run growth would result not only in higher incomes for everyone, but also in a less unequal income distribution which means that the income of the lower strata would rise more rapidly than that of the rich.

However, all this changed drastically as the end of the 1960s and the 1970s saw the emergence of two opposing trends in development thinking and practice. One trend consisted of widening the scope of development by including explicitly social considerations, such as education, health, nutrition, employment, income distribution, basic needs, poverty reduction, environmental considerations, gender, and so on. The other trend was represented by a return to neo-classical thinking.

During the 1970s, the United Nations family of organizations (including the World Bank) was heavily engaged in the elaboration of the first trend. At the end of the 1960s, it dawned upon many development economists that the economic growth pattern followed hitherto had secured high rates of growth, but had not made a real dent in the prevailing social conditions. Income distribution did not necessarily obey Kuznets' U-curve. For example, Fishlow pointed to growing income inequality in Brazil during that country's economic miracle of the 1960s (Fishlow, 1972). There was also evidence of widening dualism in developing countries — instead of lessening (as it should, according to the book), it often worsened. As early as 1970, Hans Singer pointed to the creation of a dual employment situation: small numbers are employed in the modern sector at relatively high wages, and an increasing share of the labour force is relegated to a marginal existence (Singer, 1970). The ILO and the OECD Development Centre were among the first to focus on the growing employment problem in developing countries (ILO, 1969; Turnham and Jaeger, 1971).

This body of empirical evidence on inequality, unemployment and underemployment, and dualism contributed to a growing scepticism about the reality of the 'trickle-down' mechanism. This led Dudley Seers, in a widely publicized lecture, to advocate a shift from development mainly related to growth to a wider concept encompassing reductions in poverty, unemployment and inequality:

> The questions to ask about a country's development are therefore: What has been happening to unemployment? What has been happening to poverty? What has been happening to inequality? If all three of these have become less severe, then beyond doubt this has been a period of development... If one or two of these central problems have been growing worse, and especially if all three have, it would be strange to call the result 'development', even if per capita income has soared. (Seers, 1969)

Gunnar Myrdal, in outlining his world anti-poverty programme, also stressed the objective of greater equality in proposing major reforms in agriculture, education, population and the State (Myrdal, 1970).

The role of education as an investment in human beings which is essential for economic growth became widely accepted. The 'renaissance' of the economics of education had already started in the late 1950s and early 1960s (Blaug, 1968; Tinbergen and Bos, 1965). Denison discovered the so-called residual factor — a factor combining education, technological progress, management practices — which explained a larger proportion of economic growth than the factors 'labour' and 'capital' combined (Denison, 1962; Solow, 1956)

The series of World Conferences organized by UN organizations during the 1970s brought all these issues, including environmental factors and gender issues, into sharper focus. The ILO launched the concept of a basic needs oriented development strategy; the World Bank worked out the related concept of redistribution with growth and at the end of the 1970s one might have thought that a new paradigm had been created. All this is set out in greater detail in a recent publication (Emmerij et al., 2001).

Development aid followed this important change in priorities and aid monies were now channelled into poverty projects, gender questions, the informal sector (ILO, 1972), and so on. Technical assistance took on increased prominence with the rediscovery of the importance of trained personnel and education in general. Technical assistance was now seen as bridging a temporary gap between the supply of human capital and the demand for it, just as had been the case with physical capital earlier. Consequently, the 1970s saw an important diversification of development aid: without having successfully filled the investment or the foreign exchange gaps, development aid was now directed at multiple objectives, such as increased technical assistance, poverty reduction, education, policies focused on reducing the gender gap, bringing environmental considerations into the mainstream of economic policies, etc. The flight forward had begun.

While a widening and deepening of development strategies was proposed, and correctly so, development aid became dispersed as a consequence and hence started losing focus. As development policies during the 1970s became more comprehensive and more employment and income-distribution oriented, the groundwork was laid by the followers of a neo-classical and neo-liberal approach that became the new paradigm as of the 1980s. Already at the end of the 1960s, the criticism of import-substituting policies became more precise, technical and empirical. Extensive work was undertaken by the OECD Development Centre and the World Bank (Little et al., 1970). These studies pointed to a tendency for many developing countries to protect capital-goods industries and strong anti-export bias that resulted from policies that sought to encourage heavy industrial development. The anti-export bias notably affected light manufacturing and agriculture.

This early work was followed by other studies that represented an important strengthening of the theoretical framework of the open-economy model. One illustration is the work on the methodology of project appraisal and micro-level planning. Two links between the proposed project appraisal techniques and the neo-classical approach can be identified. The first is the neo-classical assumption that agents possess complete information, that markets are fully functional, that there are no externalities, and there are no distortions in the economy. The second is the use of world prices as shadow prices. This builds a pro-trade bias in the appraisal methodology and is therefore implicitly mapping out a case for free trade and supply-side adjustment along neo-classical lines (Little and Mirrlees, 1968, 1974; for an alternative view, see Sen, 1972).

Defenders of the neo-classical resurgence have argued that whereas neo-classical economics became more precise in its use of mathematics and application of econometrics, 'development economics ... has relied on large doses of casual empiricism, fairly unrigorous theorizing and an eclectic approach to related social sciences' (Lall, 1976). Obviously, this position has been attacked: Frances Stewart was an early and typical example by the time the neo-classical resurgence was being implemented as actual policy. She brings considerable argument to bear in order to conclude: 'Taking all these (arguments) together, there is no theoretical basis for concluding that an undistorted price system will lead to a higher level of welfare than one containing various government interventions' (Stewart, 1985).

So, during the 1970s, there was both a broadening of the thinking about economic and social development, and a narrowing reflected in the neo-classical resurgence. As of 1980 the latter had the upper hand. One of its more far-reaching effects during the 1980s and beyond has been its influence on the conditionality of 'structural adjustment' lending by the World Bank and the Regional Development Banks as well as on the conditions attached to IMF loans in developing countries. This new orthodoxy, also known as the Washington Consensus, was neatly summarized by John Williamson in ten prescriptions (Williamson, 1990, 1997). These can be summed up in two major areas of policy:

1. The establishment of a healthy base for growth through macro-economic stabilization and austerity programmes. This was seen as an important step on the road to growth and prosperity. It included fiscal discipline to put an end to budget deficits, tight controls of public expenditure, and reliance on unified exchange rates in place of import controls or export subsidies.
2. The restructuring of the economy toward export- and market-oriented activities through liberalization, deregulation, and privatization. The objective was to strengthen the private sector as the main actor of growth and development through tax reform, liberalization of trade and finance, privatization, deregulation, and strengthening of property rights. Countries should also be opened to foreign direct investment.

The 'new' paradigm was of course a recycled version of trickle-down economics (which we already encountered above), with growth given greater weight than income distribution and social objectives. The underlying hypothesis was that policy reforms designed to achieve efficiency and growth would also promote better living standards, especially for the poorest (Streeten, 1987). The social costs of structural adjustment were inconvenient but temporary; in any case they were inevitable in order for countries to return to more rational and viable economic structures.

Once again, development aid followed the 'new' trend, with less enthusiasm than previously, it is true, and while maintaining much of the dispersion acquired during the 1970s, but follow it did. Thus, another layer was put on top of the already high aid cake.

As of 1990, UNDP started producing its annual *Human Development Reports* (UNDP, various issues) that were largely based on the work of Amartya Sen, the 1998 Nobel Prize laureate. Sen's academic work has encompassed welfare economics, economic inequality and poverty, on the one hand (including the most extreme manifestation of poverty in the form of famines), and the scope and possibility of rational, tolerant and democratic social choice, on the other (including voting procedures and the protection of liberty and minority rights).

Sen sees individual advantage not merely as opulence or utility, but primarily in terms of the lives people manage to live and the freedom they have to choose the kind of life they have reason to value. He came up with a universal definition of poverty, not of course in terms of purchasing power, but of *capabilities* and *functionings*. The poor are poor because their set of capabilities is small — not because of what they do not have, but because of what they cannot do. There is not very much they can do with their time.

A minimum list of capabilities would include being able to lead a healthy and productive life, to communicate and participate in the community, to move about freely, and to have a family with a partner of their choice. Sen's emphasis on freedom of choice led him naturally to attach prime importance to democracy as a preferred political system: 'A country does not have to be deemed fit *for* democracy; rather, it has to become fit *through* democracy' (Sen, 1999a). He shows empirically that there is no correlation between political rights and economic performance, but since democracy and political liberty have importance in themselves, the case for them remains a priority (Sen, 1999b).

Sen has a sound distrust of unadulterated market economics, is in favour of democratic decision-making, and calls for social support in development. He points out that in the classical writings on development, it was always assumed that economic development was a benign process, in the interest of the people. The view that one must ignore any kind of social sympathies for the underdog, and that one cannot have democracy, did not become dominant until the beginning of modern development economics, that is, as of the 1950s. Sen's 'friendly' approach to development sees it as a process in which people help each other and themselves with an emphasis on human skills and human capital, and on the role of human qualities in promoting and sustaining economic growth. Ultimately, the focus is on the expansion of human freedom to live the kind of lives people have reason to value. And, thus, the role of economic growth in expanding these opportunities has to be integrated into that more foundational understanding of the process of development: 'To reject the "hard state" that denies the importance of human rights... is thus complementary to the rejection of other forms of "hardness that view development as a terribly fierce" process' (Sen, 1997).

Amartya Sen's development as freedom and the concept of human development led to a further diversification of development aid. Democracy, freedom, human rights became new priorities on top of all the others. As a kind of perversion of Sen's thought process, the term *good governance* descended on the development milieu and particularly on the development aid community. The World Bank came to the tautological conclusion that development aid is more effective when a country has 'good governance', that is, when there is transparency in government expenditures, absence of corruption, integrity of business practices and of the civil service, freedom of trade unions and political parties, limited military expenditures, when human rights are guaranteed, and the 'right' economic policies are being pursued (Burnside and Dollar, 1997).

This emphasis on good governance as the latest conditionality has of course been attacked (Emmerij, 2001; Pronk, 2001). A country that meets all the conditions of good governance is no longer underdeveloped, and few countries would have developed if all these conditions were imposed right from the beginning. The industrial countries certainly cannot be held as examples of good governance. The USA cannot put order in its campaign finance situation; the presidential election of November 2000 was definitely not a shining example of democracy; and the robber barons of the nineteenth century were not exactly the business men of integrity required by today's good governance advocates. In some important European countries there is hardly a leading politician or business person who has not been to prison, is in prison or is about to go there.

In conclusion to this first section, it can be maintained that development aid is the repository of accumulated ideas and priorities of development theory of the last sixty years. Development aid more than development theory has been the institutional and intellectual memory of development thinking. In the multifarious layers of the development aid tree one can discover not only its age, but the successive priorities of development theory, reflecting the 'wisdom of the day'. Development aid was supposed to be temporary, but through its flight forward (moving from one priority to the next without solving the preceding one), it has turned into a permanent feature of international economic and financial relations.

FROM THEORY TO PRACTICE

Some time ago, the OECD Development Centre convened a meeting with the purpose of discovering the 'secret' of the high growth performance of dynamic developing countries, particularly in East and South-East Asia. Practitioners from Asia distilled ten 'policy secrets' that could explain the success stories in their region. These are the following (Emmerij, 1992):

1. The role of the State and its importance in governing the market, i.e. in getting the economic growth machine moving and keeping it on track. The role of leadership is very important in that respect. This also applies to the private sector.
2. For a country to get on the high road of development, there must be in the society a sense of political and economic urgency. There must be a will to move ahead.
3. There must be a feeling of belonging, a feeling of the group, of solidarity in the country. Civil wars, for example, are the death of economic growth and development.
4. For a country to move onto the high road, it must not take its comparative advantage in terms of factor endowments as given. It must set out to create its own competitive advantages — among others by giving priority to science and technology — in order to eke out niches for exports and thus connect up to the global markets. Human resources, education and training, are of the essence in this connection. And so is the entrepreneur. Countries must create an incentives system to simplify his work and thus make him more productive.
5. The fifth secret is that there must be a balance between agriculture, manufacturing and services. On the bottom rung of the economic

ladder, agriculture must surely come first, but it must also become integrated in a country's overall development strategy.

6. The sixth secret is to try to avoid the excesses of corruption. For this to happen a free press is of the essence. There must be an ethic to promote efficiency; honesty is good for business.

7. The seventh secret is that if a country wants to move ahead, it must get its initial conditions right: for example, liberalization of trade and capital flows should not come at too early a stage; the institutions must be in place (banking, property rights) before policies can have their effect.

8. Moving from one extreme to the other, policy-wise, must be avoided. Extreme ideologies are neither required nor desirable. On the continuum between extremes (export promotion versus import substitution, state versus market, growth versus income distribution), each country must decide where it should situate itself at any given point in time and, even more importantly, get its timing right for the move on the continuum towards one direction or the other, without going too far. Extremes may be spectacular but are seldom effective.

9. The ninth secret is the question of political democracy, economic democracy (in the sense of participatory decision-making processes) and economic efficiency. There is no simple relationship here. There is no clear correlation between political democracy and economic efficiency. Culture and habits are important and no one recipe can be imposed. One can be against something *ex ante*, but admire it *ex post* when and if it works. But there is agreement on one thing: in the longer run, for economic efficiency to be sustainable, political democracy, freedom, incentives are absolutely essential.

10. The final and tenth secret concerns international governance. A country that has shifted its national governance in the above sense — political will, balanced economic and financial policies without going to extremes, balance between political democracy and economic efficiency, etc. — has all its initial conditions right. But if the external environment is hostile things can be very difficult. In other words, good national governance (in the sense here defined) must be accompanied by good international governance. That was also one of the conclusions of Pronk's essay (this volume, Ch. 1).

It must be noted that there is nothing in these policy secrets that is so specific to East Asia that they cannot be transferred to other regions. This is an important conclusion because it has been alleged that East and Southeast Asia are so specific as to make the transfer of their experience impossible. But in order for other regions, like Africa, to be able to absorb this experience, capacity building is vital. The point of entry on the road to increased and sustained economic growth is capacity building, including the areas of management and leadership (Emmerij, 1992).

What lessons for development aid can be deduced from the East Asian experience, as summed up in the above ten policy secrets? The first lesson is to be distrustful of moving from one extreme to the other in terms of development strategies. Balance is the key. 'One size fits all' prescriptions are rarely good recipes. There must be a balance specific to each country between political democracy and economic efficiency, between the role of the state and that of the market, between national and international governance, between export promotion and import substitution, and so forth.

The second lesson is that capacity and institution building are crucial prerequisites for new policy moves to have a chance of success. Development aid can be of special use here. The role of leadership, of entrepreneurship, and their identification are of prime importance.

The third lesson is to help countries to create their competitive advantages, to assist them in identifying niches in regional and global markets. The creation of Centres of Excellence — particularly in science and technology, but also in management studies — must be stimulated.

The fourth lesson is that it is difficult, if not impossible, to move along a very wide front where everything must be tackled simultaneously. There is a real danger of growing paralysis in the 'flight forward' approach of development aid, culminating in the Amartya Sen 'all or nothing' development strategy, as set out above. But maybe — in order to remain within the general message of this article — the problem must be put as a choice between two possibilities. Should we assist countries that have identified one or two points of entry in their development approach and, therefore, go for a sequential policy of 'first things first', or should we favour countries that want to tackle everything simultaneously, that want to advance over a very wide front? Could it be true that the former approach would instil bad habits that tend to become permanent? For instance, if a country (like China) goes for economic efficiency first and puts political freedom on hold, could this become a permanent situation? The historical evidence in East Asia would tend to give a negative answer to this question. Korea, for example, curtailed trade unions and political parties for quite some time. But with the increase in individual incomes, the pressure in favour of political democracy and trade union freedom became stronger and Korea has moved a long way in the right direction.

The fifth lesson, also mentioned in Pronk's chapter, is that development aid must shift from project aid to sector and programme aid in order to do away as much as possible with the paradox of effective project aid and ineffective macro-economic performance. There must be consistency between micro-, meso- and macro policies. How many times has one observed the results of pilot projects being wiped out by one stroke of the macro-pen on the twelfth floor of a steel and glass ministerial building? The results of the pilot project are good, but the country is going down the drain. This does not mean that good projects in the midst of bad macro-economic and financial policies, are to be neglected. They can be important for thousands of individuals. But if good national governance has a meaning, it must also imply consistency between different levels of decision taking.

The sixth lesson raises another consistency problem, namely the consistency between development aid and other instruments of international economic and financial policy. In other words, it raises the question of international good governance. The industrial countries have been preaching liberalization of international trade, but they themselves do not practise what they preach. They apply 'pragmatic liberalism'. Pure liberalism is an exportable doctrine for use by third-world innocents (Jaguaribe, 1997). Pragmatic liberalism is reflected, for instance, in the agricultural policies of the OECD countries, in their Multi-Fibre Accord, in the import obstacles put in the way of developing countries, such as technical conditions and dumping accusations. This must come to an end, as must the pressures for premature trade liberalization on countries that are not yet ready for it. Finally, the anarchy of un-coordinated development aid must be stopped in favour of a much more united and consistent approach by countries, international organizations and non-governmental organizations alike.

CONCLUDING REMARKS

Development is decidedly possible, as many countries — although not enough — have shown. Development aid must become more effective by moving toward sector and programme forms of assistance; by becoming more co-ordinated regionally and internationally; and by becoming the catalyst for a consistent set of international economic and financial policies.

On the donor side, development aid must become more and more concentrated regionally and globally by giving a larger role to the European Union and the United Nations. On the recipient side, aid must be used more for regional projects, such as for infrastructure (communications, transport, pipelines), regional Centres of Excellence at the graduate and research levels, capacity building, and so on. The European Union must endeavour to practise what it preaches and relax agricultural policies and, in general, to liberalize its international trade policies. The United Nations must concentrate on achieving changes in global governance that advance worldwide economic growth and at the same time diminish the global income gap (Emmerij et al., 2001). This can be achieved by introducing the long debated Economic Security Council that must start its activities by setting up a global social contract (Petrella, 1995).

REFERENCES

Blaug, Mark (1968) *An Introduction to the Economics of Education*. New York: Pergamon Press.

Burnside, C. and D. Dollar (1997) *Aid, Policies and Growth*. Washington, DC: The World Bank.

Chenery, H. B. and M. Bruno (1962) 'Development Alternatives in an Open Economy: The Case of Israel', *Economic Journal* 72 (March): 79–103.

Chenery, H. B. and A. M. Strout (1966) 'Foreign Assistance and Economic Development', *American Economic Review* LVI(4i): 679–733.

Denison, E. (1962) *The Sources of Economic Growth in the United States and the Alternatives before Us*. New York: Committee for Economic Development.

Emmerij, Louis (1992) 'High Growth Performance Experience of Dynamic Developing Economies'. Paris: OECD Development Centre (mimeo).

Emmerij, Louis (2001) 'Goed Bestuur als Voorwaarde voor Ontwikkelingshulp?', in Wetenschappelijke Raad voor het Regeringsbeleid, *Ontwikkelingsbeleid en Goed Bestuur*. The Hague: Sdu Uitgevers.

Emmerij, Louis, Richard Jolly and Thomas Weiss (2001) *Ahead of the Curve? UN Ideas and Global Challenges*. Indianapolis: Indiana University Press.

Fishlow, A. (1972) 'Brazilian Size Distribution of Income', *American Economic Review* LXII(2): 391–402.

Galenson, W. and H. Leibenstein (1955) 'Investment Criteria, Productivity and Economic Development', *Quarterly Journal of Economics* (August).

Gerschenkron, A. (1952) 'Economic Backwardness in Historical Perspective', in B. Hoselitz (ed.) *The Progress of Underdeveloped Areas*, pp. 3–29. Chicago, IL, and London: Chicago University Press.

Gerschenkron, A. (1962) *Economic Backwardness in Historical Perspective*. Cambridge, MA: Harvard University Press.

Hirschman, A. O. (1958) *The Strategy of Economic Development*. New Haven, CT: Yale University Press.

Houthakker, H. S. (1965) 'On Some Determinants of Savings in Developed and Underdeveloped Countries', in E. A. G. Robinson (ed.) *Problems in Economic Development*. Proceedings of a Conference held by the International Economic Association. London: Macmillan.

ILO (1969) *Annual Report of the Director General*. Geneva: ILO

ILO (1972) *Employment, Incomes, and Equality: A Strategy for Increasing Productive Employment in Kenya*. Geneva: ILO.

Jaguaribe, H. (1997) 'Economic Development in Latin America and the Need for a Theory of Functional Elites', in Louis Emmerij (ed.) *Economic and Social Development into the XXI Century*, pp. 207–10. Baltimore, MD: The Johns Hopkins University Press.

Kuznets, S. (1955) 'Economic Growth and Income Inequality', *American Economic Review* XLV(1): 1–28.

Lall, S. (1976) 'Conflicts of Concepts: Welfare Economics and Developing Countries', *World Development* 4(3): 181–95.

Lewis, W. Arthur (1954) 'Economic Development with Unlimited Supplies of Labour', *The Manchester School of Economic and Social Studies* (May).

Lewis, W. Arthur (1955) *Theory of Economic Growth*. London: Allen and Unwin.

Little, I .M. D. and J. A. Mirrlees (1968) *Manual of Industrial Project Analysis*. Paris: OECD Development Centre.

Little, I. M. D. and J. A. Mirrlees (1974) *Project Appraisal and Planning for Developing Countries*. London: Heinemann.

Little, I. M. D., T. Scitovski and M. F. G. Scott (1970) *Industry and Trade in some Developing Countries*. London: Oxford University Press.

Myrdal, G. (1970) *The Challenge of World Poverty*. London: Penguin.

Nurkse, R. (1952) 'Some International Aspects of the Problem of Economic Development', *American Economic Review* XLII(2): 571–83.

Petrella, R. et al. (1995) *Limits to Competition*. Boston, MA: MIT Press.

Ranis, G. and J. Fei (1961) 'A Theory of Economic Development', *American Economic Review* LI(4): 532–65.

Ranis, G. and J. Fei (1964) *Development of the Labor Surplus Economy: Theory and Practice*. Irwin: Homewood.

Rosenstein-Rodan, P. N. (1943) 'Industrialization of Eastern and South-Eastern Europe', *Economic Journal* 53.

Rostow, W. W. (1956) 'The Take-Off into Self-Sustained Growth', *Economic Journal* LXVI (March): 23–48.

Rostow, W. W. (1960) *The Stages of Economic Growth: A Non-Communist Manifesto*. Cambridge: Cambridge University Press.

Seers, D. (1969) 'What are we Trying to Measure?' Lecture presented at the 11th SID World Conference, New Delhi (November).

Sen, A. K. (1972) *Guidelines for Project Evaluation*. New York: United Nations/UNIDO.

Sen, A. K. (1997) 'Development Thinking at the Beginning of the XXI Century', in Louis Emmerij (ed.) *Economic and Social Development into the XXI Century*, pp. 531–51. Baltimore, MD: The Johns Hopkins University Press.

Sen, A. K. (1999a) 'Democracy as a Universal Value', *Journal of Democracy* 10(3): 3–17.

Sen, A. K. (1999b) *Development as Freedom*. New York: Knopf.

Singer, H. W. (1970) 'Dualism Revisited: A New Approach to the Problem of the Dual Society in Developing Countries', *Journal of Development Studies* 7(1): 60–75.

Solow, R. M. (1956) 'A Contribution to the Theory of Economic Growth', *Quarterly Journal of Economics* 70: 65–94.

Stewart, Frances (1985) 'The Fragile Foundations of the Neoclassical Approach to Development: A Review of Deepak Lal "The Poverty of Development Economics"', *Journal of Development Studies* 21(2): 282–92.

Streeten, Paul (1987) 'Structural Adjustment: A Survey of the Issues and Options', *World Development* 15(12): 1469–82.

Tinbergen, J. and H. C. Bos (1965) 'A Planning Model for the Education Requirements of Economic Growth', in *OECD Econometric Models of Education*. Paris: OECD.

Turnham, D. and I. Jaeger (1971) *The Employment Problem in Less Developed Countries: A Review of Evidence*. Paris: OECD Development Centre.

UNDP *Human Development Report* (annual publication). New York: Oxford University Press.

Williamson, John (1990) *Latin American Adjustment: How Much Has Happened?* Washington, DC: Institute of International Economics.

Williamson, John (1997) 'The Washington Consensus Revisited', in Louis Emmerij (ed.) *Economic and Social Development into the XXI Century*, pp. 48–61. Baltimore, MD: The Johns Hopkins University Press.

Chapter 4

Aid is an Unreliable Joystick

Gus Edgren

It is easy to agree with Jan Pronk (Chapter 1) that aid is not a primary agent of development but more like a catalyst. If one wants to be self-critical, full awareness of this truth did not penetrate the aid agencies until the late 1970s, when some major aid recipients began to produce deteriorating outcomes in terms of governance and growth. Awareness of the second great truth came much later — that a positive effect from this catalyst can be achieved only in the circumstances of macro policies which create a positive framework of incentives for development. As in the field of chemistry, from which the parallel is drawn, aid can be completely useless and sometimes even harmful if the proper conditions for catalysis do not exist.

Forty years of experience in development co-operation ought to have taught us to define these conditions, and to avoid repeating the mistakes made in the years of innocent and idealistic experimentation. In some fields, such organizational learning has taken place both among aid agencies and their counterparts in developing countries. But it is striking that a number of the cardinal mistakes in development aid keep being repeated time and again, despite overwhelming evidence of past disasters (Berg, 2000; Edgren, 2000). One reason for this is the political element at all levels of the aid relationship, which economists until rather recently tried to define away as 'institutional factors' or 'market imperfections'. It is impossible to understand the low effectiveness of the global foreign aid industry if these political elements are not fully integrated into our model for analysing the role of aid in support of development. Together with economic and institutional factors, they have created a very complex and partly perverse incentive structure for the whole industry, and this structure exercises a heavy influence on the outcome of the catalytic process.

The incentive system works in different directions at different levels of the development co-operation industry. Jan Pronk mentions foreign policy objectives such as maintaining peace, stability and spheres of influence. While many of us in the OECD group of donors were preoccupied with development objectives like the ones which are the main focus of Pronk's paper, it was evident that foreign policy objectives had such an impact on aid flows that more funds went to strategically important countries (Israel,

Egypt) than to the least developed recipients. At the end of the Cold War some observers (particularly in the US) saw the end of foreign aid as we know it, since there was no longer any need to prop up weak allies. But the political counterweight to performance-based aid allocation is still strong. Spheres of interest are still being maintained, although with less largesse. Within the EU, aid is often seen as a compensation to former colonies for their lack of access to European export markets. And three or four decades of development co-operation have created bonds which are even stronger than the old colonial ones. The Nordic countries, for instance, have great qualms about pulling out of even the worst-performing African partner countries in view of all the material resources and 'social capital' that have been invested in the relationship. From the social scientist's point of view, all of this will reduce effectiveness in reaching development objectives like economic growth, poverty reduction, gender equity and good governance.

The aid industry is very fragmented and is characterized by a host of 'market imperfections'. Donor agencies have an upper hand in determining which products should be sold and at what price, and the recipients often have a vested interest in accepting less than optimal solutions. If one looks at the industry as a global mechanism for transferring resources from rich countries to poor, one could be excused for thinking that the Devil himself could not have created a more infernal system. Each donor agency is trying to reach its own objectives, which often differ to some degree from those of other donors, and from those of the recipient government. When all agents are simultaneously trying to get the most out of the system for themselves, the results produced by the system as a whole are bound to be less than effective. It is particularly counter-productive that the system allows individual agencies to boast of good results for their own projects while these 'successes' are being achieved at the expense of the total outcome. International agencies like the UN and the IFIs have done a lot to bring about correspondence of both objectives and approaches, but the fact remains that the aid industry is a very flawed instrument for the task of promoting development.

Political factors weigh heavily in the explanation of development outcomes, more heavily than could be imagined by economists in the 1960s and early 1970s — even Myrdal's *Asian Drama* (1968) underestimated or misjudged them. Development-oriented governments were often supported by weak coalitions of interests, which soon found it more profitable to resort to predatory practices, leading to war and instability. When donors and IFIs used their aid leverage to force economic reforms on weak coalitions or predatory tyrants, it often backfired, since powerful groups were better served by more accommodating policies. Only in the late 1980s did the development agencies begin to include the political power structures in their analytical framework. UN agencies and IFIs still had difficulties into the 1990s in speaking openly about governance and power structures, but both

UNDP's *Human Development Reports* and the World Bank's *World Development Reports* now explicitly examine political aspects and foundations for poverty reduction and good governance. Building stable political coalitions in support of development is a painstaking task with a very long time perspective, and it rarely involves large transfers of money. In fact, large aid transfers may sometimes even counteract the building of such coalitions by allowing leaders to postpone difficult but necessary decisions on the distribution of resources.

After the end of the cold war, with political collapses leading to famines, the big powers allowed wars and large refugee movements to run their course longer and more often than before. This had two important consequences for development co-operation. First, even donors that gave high priority to development objectives felt obliged to step up their support to poor performers, in order to protect their earlier investments in those countries. Second, aid was increasingly attracted to humanitarian purposes like disaster relief and support of refugees. Such human disasters of course occurred more often in countries with a poor governance record. In these circumstances, it was easy for Peter Boone (1994) to show that aid was negatively correlated with performance.

The poor performance of major African aid recipients like Tanzania and Zambia in the late 1980s and early 1990s did eventually influence political opinion in development-oriented donor countries like Sweden. But it coincided with reduced public support for foreign aid among the younger generations and led to generally reduced aid allocations and to a shift from development aid to humanitarian causes, some of which were found closer to home in the Balkans and the former Soviet Union. Although it was a declared Swedish aid policy to favour low-income countries, particularly in Africa, the 1990s saw a dramatic shift of bilateral aid flows from poor to middle-income countries. Africa's share, which had remained around 50 per cent during the 1980s, dropped to 40 per cent during the 1990s, and the share of LLDCs in Swedish aid disbursements also fell. The conflicts and disasters during that decade increased the political pressure on donor agencies to allocate more of their funds to humanitarian aid than to development purposes. This tendency has not weakened, and it may well be argued that it has already changed the business of foreign aid forever — or at least, for the foreseeable future.

After four decades of development co-operation, a syndrome of *aid dependency* has emerged as a development problem of its own. The majority of low-income economies have become heavily dependent on foreign aid in the sense that most of their public investments and a large share of the current expenditure is regularly financed by concessional resource transfers (Lensink and White, 1999). Economists tend to treat this problem as a simple lack of resources, a variant of the two-gap model of the 1960s. Increased domestic resource mobilization or foreign direct investment could reduce and eliminate dependency in a matter of years, as in the case of South

Korea in the 1960s. But the present syndrome involves behavioural patterns which deepen the problem beyond a mere lack of resources.

In chemistry, a catalyst is a substance which changes the velocity of a chemical reaction while not being changed itself. Clearly, the parallel between foreign aid and chemistry does not cover the last clause: development co-operation has had considerable impact on the donors, as well as on the aid relationship itself. The impact has important positive aspects, such as learning about development problems and understanding other cultures. But there is another side to the influence that aid has exercised on the donors. Agencies have developed vested interests in showing success in partner countries, and they depend on their government counterparts in those countries to produce the 'indicators' of this success. Agency officials feel under pressure to disburse resources allocated to their programmes, and this pressure is passed on to their counterparts and to project personnel. A principal–agent analysis of this system suggests that the incentives in this relationship are perverse and information flows asymmetrical (Killick et al., 1998). Donor agents are as dependent on continuing an activity as the recipient agents, and their principals find it increasingly difficult to bring about policy changes.

On the recipient side, the dependency syndrome expresses itself through a pattern of behaviour which leaves all initiative to the donor and where donors are expected to pay for everything, including the salaries of civil servants acting in their normal course of duty. Recipients share the donor agents' interest in fast disbursements, positive reports on activities and a continued provision of external support. No plans are made for replacing aid with domestic financing — in fact government officials are under instruction to secure continuation of all major programmes (Catterson and Lindahl, 1999). Even the growing NGO bureaucracy is subject to dependency syndrome, which makes the hope of building independent institutions of civil society ever more remote.

This sketch of how the dependency syndrome works is stereotypical and it is not patterned on any particular country. But forces like these are at work in poor and aid-dependent recipient countries, and they affect the way foreign aid functions in support of development. They also affect the chances of using aid as a reward for policy reform, regardless of whether this reward is given *ex ante* as in the case of the IFI's adjustment lending, or *ex post* as advocated by some economists who are displeased with the large number of governments which sign up for an adjustment programme, take the first tranche and then revert to their bad old ways (Svedberg, 1995). The dependency syndrome has a strong tendency to reward poor performers rather than good ones (Sobhan, 1996), which adds to the biases already mentioned.

A remedy for some of these ills is already well-known, namely programme aid or sector-wide approaches (SWAPs). Debt cancellation is the simplest of those methods, easy to administer and potentially with a direct link between performance and reward. The problems in applying this measure are mostly external: the burden sharing among donors and the potential moral hazard in giving the wrong incentives to other borrowers. Programme lending triggered by agreed policy reforms (a more palatable form of the conditionality-leveraged SAPs of the 1980s) is probably the most effective instrument for linking aid disbursements to good development governance, but if it is to deliver such results, all major donors have to support it, either through joint financing or by adapting their own operations to an agreed policy framework. A disadvantage that many donors see in this approach is that it does not easily identify their aid with specific development outcomes. The SWAP could accommodate this interest, representing a compromise between policy lending and project support. A SWAP could be designed in ways which allow the partners to do away with many of the donor-specific niches and regulations on which perverse incentive structures are currently based.

This has all been common knowledge for many years, and yet these approaches to development co-operation have so far attained very limited coverage. Some donor agencies are very enthusiastic about them, while others are reluctant or even hostile, and some are prohibited by their principals from taking part in such exercises. On the recipient side, resistance is often strong at the operational level, where departmental rivalries and financial interests manifest themselves in delaying tactics. These obstacles will not go away just because we make solemn declarations in DAC or the UN: they are deeply embedded in the political setting as well as in the administrative structures on both sides. Hence, how to deal with those obstacles remains a more urgent question than what we may be able to achieve when they have been completely overcome.

Meanwhile, the real world continues to show cases where rewards have been given either too late, too soon, or for the wrong reasons. David Dollar (1998) showed how aid flows to Zambia grew while the policy framework steadily deteriorated during the 1980s. In Vietnam, the reverse was true: dramatic economic reforms took place in 1989–93, coinciding with a drastic fall in foreign aid as the Soviet Union folded up and only UN agencies and a few Western donors remained.

The case of Vietnam is a good illustration of the difficulty the donor community faces in using foreign aid to reward or punish recipient performance. Vietnam carried out a major reorientation of its external trade from the Soviet Bloc to the convertible area, liberated its price and production controls to fend off a threatening hunger crisis, and changed the management of its monetary system to become compatible with the market economies of the region, all without any major concessional aid transfers. UNDP gave crucial help in bringing Vietnamese economic managers in contact with Western expertise, but the hard and risky decisions on transforming the economy were taken by the Vietnamese leaders themselves, and without any help of soft credit facilities.

Would this transformation have been faster or less painful if it had been facilitated by large aid transfers? Ironically, such transfers started to pour in from 1994 onwards, when the *doi moi* reforms were all but completed, and some observers were in fact concerned that the surge of new aid helped the government to postpone a necessary second round of reforms (Dapice, 1999; Edgren, 2001). The sense of urgency that was present among decision-makers during the 1989–93 reform period might not have been so acute if foreign aid had been as ample as it is today. The economic managers were aware that the reforms *must* succeed, or the country would slide deeper into an already serious crisis. The reforms moved very quickly, and it is hard to believe that new sources of aid could have been injected fast and accurately enough to act as an incentive for deeper reforms, even if adjustment facilities had been available.

On the other hand, the reforms had serious negative effects on the social sectors, where Vietnam had earlier been one of the best performers among the low-income countries. The dissolution of the commune system led to a near-collapse of the rural health services, which did not pick up until seven years later, when both the economy and external aid to the health sector had grown. Considerable suffering could probably have been avoided if the donor community had been able and willing to support the economic reforms with transition aid to the health sector. But again, political factors weighed in. At the time, Vietnam was out in the cold because of its military presence in Cambodia. As so often before, the donors gave priority to their own domestic politics over the objectives of development.

My conclusion from all these ponderings is that foreign aid is much too unwieldy an instrument for providing sharp and timely incentives to policy reform. It is not a joystick by which donors can manipulate macroeconomic or political outcomes. Too many diverse objectives drive too many donor agencies, and their working methods are slow and complicated. The aid relationship often provides signals which run counter to the reform agenda. Donor agencies can indeed help increase the understanding of how the economy works and what will be the outcomes of different policies, and they can advocate strategic approaches to any development problem at hand. But aid flows cannot be turned on and off like a faucet, and very rarely can they be directed to projects and programmes with an accuracy that sends clear signals to policy-makers and economic managers. Only in a medium-to long-term perspective can aid flows respond to changes in performance. And as experience shows us, this time perspective is often very long indeed.

REFERENCES

Berg, E. (2000) 'Why aren't Aid Organizations Better Learners?', in J. Carlsson and L. Wohlgemuth (eds) *Learning in Development Cooperation*, EGDI 2000:2. Stockholm: Swedish Ministry for Foreign Affairs.

Boone, P. (1994) 'The Impact of Foreign Aid on Savings and Growth'. London: London School of Economics (mimeo).

Catterson, J. and C. Lindahl (1999) *The Sustainability Enigma: Aid Dependency and the Phasing out of Projects, The Case of Swedish Aid to Tanzania.* EGDI 1999:1. Stockholm: Swedish Ministry for Foreign Affairs.

Dapice, D. (1999) 'Debt Prospects for Vietnam — Problems Ahead Without Better Policies'. HIID paper prepared for OECF mission to Hanoi, Hanoi.

Dollar, D. (1998) *Assessing Aid: What Works, What Doesn't, and Why,* New York: Oxford University Press for the World Bank.

Edgren, G. (2000) 'Fashions, Myths and Delusion: Obstacles to Organisational Learning in Aid Agencies', in J. Carlsson. and L. Wohlgemuth (eds) *Learning in Development Cooperation,* EGDI 2000:2. Stockholm: Swedish Ministry for Foreign Affairs.

Edgren, G. (2001) 'How Effective is ODA in Vietnam?' Department of Evaluation and Internal Audit Working Paper 2001:1. Stockholm: Sida.

Killick, T., R. Gunatilaka and A. Mar (1998) *Aid and the Political Economy of Policy Change.* London and New York: Routledge.

Lensink, R. and H. White (1999) *Aid Dependence: Issues and Indicators,* EGDI, 1999:2. Stockholm: Swedish Ministry for Foreign Affairs.

Myrdal, G. (1968) *Asian Drama: An Inquiry into the Poverty of Nations.* New York: Pantheon.

Sobhan, R. (1996) 'Aid Dependence and Donor Policy', in *Aid Dependency: Causes, Symptoms and Remedies.* Stockholm: Sida.

Svedberg, P. (1995) *Kan bistånd till Afrika bli effekivt? (Can aid to Africa become effective?),* Ekonomisk Debatt 23:6. Stockholm: Elanders Gotab.

Chapter 5

Development Goals, Governance and Capacity Building: Aid as a Catalyst

John Degnbol-Martinussen

The essay by Jan Pronk provides an excellent point of departure for discussing a wide range of issues relating to aid and international development co-operation. I find it difficult to disagree with Pronk on any of his major explicit points. However, it may be useful to discuss some of his arguments in greater detail and add new perspectives that emerge from approaches proposed by UNDP as well as from the policies adopted by Denmark and the other Nordic countries.

GROWTH AND OTHER DEVELOPMENT OBJECTIVES

A substantial part of Pronk's essay deals with aid impact in terms of aggregate economic growth. Several studies are reviewed, some of which have focused on the direct linkages between the quantity of aid and indicators of economic performance, while others have incorporated the effects of 'good' and 'bad' policies. Pronk argues that it is not possible to establish an unequivocal relationship between aid and a net increment to overall economic growth in developing countries. Similarly, there are no simple causal relationships between types of policies and economic performance. In his opinion it is preferable to look at specific forms of aid, to specific countries, in specific circumstances, in order to reach specific objectives: 'These are the only aid evaluations that make sense'.

With these observations Pronk helps set an agenda for broader studies of aid impact. What I would like to add in this context is that much of the international debate so far has been focusing far too much on impact in terms of aggregate growth and income growth. The impact of aid should also be assessed against other development objectives — those adopted by donors as well as by recipient countries. As there is no universal agreement on development objectives this calls for much greater variation in the design of impact studies. However, considering the broad consensus today among many donors, both bilateral and multilateral, on human development as the overriding goal it may be appropriate to elaborate on the above points with reference to this development objective.

The concept of human development has been worked out by prominent economists including Amartya Sen, Paul Streeten and Mahbub ul Haq, who believed that increased incomes should be regarded as a means to improve human welfare, not as an end in itself (Haq, 1995; Sen, 1988; Streeten, 1981, 1994). Under the leadership of Mahbub ul Haq a group of scholars prepared the first comprehensive report on human development, for UNDP, in 1990 (UNDP, 1990). They defined development as a process of enlarging people's choices. According to Haq, the defining difference between the concepts of economic growth and human development is that the former focuses exclusively on the expansion of only one choice — income — while the latter embraces the enlargement of all human choices, whether economic, social, cultural, or political (Haq, 1995: Ch. 2). It could be argued that an increase in income would enhance all other choices as well, but this is exactly what Haq and others have questioned by asserting that the causal link between expanding income and expanding human choices depends on *the quality and distribution of economic growth*, not only on the quantity of such growth. They have argued that a link between income growth and human welfare has to be created consciously through public policies that aim at providing services and opportunities as equitably as possible to all citizens. This cannot be left to market mechanisms, which are of their essence unfavourable to the poor, to the weak, and to the vulnerable (ibid.: Ch. 12).

Rejecting the automatic link, however, should not be taken to imply a rejection of the importance of economic growth. Haq very carefully tries to balance the argument by pointing, on the one hand, to the need for growth in poor societies, in order to reduce mass poverty, and on the other, to the fact that the distribution of growth and the manner in which available resources are being utilized often matter more to the poor than aggregate growth of national income and production.

The human development school initially drew attention primarily to choices in three essential areas: the opportunity to lead a long and healthy life; the opportunity to acquire knowledge; and the opportunity to have access to resources needed for a decent standard of living. To these, a number of other dimensions and aspects were later added, and the name of the concept itself grew from 'human development' to 'sustainable human development', in order to highlight the importance of sustaining all forms of capital and resources — physical, human, financial, and environmental — as a precondition for meeting the needs of future generations.

Adopting human development in one form or another as the overriding goal has wide-ranging implications for international development co-operation as well as for the design of impact studies. There is no space here to go into detail, but some of the implications will be noted in the following discussions of governance issues and criteria for allocating aid among countries.

Governance — For Growth and Human Development

As Pronk argues, better governance should be seen not only as a precondition for effective utilization of aid and development, but also as a development objective in itself. With the broadening of the perspective from growth to human development, however, the issue of 'good governance' becomes more complex.

Much of the debate on governance in the 1980s focused on government in the narrow sense and on *outcomes*, rather than *processes*. The emphasis both in economic analyses and among the major donor agencies, including the World Bank, was on questioning the relevance and effectiveness of the state for the advancement of economic development. A prevailing view looked at the state as part of the problem, rather than as part of the solution to the challenges faced by developing countries. The economic role of the state should be minimal with as much as possible left to the market and the private sector. To the extent that the state was required to play a role in economic development it should be restricted to providing 'good' (or 'sound' or 'prudent') macroeconomic policies. In social development, poverty alleviation and environmental protection, this prevailing view allowed for some necessary state interventions, but only where the market and private initiative were clearly lacking in terms of pursuing these objectives.

Since about 1990, the debate has changed markedly in at least four major respects (cf. *IDS Bulletin*, 1998; UNDP, 1999; World Bank, 1997):

(a) Issues of governance are now dealt with in a broader perspective, in the framework of rules, institutions and practices that set limits and provide incentives for individuals, organizations and firms. Positions in the debate are argued not only in terms of the appropriate role of the state, but also in terms of the nature of the institutional arrangements that promote or obstruct development.

(b) Governance is now seen as *both outcomes and processes*. The technocratic approach with its emphasis on 'good policies' and economic effectiveness is still there, but much more attention is paid to processes through which policies are shaped and implemented. New issues have been added, such as people's participation, the ways in which governments interact with citizens, and responsiveness, along with concern for transparency, accountability and the combating of corruption.

(c) The acknowledgement of the diversity of development goals that was already present in the 1980s has been taken more systematically into account when discussing governance. Hence, it is now more widely recognized that different types of governance are required for promoting different types of development goals. The policies and institutional arrangements best suited to promote aggregate economic growth are not necessarily the same as those required for promoting human development and poverty alleviation.

(d) Democratization and the observance of human rights have been assigned much higher priority as development objectives in their own right. Several bilateral donors, including the Nordic countries, have explicitly stated these objectives in their development policies. Others apply somewhat different terminology such as 'people's participation' or 'bringing the state closer to the people', but basically the approaches adopted by most donor agencies reflect a genuine concern for promoting democratization as well as increasing the capability and capacity of the state for advancing economic and social development.

UNDP, among other agencies, has contributed to these changes in the prevailing discourse on governance. In particular, UNDP has played a major role in shaping the agenda for governance that comprises two major elements: a concern for the processes of citizen participation and involvement in decision-making; and a concern for outcomes in terms of policies and institutional arrangements that promote human development. Moreover, while the World Bank and some other agencies have remained sceptical about decentralization and devolution of powers to local authorities, UNDP strongly promoted the idea of pursuing people-centred, participatory development also at the local level.

The discourse on governance has changed significantly since the early 1990s. The same applies to the practices pursued in several countries, as reflected primarily in the wave of democratization observed in both developing countries and societies in transition. However, there is little indication that governance practices have improved in any general manner as seen from a human development perspective. Most governments pursue policies that are not conducive to promoting human development. Most states remain weak and incapable of implementing effectively the human development policies that they may have formally adopted. Some states have essentially broken down, or are close to breaking down as a result of serious internal conflicts and civil strife. Consequently, there is a widespread need for advocacy in order to promote the adoption of human development policies and an even greater need for institution- and capacity-building for improved governance in support of human development. Countries torn apart by internal conflicts need special types of comprehensive support.

UNDP has, in recent years, worked within a general definition of governance as the exercise of political, economic and administrative authority in the management of a country's affairs at all levels; comprising the complex mechanisms, processes and institutions through which citizens and groups articulate their interests, mediate their differences and exercise their legal rights and obligations (UNDP, 1997). Within this general definition of governance, UNDP has focused on aspects of particular relevance for promoting broad-based human development.

Moving beyond the explicit formulations proposed by UNDP (and other organizations adhering to the human development approach), one may summarize the types of foreign aid to governance and institutional development in three broad categories:

(a) *Enhancing state capacity* for 'reaching down and reaching out' to citizens and providing services in support of human development. Focus areas may include improved public administration; resource mobilization; better utilization and management of public resources; and decentralization and strengthening of local self-governance.

(b) *Strengthening state–society linkage institutions and procedures*, especially those that provide for broader popular participation and dialogue between the authorities and organizations representing civil society. Focus areas could include consolidation of democratic institutions and procedures, comprising electoral systems and parliament; and judicial reform, rule of law and observance of human rights.

(c) *Empowerment of civil society organizations* that give people a voice and provide them with instruments of collective action. In a sense, this implies enabling citizens and their representatives to 'reach up' to the authorities and influence decision-making.

With the added attention to governance and institutional development, the whole discussion of selectivity and conditionality that Pronk takes up in Chapter 1 of this volume is seen in a different context.

PERFORMANCE-BASED VERSUS NEEDS-DRIVEN APPROACHES

In much of the previous debate on criteria for allocation of aid among countries the focus was on 'good' policies. The extreme position implied that aid should be provided only to countries with 'good' macro-economic policies. This was justified with reference to studies which indicated that foreign aid was only effective in countries with such policies. In recent years, other types of conditionalities referring to economic performance have been added. Pronk provides an excellent review and discussion of these policy- and performance-based approaches. He ends up by arguing against pre-selection of countries based on what they have already done and achieved. Instead, he argues in favour of a special type of conditionality that implies assisting countries to improve policies and performance (cf. also Dijkstra, 1999).

While I agree with his conclusion, I would like to add two points. First, the narrow approach proposed by, especially, the World Bank and USAID cannot be justified within the broader conception of development goals outlined above. Giving preference to growth-promoting policies and performance in terms of aggregate growth implies disregarding, at least to some extent, other development goals such as poverty alleviation, human development and democratization. Second, favouring the 'good performers', although often increasing the effectiveness of aid in narrow economic terms, cannot be justified based on a needs assessment. The developing countries which are in greatest need of foreign aid are generally characterized by mass poverty, weak states, and weak institutional foundations for a market economy and a democratic political system. Rather than punish these countries for their poor performance, they should be offered comprehensive assistance to establish the basic conditions for both 'good governance' and socio-economic development. Considering the very different requirements in developing countries this further implies a differentiating approach, as also argued by Pronk with respect to policy advocacy. What is good policy in one country may not be appropriate in another where conditions, problems and potentials are different. The same applies to aid in support of institutional development (for a more elaborate discussion, see Degnbol-Martinussen and Engberg-Pedersen, 1999: Ch. 13).

It seems that thinking within the World Bank has been moving in similar directions in recent years, with more attention given to the need for different types of policies (for example Stiglitz, 1998). At the same time, the Bank is increasingly helping to build or strengthen the institutions so that they become more capable and better-equipped to provide services efficiently and equitably, rather than just focus on direct supply of physical infrastructure and social services.

Several bilateral donors have been moving in the same directions within the framework of sector-support programmes. With this new modality of development co-operation, donors can concentrate on certain sectors that are worthy of support even where macroeconomic policies are not in keeping with donor priorities. Sector-support programmes further provide a basis for more comprehensive assistance, ranging from policy advice through capacity building to actual implementation and provision of services. Danish foreign aid in these areas may be used as an illustration of both the inherent strengths of sector-wide approaches and the challenges faced.

Sector-Wide Approaches: Challenges Facing Danida and Other Donors

According to Danida's 'Guidelines for sector programme support' this kind of development assistance strategy pays more attention than the traditional project approach to comprehensive and sector-wide policy development and institutional, organizational and financial management issues. The sector-support strategy emphasizes the processes necessary to achieve sustainable results and impact (Danida, 1998).

The decision to move away from project assistance and instead concentrate on sector programme support is commendable from several points of view. Heavy reliance on donor-driven and donor-managed projects in the past often prevented Danish aid from having its intended impact, because it was not sufficiently integrated into national policies and programmes, and because the projects were generally too small to really affect the administrative and socio-economic setting in which they were implemented. As a corollary, it was difficult to achieve sustainability. Moreover, project assistance could often be 'captured' by ruling elites and used by them to promote their own special interests. This form of targeted intervention, with a limited geographical coverage and specified target groups, could be used to reward friends and supporters, or to buy goodwill from powerful opposition groups upon whose support the ruling elites were dependent. The implied submission of economic development considerations under political power considerations was regularly addressed by Danida through careful appraisals and project design, but the potential capture of projects by ruling elites put constant pressure on resources, even in the course of implementation.[1] Sector programme support is much less exposed in this regard, because of its size and complexity, and at the same time it is more likely to achieve a sustainable impact.

On the other hand, successful sector programme support depends heavily on national policies and the administrative and institutional set-up in recipient countries. In this respect, Danida's task is not easy, because the overwhelming majority of the selected programme countries have weak states.[2] These states are characterized by incoherent and inefficient administrative agencies with little capacity to promote economic and social development. They are weak also in the sense that they are unable to implement in a consistent manner the policies decided. Moreover, they are often controlled by small political power elites. For sector programme support to become effective, such states need considerable capability and capacity development and significantly improved accountability. We will return to this below.

Another challenge facing Danida in societies with weak states is how to promote national ownership and responsibility for development assistance efforts without compromising the poverty alleviation objective and the cross-cutting priorities concerning gender equality, environment, and democratization. Very few of the weak states with which Danida co-operates share the priorities of Danish aid policies. This is clearly evident with respect to the poverty alleviation objective — which should not surprise donor agencies, since the governing elites in poor societies are generally not dependent on the poor majorities of their populations, not even in formally democratic societies. The governing elites have no vital interests in transforming their states into pro-poor developmental states. Rather, they have vital interests in using the public resources at their command to retain power. For this they depend on the military, the civil bureaucracy and other politically and economically powerful groups. Poor, uneducated and

---

1. Several development researchers, including Robert Bates and Göran Hydén, have emphasized the tendency for projects to be captured by elites and used by them in their patronage systems (cf. Martinussen, 1997: 17).
2. The terminology used here is taken from Evans (1989). The concept is similar to Gunnar Myrdal's 'soft state'.

unorganized people are of little relevance in this context. The real options for Danida, therefore, are either to compromise on Danish aid objectives or to pressure recipient country authorities to change their own priorities. Similarly, with respect to institutional development strategies, Danida may either accept continued poor performance of the public institutions or interfere with their structures, procedures and priorities, again possibly undermining national ownership.

These are challenges faced not only by Danida but by aid agencies in general, since societies with weak states are also the societies most dependent on foreign aid. With the intensified demands from donors concerning both policies and institutional structures and procedures, there is a tendency to reduce the room for manoeuvre of the political leadership of weak and poor states. This may be fully justified from a perspective of poverty alleviation, but the outcome is difficult to accommodate within the ideology of national ownership.[3] Paradoxically, the specific demands concerning recipient government policies and their administrative set-up may further interfere with processes of democratization, because weak states may be forced to pay more attention to accommodating donor demands than to demands from their own citizens and their (often weak) organizations. When aid accounts for a substantial proportion of government income, often more than half, accountability may easily shift from citizens to donors.

There is little doubt that sector programme support must give much more emphasis to institutional development and capacity strengthening in the large majority of recipient countries. What these countries need is not only more resources but also institutions, procedures and incentive structures that can help them utilize the resources more effectively and efficiently. This implies a shift of attention in aid strategies from transferring resources to building capabilities and capacities. This is in line with Pronk's emphasis on aid as a catalyst, but in a somewhat different sense than in his essay. Given the above paradox, it is important that institutional development strategies also aim at strengthening interaction between state and society.

INSTITUTIONAL DEVELOPMENT AND CAPACITY BUILDING

The basic idea embodied in institutional development assistance is to strengthen institutional capabilities (in a qualitative sense) and capacities (in a quantitative sense) to perform the functions assigned to them. What this means in detail varies considerably, depending on the functions assigned, the development objectives, and the strengths and weaknesses of the institutions and organizations concerned. Certain basic differences relate to the two main stages of *policy formulation* and *implementation*.

---

3. These issues have been discussed more thoroughly by Doornbos (1995).

Decision-making and policy formulation comprise several logical steps such as articulation of demands, selection and aggregation of demands, setting of objectives and priorities, and elaborating strategies for implementation. The important issues for the elaboration of institutional development strategies include the following. What are the most important institutions that shape decision-making and policy formulation in the sectors given priority by the donors? How can the donors provide assistance to strengthen the institutions concerned?

In keeping with most donors' development assistance policies and priorities, special attention must be given to how best to contribute to making the institutions (a) more open to citizen involvement in decision-making; (b) more transparent and accountable; (c) more responsive to the needs of poor people; (d) more attentive to the needs of women; and (e) more attentive to environmental considerations. Again, however, these donor concerns should not be transformed into conditionalities. Rather, as Pronk argues at a more general level, they should be embodied in the kind of assistance offered to the recipient countries.

In the second major stage of the policy process, the focus shifts to the implementation of agreed policies and the institutions involved here. This implies looking at the government agencies at national and local level that play a role in policy implementation; this may include resource mobilization, allocation of resources, and service delivery. It also implies, however, looking at private sector institutions and civil society organizations to the extent that these contribute to — or in different ways affect — implementation and service delivery within the sectors concerned. Poorly functioning public sector institutions are often major constraints at the stage of policy implementation, and in some cases these institutions may even pursue strategies of their own. They may obstruct implementation of agreed policies. They may distort implementation by acting in accordance with narrow interests of the government officials involved, for instance when bribes are demanded for providing services to citizens. Similar distortions may be brought about by agents in the private sector and even in civil society organizations.

Based on this, institutional development assistance must aim at improving the effectiveness and efficiency of policy-implementing institutions and organizations and thus render them more capable of delivering services, especially to the poor. Further, they should promote service- and client-oriented behaviour and help reduce the scope for corruption and other distortions in policy implementation.

When addressing these issues it needs to be borne in mind that effectiveness and efficiency cannot be treated as socially neutral. Improving service delivery needs to be tackled in a differentiating manner — as seen from the perspective of the rich as well as from the perspective of the poor. It is evidently more costly for the state to deliver services to the poor, whose financial contribution may be marginal at best. Moreover, the commonly adopted institutional development strategy of relying on external pressure to improve institutional performance may not be very helpful in developing countries where the resource-weak segments of the population are not in a position to exert any major pressure on the state agencies or, especially, on commercial undertakings. In other words, external pressure — although in principle one of the available means to enhance institutional performance — may in practice result in socially biased delivery. This must be taken into account when designing sector programmes. More specifically, it may lead to continued direct involvement of donors in service delivery to the poor.

CONCLUDING REMARKS

I have argued here that more attention should be paid to other development goals, beyond aggregate growth and increasing per capita incomes. This implies that the impact of aid should also be assessed against these other goals, particularly against the goals of poverty alleviation, human development, gender equality, sound environmental management, and democratization. I have further argued that aid should be seen as a catalyst and as co-operation aimed at bringing about the conditions for sustained economic and social development rather than as a reward for compliance with donor-recommended policies. Consequently, aid should be allocated mainly in accordance with needs. These needs relate to both access to resources, and capabilities and capacities for utilizing the resources available which, by implication, means that more attention should be given to institutional development. Comprehensive sector-wide support is preferable to project assistance and is feasible even in an environment where macro-economic policies are not optimal. Pronk covered these aspects and issues in his essay: this article has merely sought to elaborate on some of them with particular reference to the aid policies and institutional development strategies of UNDP and the Nordic countries.

REFERENCES

Chenery, Hollis and T. N. Srinivasan (eds) (1988) *Handbook of Development Economics*, Vol. I. Amsterdam: North Holland.

Danida (1998) *Guidelines for Sector Programme Support*. Copenhagen: Ministry of Foreign Affairs.

Degnbol-Martinussen, John and Poul Engberg-Pedersen (1999) *Bistand. Udvikling eller afvikling. En analyse af internationalt bistandssamarbejde*. Copenhagen, Mellemfolkeligt Samvirke.

Dijkstra, Geske (1999) 'Programme Aid, Policies and Politics. Programme Aid and Conditionality'. Stockholm: Sida.

Doornbos, Martin (1995) 'State Formation Processes under External Supervision: Reflections on Good Governance', in Olav Stokke (ed.) *Aid and Political Conditionality*, pp. 377–91. London: Frank Cass in association with EADI.

Evans, Peter (1989) 'Predatory, Developmental and Other Apparatuses: A Comparative Political Economy Perspective on the Third World State', *Sociological Forum* 4(4).

Haq, Mahbub ul (1995) *Reflections on Human Development*. New York: Oxford University Press.

IDS Bulletin (1998) Special Issue 'The Bank, the State and Development. Dissecting the 1997 World Development Report' in Alison Evans and Mick Moore (eds), *IDS Bulletin* 29(2).

Martinussen, John (Degnbol) (1997) *Society, State and Market. A Guide to Competing Theories of Development*. London and New Jersey: Zed Books.

Sen, Amartya (1988) 'The Concept of Development', in H. Chenery and T. N. Srinivasan (eds) *Handbook of Development Economics*, Vol. I. Amsterdam: North Holland.

Stiglitz, Joseph E. (1998) 'More Instruments and Broader Goals. Moving towards the Post-Washington Consensus'. WIDER Annual Lecture 2. Helsinki: World Institute for Development Economics Research.

Streeten, Paul P. (1981) *First Things First. Meeting Basic Human Needs in Developing Countries*. New York: Oxford University Press for the World Bank.

Streeten, Paul P. (1994) *Strategies for Human Development. Global Poverty and Unemployment*. Copenhagen: Handelshøjskolens Forlag/Munksgaard International Publishers.

UNDP (1990) *Human Development Report 1990*. New York: Oxford University Press.

UNDP (1997) 'Governance for Sustainable Human Development'. New York: UNDP Policy Document.

UNDP (1999) *Human Development Report 1999*. New York: Oxford University Press.

World Bank (1997) *World Development Report 1997*. New York: Oxford University Press.

Chapter 6

Age of Reverse Aid: Neo-liberalism as Catalyst of Regression

James Petras and Henry Veltmeyer

INTRODUCTION

From the outset the study of international economic development has been closely tied to questions about the need for, and the potential contributions of, what has become known as 'overseas development assistance' (ODA) or, in more common parlance, 'foreign aid'. Connected to the central question that has been raised in the literature about the link between development and aid are questions about the motivations behind the giving of aid, the link between aid and political power, and evaluations as to the positive and negative benefits to recipients. Within the debates that have surrounded these and other such questions,[1] two analytical perspectives can be distinguished, each with numerous permutations, one based on what could be termed *realism*, the other *idealism*. In addition, there is a less scientific, more ideological tradition, with little reference made to substantive empirical findings or the need to explain the dynamics of ODA. In this tradition the discourse on foreign aid takes the form not so much of description and explanation as policy prescription, focusing less on donor motivations or the politics of aid, and more on programme/project objectives and presumed benefits to recipient countries. Such works tend to refer only loosely to the analytical or evaluative literature, and then only to seek justification for prescribed policies. It is in this tradition that we would place the essay of Jan Pronk (this volume, Ch. 1), although his ideas and theoretical perspective are suggestive of both idealism and structuralism. In this tradition we also find countless position papers that rehearse the familiar litany of World Bank

---

1. There are other issues that are periodically addressed in the literature. They include questions as to where and how aid should be allocated, the relative merits of (micro) project versus (macro) programme aid, the so-called 'fungibility' of aid, and questions as to the most appropriate or effective agency, partnerships, etc. However, these and other such questions (see, for example, Chenery, 1967; Chenery and Carter, 1973; Little and Clifford, 1969; Singer, 1965) generally do not arouse much debate or controversy.

(and IMF) doctrine: that all developing countries' problems are internal; the aim of policy reform is to get the prices right and to roll back the government sector. This kind of 'reform', it is asserted, 'increases equity as well as efficiency', and 'conflict between stabilisation and structural adjustment goals is minimal' (Mosley et al., 1991: xvi).

ODA entails critical issues that re-surface from time to time, in a seemingly never-settled academic and policy debate among liberals and structuralists, neo-liberals and neo-structuralists. To join this debate in its latest twist, this paper places aid in an alternative theoretical perspective, one based in part on a politically *realist* view of the process involved and in part on a critical perspective on the agency of bilateral and multilateral aid as well as the international flows of private capital. In this regard we reflect critically on the ideas advanced by Pronk and the broader community of policy-makers and academics of which he is a part. In terms of these ideas, the issue is not whether aid contributes directly to the development process but its role in promoting and ensuring the adoption of neo-liberal free market reforms. In this connection, we argue that if 'aid' is a catalyst of anything it is not of development but of regression. What are viewed as 'good policies' by both neo-liberals and self-styled 'truly confident' social liberals (or idealists) like Paul Mosley et al. (1991) and Jan Pronk in effect, if not by design, serve as an aid to imperialism, and they have served as such at a social cost borne primarily by people in the developing countries.

AID AS A CATALYST OF REGRESSION

The term 'foreign aid' is at best ambiguous, disguising more than it reveals. Bilateral and commercial loans, as well as loans from the international financial institutions (IFIs), require the payment of principal and interest. Even if interest rates on IFI loans are lower than those of the commercial banks, the onerous repayment conditions have had a devastating impact on policy-making in developing countries.

Jan Pronk's essay argues that aid is not the prime mover of development but a catalyst. However, the fundamental question is: aid as a catalyst for what and for whom? For an answer to this question we turn to what could be termed a politically 'realist' approach to aid (Hayter, 1971, 1985; Magdoff, 1969). In this approach the role of aid is examined in its historical context, looking at how foreign aid is part of the arsenal of policy instruments used by aspiring hegemonic states to conquer markets and promote the interests of their capitalist classes against competitors and their nationalist and socialist opponents. The 'idealist' view, in contrast, conceives of aid as a disinterested policy, divorced from the interests of the capitalist class and guided by humanitarian concerns, democratic values and economic well-being. More often than not, idealists dissociate their discussion of aid from the historical–structural context in which it is embedded and argue in terms of normative values and the degree of compliance with those values by the recipient country.

There are two types of realist critics of the 'idealist' approach. Market fundamentalists like Milton Friedman (1982) condemn foreign aid because it is said to subsidize 'statism' and hinder market forces that are better able to deal with economic and social problems. Some critics, on the other hand, argue that 'aid' from hegemonic countries undermines Third World development by catalysing structural changes that undermine popular sovereignty, facilitate vast outflows of funds and undermine locally based productive units.

In the following we adopt the *realist* perspective that foreign loans and grants are a catalyst of 'reverse aid' — designed to benefit the donor countries. In the context of widespread implementation of a neo-liberal model of capitalist development, aid has contributed towards what could be termed 'bad governance' (neo-authoritarianism, large-scale chronic corruption and external subordination), extending and deepening social inequalities, and generating conditions of global poverty as well as economic stagnation and volatility in the international flows of capital.

Historical–Structural Context of Aid

In the colonial era, following the initial period of bloody conquest and pillage, the 'authorities' set about to combine 'normal' capitalist exploitation with foreign aid to educate and train a class of indigenous clients in the lower levels of the colonial administration and armed forces. The purpose was to maximize the extraction of surplus while reducing the level of conflict and the costs of empire. While the colonial state incurred these costs, private investors reaped the profits. The point is that 'aid' can only be understood in the context of pillage and exploitation — of extractive colonies and industrializing empires, of underdevelopment and development (Hayter, 1971, 1985; Magdoff, 1969). Aid, in this context, served as a catalyst for stabilizing imperial rule and facilitating the transfer of riches, with the overall result of what we call 'reverse aid' — net gain for the imperial country or centre at a cost borne by the colonies.[2]

The targets of aid were usually not the peons in the plantations and mines but local collaborators. The beneficiaries of aid were usually not some undifferentiated 'colony' or 'nation' but village chieftains, tribal leaders,

---

2. In its Final Resolution, the recent UN Conference on Racism held in Durban, South Africa, indicted various forms of colonialism and imperialism, including slavery, the slave trade, and the dispossession and super-exploitation of indigenous peoples, as the original or underlying 'cause' of the racist structures and practices in place today all over the 'developing world'.

landlords and, more recently, trained military officials. This colonial experience of conquest and aid raises several theoretical issues of continuing relevance. First, 'aid' subsumes commercial transactions beneficial to the 'donor' (or, more precisely, the colonial power). Secondly, the 'benefits' of aid to the recipient (colonized) countries are not equitably distributed among the different classes, social strata, gender-based or ethnic groups; most benefits accrue to collaborators of the elite. Thirdly, the asymmetrical political and economic linkages between 'donors' and 'recipients' lead to long-term, large-scale transfers of wealth, property and power that favour donors, while the transfer of any benefits to recipient regimes is independent of the claims and perhaps 'good intentions' involved. Under the systemic forces (unequal power and exchange) at work, the class nature of the 'donor' regimes (the dominance of multinational corporations and financial institutions), the political–economic matrix of aid (protectionism and subsidies in the 'donor' country and 'neo-liberalism' in the recipient country) and the subordinate nature of the recipient or client regime (macroeconomic policy dictated by IFI technocrats), foreign aid serves as a catalyst for aid reversal — a transfer of wealth to the 'donor countries'.

Neo-Mercantilist Imperialism, Catalyst of Regression

While academics of the Left and Right write of 'neo-liberalism' or 'free markets', interstate relations between Europe and the US, on the one side, and the Third World and ex-Communist countries on the other, are characterized by neo-mercantilism. Euro-US state interventionist policies generally protect, subsidize and advance the interests of 'capital' while the so-called 'developing countries' are constrained to reduce subsidies, eliminate trade barriers, privatize state enterprises and end state regulation.[3] Aid is conditioned on the compliance with this neo-mercantilist agenda.

Euro-US takeovers of lucrative assets and current account deficits lead to increased borrowing and spiralling overseas debt payments, with predictable social consequences. There is also abundant evidence that the elite members of the donor countries' multinational banks and corporations have benefited enormously from this new imperial neo-mercantilist system. If we look at the relations between the US and Latin America over the last quarter of a century in terms of the political–economic matrix of aid, we find considerable evidence of 'reverse aid'. The new imperial mercantilist order is built on five pillars: large-scale, long-term interest payments on external debt; massive transfers of profits derived from direct and portfolio investments; buy-outs and takeovers of lucrative public enterprises and financially

---

3. This bias is clearly reflected in the rules of trade set up by GATT and, since 1994, by the WTO.

troubled national enterprises, as well as direct investments in sweatshops, energy resources and low wage manufacturing and service industries; the collection of rents from royalty payments on a wide range of products, patents (especially pharmaceuticals) and cultural commodities; and favourable current account balances based on the dominance of US corporations and banks in the region (Petras and Veltmeyer, 1999). Between 1990 and 1998 US banks received over US$ 329 bn in interest payments, while the total debt grew from US$ 476 bn to US$ 698 bn, debt payments amounting to about 30 per cent of total export earnings.[4]

Foreign direct investments (FDI) during the 1990s increased 600 per cent over the previous decade. Most of this FDI has been used to purchase the assets of privatized public enterprises and private firms. Together such acquisitions account for 68 to 75 per cent of all FDI in the region. Conditionality[5] imposed by bilateral and multilateral lending agencies facilitated the purchase of Latin American enterprises. Aid, in other words, was the catalyst for the transfer of national public to private foreign monopolies. In a three year period, 1995–97, over US$ 157 bn in profits were repatriated, according to the Economic Commission for Latin America (Petras and Veltmeyer, 1999). Thus aid and the conditions imposed on aid recipients facilitate the takeover of lucrative enterprises and the repatriation of billions of dollars to aid the global accumulation process and the expansion of the US empire.

Royalty payments and licence fees are another source of reverse aid. During the 1990s approximately US$ 13 bn was transferred from Latin America to the US. Royalties are the fastest growing sector of US returns (Petras and Veltmeyer, 1999). Foreign aid is conditioned on Latin American regimes accepting the US definition of 'intellectual property rights' and supporting Washington's battle to include 'intellectual property' clauses in the GATT or World Trade Organization.

The role of trade between the US and Latin America is of equal importance as the cumulative returns to US investors and lenders. Close to a fourth of US exports are directed towards Latin America, which is the only region in the world that provides the US with a significant current account surplus. Foreign aid or loans by the IFIs influenced by the US (World Bank, the IMF, IDB) is conditioned on the lowering of trade barriers in Latin America, ending subsidies and cutting back public spending on social services. The result has been a loss of market shares by local enterprises, rising unemployment and underemployment, and the de-industrialization of some

---

4. Both these figures and the data that follow, together with their sources, are presented and analysed in Petras and Veltmeyer (1999).
5. As noted by Mosley et al. (1991: xiii) conditional aid (particularly in the form of the concessional loans provided by the World Bank) entails not just the usual conditions of repayment but rather conditions that the recipient government must perform by changing some of its previously chosen or preferred policies.

countries with the proliferation of sweatshop or low wage assembly plants where the workers are denied the right to organize, access to social welfare benefits and protection of labour legislation. Thus the meagre flows of foreign aid not only fail to compensate for the outflow of wealth; they are a catalyst of reverse aid.

The cumulative benefits of profits, royalty and interest payments, favourable trade balances and takeover of public enterprises form the matrix in which foreign aid is embedded and shape its function and impact. The trade limitations explicit in the US neo-mercantilist relations to Latin America are evident in the controls and quotas imposed on the importation of beef, textiles, steel, sugar, and a host of other commodities from Latin America that compete with US producers. In contrast, US aid is tied to Latin American purchases of US products which are priced as much as 30 per cent higher in some cases. Thus aid is a catalyst for promoting uncompetitive 'first world' enterprises and mercantilist relationships.

As for the social impact on Latin America of aid it is clear that neo-mercantilism, and the flow of private capital and foreign aid, have had a regressive impact on developments in Latin America. From the perspective of the recipient countries, particularly the working classes, the urban poor and peasants, ODA, like other international resource flows, has led to economic stagnation, poverty and declining income. Under the facilitating conditions of what Pronk and others regard as 'good policy', aid, in both its multilateral and bilateral forms, has led to what realistically can be termed 'pillage', and to a drastic deterioration of living conditions for much of the population. This regression is evident in a whole range of indicators of socio-economic 'development', including a general decline and at times steep fall in the value of wages,[6] a deepening and extension of social inequalities in the distribution of wealth and income,[7] and the further spread of poverty.

With regards to the latter, not even the World Bank's efforts to reduce the incidence of poverty by statistical fiat (defining as poor only those with incomes of less than two dollars a day — one dollar for those in extreme poverty) have succeeded in disguising either the extent and scope of the problem, or its root causes.[8] Even by the Bank's controversial and con-

---

6. The fall relates to both average and minimum wage rates, which, according to the ILO (see Khor, 1995: 45) fell a minimum of 40 per cent in one decade (from 1985 to 1995) for most countries, up (or down, rather) to 94 per cent in the case of Colombia and 67 per cent in Brazil.

7. On the growth of social inequalities in the distribution of income over the course, and as a result of, IMF and World Bank policies of stabilization and structural adjustment see, inter alia, ECLAC (1998), Khor (2000) and Morley (2000).

8. In the literature on this issue, a distinction is sometimes made between old forms of poverty rooted in structures deeply embedded in Latin America's history and new forms that are clearly associated with the stabilization and structural adjustment policy measures implemented over the past two decades. On this see Bulmer-Thomas (1996), Lustig (1995), and Veltmeyer and Petras (1997, 2000).

Table 1. Share of Wages in National Incomes, Selected
Countries Latin America (percentages)

	1970	1980	1989
Argentina	40.9	31.5	24.9
Chile	47.7	43.4	19.0
Ecuador	34.4	34.8	16.0
Mexico	37.5	39.0	28.4
Peru	40.0	32.8	25.5

Source: CEPAL (various years).

servative new measure, poverty affects over 40 per cent of the growing population in Latin America, a considerable increase over the rate of poverty in 1982, on the threshold of Latin America's turn towards the World Bank's 'new economic model'.[9]

Underlying these and other regressions in living or social conditions can be found a number of 'structural' changes associated with the shifts in government policies induced by the policy conditions of aid. Table 1 presents one of these changes for the first decade of neo-liberal structural reforms.[10] Other changes are reflected in widespread social conditions associated with increasing disparities in the distribution of wealth and income, falling wages, deteriorating health, a rise in the rate of unemployment and the proliferation of low incomes that UNRISD (see Khor, 1995), among others, attributes to the social effects of globalization and structural adjustment, the policy conditionalities of 'aid' in access to 'international financial resources'. Even economists associated with the World Bank and the IMF have admitted the general failure of structural adjustment policies — and

---

9. Over the entire period of structural adjustment and globalization, 1983–2000, Latin America has produced poor people at twice the rate of total population growth: 44 per cent and 22 per cent respectively. According to the UNDP (1996), those living in poverty increased from 40 per cent of the total population in 1980 to 44 per cent in 1986 and a staggering 62 per cent in 1993, after ten years of structural adjustment and five years of a widely-declared war on poverty — viz. the 'new social policy' (NSP) targeted at the extremely poor.

10. In this context, the transfer of income from wage-earners to non-wage earners in most countries in the region has been dramatic: in 1980 wages represented almost 40 per cent of the national income, 34 per cent in 1990 and 32 per cent by 1996 (CEPAL, various years). Table 1 shows that in some countries the process has been particularly brutal, the share of wages in national income falling below 20 per cent. This 'development' is reflected in the relative regression in living standards for the majority of working people in the region over the course of the past two decades of free market 'structural reform'. In this connection, by the end of the 1990s the standard of living for most of the population in virtually every country was lower than that achieved in the 1970s.

the associated 'marriage of the free market and liberal democracy' (Dominguez and Lowenthal, 1996) — in terms of economic growth, increased indebtedness[11] and a pronounced tendency towards 'social exclusion', or the restriction of 'benefits' to a relatively small privileged part of the population (Bengoa, 2000: 44ff).[12] What can be said with confidence is that the 'good policies' adopted by so many governments in Latin America and elsewhere in exchange for/as a condition of, aid are to a large degree responsible for the evident regression in social conditions across the region.

The neo-mercantilist/neo-liberal model has provoked greater inequalities, decreasing the share of labour and increasing the share of corporate wealth, especially foreign capital, in national incomes. In this context, foreign aid has served as a catalyst for hastening the introduction of the free market policies responsible for the maldistribution of national income. The social component of foreign aid had little, if any, effect in compensating for the loss of income shares and for the slashing of social allocations in national budgets.

The tendency for donors to channel funds for poverty alleviation through NGOs also has had little positive effect, as an earlier study by one of the authors demonstrated in the case of Bolivia (Arellano and Petras, 1994). On the contrary, foreign aid directed toward NGOs has undermined national decision-making, given that most projects and priorities are set out by the European or US-based NGOs. In addition, NGO projects tend to co-opt local leaders and turn them into functionaries administering local projects that fail to deal with the structural problems and crises of the recipient countries. Worse yet, NGO funding has led to a proliferation of competing groups, which set communities and groups against each other, undermining existing social movements. Rather than compensating for the social damage

11. A 1999 study by the Washington-based group, Development Gap, found that for more than 70 African and Asian countries during the 1990s, the longer that a country operates under structural adjustment the worse the debt burden, leading it to conclude that SAPs 'are likely to push countries into a tragic circle of debt, a weakened domestic economy and greater debt' (Development Gap, 1999).

12. Most analysts here (see, for example, Lustig, 1995; Rodrik, 1999) take the view that this regression of socio-economic conditions is directly attributable to the neoliberal policies of structural adjustment promoted by the World Bank. The solution — from the point of view of the World Bank's 'friendly critics' such as the scholars associated with UNDP and UNICEF — is a 'redesign of these policies' to reflect this 'new understanding' (see Salop, 1992) or the creation of a social investment fund, a new poverty-targeted social policy, or a social net to 'protect the most vulnerable groups' — those likely to be most deeply hurt and unable to defend themselves from the inevitably negative effects of the structural adjustment process (Morales-Gómez, 1999; Tulchin and Garland, 2000). Others, such as De Soto (2001: 33), President of the Institute for Liberty and Democracy and author of *El Otro Sendero*, see the 'mystery of capital' ('what makes capitalism a private club open to only a privileged few?') not in policy terms but as Karl Marx did — as a built-in structural feature of all capitalist systems: the legal institution of formal property relations that restricts access to society's productive resources to members of one social class.

inflicted by free market policies and conditions of debt bondage, the NGO-channelled foreign aid[13] complements the IFIs' neo-liberal agenda.

Policy Improvement and Good Governance

The implementation and administration of neo-liberal policies and foreign aid has provoked the protest of great masses of people. Conditionality loans from the IMF and World Bank have provoked general strikes and popular uprisings in the interior of Argentina, marches and highway blockages by peasant and Indian organizations in Ecuador and Bolivia, and numerous other forms of mobilization. In order to avoid public debate and popular consultations, which would be likely to reject the neo-liberal package of foreign takeovers and foreign aid, regimes have frequently resorted to ruling or legislating by decree. Ex-Presidents Menem, Salinas and Mahuad of Argentina, Mexico and Ecuador, privatized thousands of public firms by decree. Most of Latin America's macroeconomic policies are designed and enforced by foreign functionaries of the IFIs. Threats and psychological intimidation accompany the implementation of harsh anti-popular, so-called 'economic reforms' and accompanying loans — foreign aid. There is a growth of neo-authoritarianism in which non-elected foreign functionaries and local executive officials (most of them non-elected or representing a small fraction of the electorate) govern. In short, foreign aid strengthens authoritarian tendencies in the executive branches of government, under-mining popular support for the electoral process and representative government, and thus 'democracy'.

To the publicists and promoters of free markets in Europe and the US, effective government and good governance is measured by the ability of client regimes to implement 'unpopular' pro-corporate policies while limiting political protest. In this context, the basic question that needs to be raised regarding 'good governance' is: who governs and for whom? According to the technical criteria of today's 'good governance' theorists, Mussolini's success in making the trains run on time would qualify him as a 'good governor' and qualify his government for foreign aid because of the 'policy improvement' effected.

Foreign aid helps grease the wheels of corruption. For example, aid ostensibly directed to curtail the growth of coca in Bolivia, Colombia and

---

13. According to a recent OECD study (Woods, 2000: 12), in the EC up to US$ 7.3 bn of bilateral aid in 1993 was channelled through NGOs. However, the critical factor is not the volume of aid channelled in this way — at the 1994 UN World Summit for Social Development, then US Vice-President Al Gore announced that half of all US ODA would be so channelled within five years — but the fact that NGOs both in the EC and the US are the executing agents of an aid policy that is closely aligned with the World Bank. On this point see Petras and Veltmeyer (2001a).

Peru and encourage alternative crops is pocketed by corrupt military and civilian elites. Large-scale, long-term corruption has exceeded the high historical benchmarks in the past. Bribes to state officials paid by leading US and European CEOs to secure favourable terms during privatization proceedings are the norm. Foreign aid is not the cause of corruption in many cases but the catalyst. Aid is based on policy improvements and 'good governance', essentially the implementation of the free market agenda. It is the large-scale transfer of public property that is the source of corruption. In that sense, aid serves as a catalyst for policies that have almost inevitably been accompanied by corruption (Bounds, 2001).[14]

Foreign Aid and Land Reform

Despite occasional official rhetoric, foreign aid has never financed a comprehensive land reform programme in Latin America. In fact, most loans by the IFIs and bilateral financing are directed at 'modernizing' large-scale commercial landlords at the expense of landless farm workers and peasants. Brazil is a case in point. Loans from USAID, the World Bank and the IDB led, during the decade of the 1990s, to the reconcentration of land, the displacement of over one million peasant families and an increase in the unemployment of landless rural workers. Given the free market farm policies, the number of bankrupt small farmers has increased geometrically, undermining the micro-projects of European funded NGOs. The major group attempting to reverse the tendency toward land concentration and promote land reform is the Rural Landless Workers Movement (MST) which receives no official aid because of its organized land occupation policy which has benefited over 250,000 landless families. In order to undercut the MST, the Brazilian government has used the stick and the carrot: on the one hand, over fifty rural landless worker activists have been assassinated by the military police under the regime of Fernando Cardoso, scores have been jailed and tortured and thousands of squatter families have been evicted; on the other hand, the World Bank has designed and financed an Agrarian Bank which lends money to peasants to facilitate their purchase of land.[15] The commercial or market driven 'land reform', however, puts heavily indebted 'family farmers' in a disadvantageous position in relation to the flood of cheap imports resulting from the free market policies and without

---

14. See also a recent study on corruption and development in the Congo-Zaire by Bamuamba (2001), who takes issue with the World Bank's view (see, for example, Rose-Ackerman, 1998) that the development process, particularly in sub-Saharan Africa, is vitiated by problems of mis-management and corruption rather than structural problems generated by neoliberal policies of structural adjustment.
15. On this triple offensive of the Brazilian government against the MST see Petras and Veltmeyer (2001b).

resources to purchase inputs to become competitive. Foreign aid here has a political purpose in undermining successful indigenous social movements.

Neo-Structuralism, Aid and the Contemporary Crisis in Latin America

In the early 1990s many neo-liberal regimes and IFIs, particularly the World Bank, recognized that market excesses led to increased social polarization and poverty and threatened to bring down the free market architecture. Policy-makers and agency heads argued that the state had a role to correct the excesses by securing financing loans to finance micro-economic projects, poverty programmes and self-help community development. This new approach, dubbed 'neo-structuralism' by its practitioners, has been in place in varying degrees in all Latin American countries for a decade. Yet unemployment in Brazil and Argentina is at its highest levels since the Great Depression. At the time of writing, the Argentine economy is on the verge of collapse. Brazil, Colombia and Mexico are in a deepening recession. Under-employment and the informal sector range from 30 to 80 per cent in most of the Andean countries. The outflows of capital accumulated by the rich are fuelled by bailouts financed by overseas funding agencies. Exorbitant interest rates to attract foreign investors to pay an unpayable foreign debt exclude any credit to small and medium size producers.

The reason for the social and economic failures of 'neo-structuralism' is that it accepted the basic postulates of the free market economy and believed that loans to 'civil society' could ameliorate local conditions and spread throughout the economy. In reality, the social problems the neo-structuralists addressed were not on the margins of the free market policies and, therefore, could not be corrected via microeconomic projects. Rather, the problems were found on the very free market model: the elite class configuration of the state, the monopoly economic organization of the productive system and the polarized class structure, all of which required comprehensive transformations in order to achieve the general goals of equity, good government and economics. Neo-structuralists choose not to confront these deep structural conditions, seeking instead to work within the free market system and provide it with a social dimension and a human face (ECLAC, 1998). The evidence to the contrary is increasing throughout the region: Latin America's living standards are declining, the economy is regressing, debt default is pending and extra-parliamentary popular opposition to neo-liberalism, neo-authoritarianism and neo-mercantilism is growing.

CONCLUSION

The essay by Pronk at best provides a limited and flawed perspective on the dynamics of foreign aid. At worst, it helps obfuscate the real issues involved.

Aid from the hegemonic regions has a long and inglorious history as a policy tool, from colonial times to the present, to facilitate the conquest of markets, finance compliant elites, undermine indigenous insurgence and substitute ineffectual small-scale projects for comprehensive and needed egalitarian structural changes. In the present period, loans and aid have operated as catalysts for dismantling public social welfare programmes, undermining national markets and facilitating the Euro-American takeover of strategic sectors of the economy. Aid is not the 'cause' of crises and regression; rather it sets in motion a series of policies that are promoted by, and benefit, the elite — policies that can only be viewed as 'good' from the perspective of these elites. In the current matrix of power and corporate economic interests, aid has been successful in promoting Euro-American expansion and the regression of living standards in Latin America. In this context, the issue is not aid or no aid, but aid under what conditions and in what socio-historical and political context?

REFERENCES

Arellano, Sonia and James Petras (1994) 'Non-Governmental Organizations and Poverty Alleviation in Bolivia', *Development and Change* 25(3): 555–68.
Bamuamba, Clement (2001) 'Political Corruption in Congo-Zaire: Its Impact on Development'. MA Thesis, Halifax: St. Mary's University.
Bengoa, José (2000) *La emergencia indígena en América Latina*. México/Santiago: Fondo de Cultura Económico.
Bounds, Andrew (2001) 'Costly Lessons of Central America Bank Reform', *Financial Times* 11 July: 6.
Bulmer-Thomas, Victor (1996) *The New Economic Model in Latin America and its Impact on Income Distribution and Poverty*. New York: St. Martin's Press.
CEPAL (Comisión Económica de America Latina y el Caribe) (annual, various years) *Anuario Estadístico de América Latina y el Caribe*. Santiago: United Nations, CEPAL.
Chenery, Hollis (1967) 'The Effectiveness of Foreign Assistance', in H. B. Chenery et al. *Towards a Strategy for Development Co-operation*, pp. 9-18. Rotterdam: Universitaire Pers Rotterdam.
Chenery, Hollis B. and Nicholas G. Carter (1973) 'Foreign Assistance and Development Performance, 1960–1970', *American Economic Review* LXIII (2): 459–68.
Development Gap (1999) 'Conditioning Debt Relief on Adjustment: Creating Conditions for More Indebtedness'. Report. Washington, DC: Development Gap.
Dominguez, Jorge and A. Lowenthal (1996) *Constructing Democratic Governance in Latin America and the Caribbean in the 90s*. Baltimore, MD: Johns Hopkins University Press.
ECLAC (United Nations Economic Commission for Latin America and the Caribbean) (1998) 'Social Dimensions of Economic Development and Productivity: Inequality and Social Performance'. Santiago: ECLAC (December).
Friedman, Milton (1982) *Capitalism and Freedom*. Chicago, IL: University of Chicago Press.
Hayter, Teresa (1971) *Aid as Imperialism*. Harmondsworth, UK: Penguin Books.
Hayter, Teresa (1985) *Aid: Rhetoric and Reality*. London: Pluto.
Khor, Martin (1995) *States of Disarray: The Social Effects of Globalization*. Geneva: UNRISD.
Khor, Martin (2000) 'Globalization and the South: Some Critical Issues'. UNRISD Discussion Paper No. 147 (May). Geneva: UNRISD.
Little, I. M. D. and J. M. Clifford (1965) *International Aid*. London: Allen and Unwin.

Lustig, Nora (ed.) (1995) *Coping with Austerity: Poverty and Inequality in Latin America.* Washington, DC: Brookings Institution.

Magdoff, Harry (1969) *The Age of Imperialism.* New York: Monthly Review Press.

Morales-Gómez, Daniel (ed.) (1999) *Transnational Social Policies: The New Development Challenges of Globalization.* London: Earthscan Publications.

Morley, Samuel (2000) 'Efectos del crecimiento y las reformas económicas sobre la distribución del ingreso en América Latina', *Revista de la CEPAL* 71: 32–41.

Mosley, Paul, Jane Harrigan and John Toye (1991) *Aid and Power: The World Bank and Policy-Based Lending.* London and New York: Routledge.

Petras, James and Henry Veltmeyer (1999) 'Latin America at the End of the Millennium', *Monthly Review* 51(3): 31–52.

Petras, James and Henry Veltmeyer (2001a) *Globalization Unmasked: Imperialism in the 21st Century.* London: Zed Press; Halifax: Fernwood Books.

Petras, James and Henry Veltmeyer (2001b) *Brasil de Cardoso: Expropriação de un pais.* Petropólis: VOZES.

Rodrik, Dani (1999) *The New Global Economy and Developing Countries.* Washington, DC: Overseas Development Council.

Rose-Ackerman, Susan (1998) 'Corruption and Development', in B. Pleskovic and J. Stiglitz (eds) *Annual Conference on Development Economics,* pp. 35–57. Washington, DC: The World Bank.

Salop, Joanne (1992) 'Reducing Poverty: Spreading the Word', *Finance & Development* 29(4): 2–4.

Singer, H. W. (1965) 'External Aid: For Plans or Projects?', *The Economic Journal* 75(299): 539–45.

De Soto, Hernan (2001) 'The Mystery of Capital', *Finance & Development* 28(1): 29–33.

Tulchin, Joseph and Allison Garland (eds) (2000) *Social Development in Latin America.* Boulder, CO: Lynne Rienner.

UNDP (United Nations Development Programme) (1996) *Human Development Report.* New York: Oxford University Press.

Veltmeyer, Henry and James Petras (1997) *Economic Liberalism and Class Conflict in Latin America.* London: Macmillan Press.

Veltmeyer, Henry and James Petras (2000) *The Dynamics of Social Change in Latin America.* London: Macmillan Press.

Woods, Adèle (2000) *Facts about European NGOs Active in International Development.* Paris: OECD.

Chapter 7

Aid, Conditionality and Development

Ajit Singh

INTRODUCTION

Jan Pronk is an accomplished economist and a highly distinguished public servant. His reflections on aid and development are therefore of particular interest. There is much that I agree with in what he says. However, I find his perspective in the opening essay of this volume too narrow, as he looks at the problem essentially from the standpoint of aid-providing nations. This is of course very useful, especially as it comes from someone of his standing from a small north European country which has a respectable record as a donor. However, Pronk's piece, by and large, omits the concerns of aid-receivers — the developing countries.

These notes aim to complement Pronk's analysis by looking at the question of aid largely from a Third World, but also from a global perspective. While Pronk suggests that the effectiveness of aid depends on the institutions, circumstances and policies of the recipient country, a central argument of this paper is that it depends to a large extent also on the international economic environment which is primarily the creation of developed countries because of their power and economic weight in the world economy. In sum, as will become clear below, my differences with Pronk are not so much about what he has written but rather about what he has not.

POINTS OF AGREEMENT AND DISAGREEMENT

I start with points of agreement. I fully support Pronk's contention that private capital, for the reasons which he gives, cannot wholly replace publicly provided capital, whether the latter is offered in the form of grants or loans. I also agree with his view that aid can have a positive or a negative

---

It is a pleasure to acknowledge my intellectual debt to Ann Zammit in preparing this paper. However, I alone am responsible for the views expressed and the errors which still remain.

impact on the desired goals, by for example, crowding in or crowding out
private investment, but with appropriate policies it can generally be made
positive.[1] I also share his scepticism as to whether econometrics can shed
much light on the effectiveness of aid. This is partly because of the non-
availability of the necessary information, the difficulties of being able to
perform controlled experiments, and changing conditions and circumstances
which cannot always be proxied by econometric variables. Detailed historical
case-studies are more likely to be useful, but of course it is difficult to
generalize from them.

However, on closer analysis, I also have some misgivings about Pronk's
central concept of aid as a catalyst, 'no more, no less'. He concludes his
analysis in the following terms:

> Aid should, therefore, be used primarily as a catalyst, sometimes to help generate other
> resources or gain access to them, sometimes to help create domestic capacity or manage
> conflicts resulting from various forms of unsustainable development. At this juncture, what
> is required is a special focus in aid policy on social harmony, political stability and peace,
> as preconditions for economic growth and development — not the other way round. (this
> volume, pp. 17–18)

This conclusion may, at first sight, seem unexceptional and nothing but
common sense. However, on reflection it raises difficulties from the developing country perspective.

First, for aid to be given as a catalyst there would generally need to be a
presumption that the donor and the recipient agree on some proximate goals
and processes to achieve them.[2] However, what happens to countries which
may require aid because of their poverty, and have either different proximate goals, or wish to use means other than those approved by donors to
achieve them?[3] Will the international community provide no aid at all in
those circumstances? Secondly, and equally importantly, suppose some
particular groups in the recipient country share the donors' aims while many
others do not. As Pronk remarks elsewhere in his article, the process of
development is one which often engenders strife and conflict, and, as he
rightly says, this conflict could be quite intense, sometimes bordering on
civil war. Are the donors to take sides in this political conflict, instead of
letting it be played out on its own terms? Such involvement in another
nation state's political processes requires some ethical or moral justification

---

1. Following Pronk, the term 'aid' is used in this article to connote any form of financial
   assistance, rather than referring to ODA only.
2. Since all governments will say that they have the same ultimate goals as those of the
   donors (for example, reducing poverty), reference here is to proximate objectives such as
   targeting the urban poor for assistance. The processes refer to the means for reaching these
   immediate goals, for example through income supplements, subsidizing urban food prices,
   etc.
3. For example, a country may wish to target peasants instead of the urban poor and use an
   agricultural price-support programme for this purpose.

(discussed further below), particularly in view of the practical reality that foreign intervention may be resented and may lead to opposite results to the ones intended. Pronk is silent on these questions.

I am also somewhat perplexed by Pronk's claim (p. 3) that, in view of donors' lack of knowledge about the countries, incomplete understanding of the processes and other similar features, it is a 'miracle' that aid at times has been a 'spectacular success' as reported by the World Bank (1998). This 'miracle' would, however, appear to have a simple explanation when it is considered in historical perspective, in the light of important elements in the history of the international economy during the second half of the twentieth century. Between 1950 and 1980, developing countries achieved historically unprecedented economic growth, arguably a greater expansion of output during these thirty years than they had in the previous 300 years. The average rate of economic growth of Third World countries rose from 0.5 per cent during the first half of the twentieth century to almost 5.5 per cent between 1950 and 1980 (Patel, 1992). This is what led to the phenomenon of 'emerging markets' and their demonstrated capacity to make effective use of capital and human resources, and to grow at a fast pace. Not only was overall economic growth spectacular, there were impressive gains in health, education and quality of life. The average life-expectancy of a Third World citizen rose from forty to sixty years during this period. Not all developing countries were equally successful in achieving this economic and social progress, as one would expect. However, it is notable that even African countries, which started with much worse initial conditions after their independence from colonialism in the 1950s and 1960s, did quite well for much of this period. Between 1960 and the first oil shock of 1973, GDP per capita in fifteen sub-Saharan African countries grew at a rate of more than 2.5 per cent per annum, and six of these countries were among the twenty fastest growing economies in the developing world (Levitt, 2000).

In these circumstances of fast overall economic growth and social improvement in the South, it would be astonishing if the North's public aid agencies would not be highly successful in some developmental sphere or the other.[4] However, this situation greatly changed with the debt crisis in the 1980s and the much less propitious economic and political climate in the 1990s following the end of the Cold War, as outlined below. For this later post-1980 period, Pronk could well be right but, in the context of his article, his observations about the aid miracle would seem to refer to the earlier period following World War II and the end of colonialism.

---

4. There is no suggestion that aid caused the economic growth, but rather that faster economic growth would have made it more likely that some aid would have had very high social rates of return. However, it is important to note that, at least at the macroeconomic level, evidence and analysis suggest that aid during this period was not inimical to economic growth as some people contend. This issue is discussed further below

AID AND THE EVOLUTION OF THE INTERNATIONAL ECONOMY, 1950–2000

Why were developing countries so outstandingly successful during the first period, that is 1950–80, and what role did aid play in this process?

It is important to recall that the Third World's economic progress was not only exceptional with respect to its own record under colonialism in the previous half century, but also in relation to the historical record of today's developed countries during their period of industrialization, between 1820 and 1900. It is also useful to remember that nobody at the beginning of the period (that is, in the 1950s) expected the South to do so well. Professional economic opinion at the time suggested that, because of their low savings ratios, these countries would barely be able to reach subsistence-level growth rates, or keep in step with the growth of population. As the late W. Arthur Lewis reminded us:

> In 1950...these people (economists and policy-makers) were sceptical of the capacity of LDCs to grow rapidly because of inappropriate attitudes, institutions or climates. The sun was thought to be too hot for hard work, or the people too spendthrift, the government too corrupt, the fertility rate too high, the religion too other worldly, and so on. (W. Arthur Lewis, quoted in Singh, 1994)

Arguably, an important reason for the quantum jump in the South's economic progress during this period lay in the policy autonomy which developing country governments were able to exercise in the post World War II period. Not only did the achievement of political independence help in this process, a critical factor bearing on questions of aid, trade and the whole complex of other elements in North–South relations was the open contention between the liberal capitalist system supported by the US and the Stalinist command economy of the former Soviet Union. This confrontation between the two systems provided space for developing countries to industrialize. It allowed, for example, the latter to play one side off against the other to obtain aid. Thus, when the United States in the early 1950s refused an Indian request for aid to establish a large steel plant, the Soviets stepped in with an offer of an even bigger plant at Bhilai which was to be established in the public sector as the Indian government wished. Subsequently, the UK and Germany helped India with two further public sector steel plants. Even the US relented and helped train hundreds of Indian technicians at US steel plants.

Similarly, Soviet aid to China during the 1950s can be regarded as being given for geo-political reasons. Although in financial terms the total amount of this aid was relatively small, in real terms it must have had a significant impact as it involved training tens of thousands of Chinese students and technicians in Soviet universities and factories. This aid did not compromise China's economic or political autonomy. When there was any danger in that direction in the late 1950s the Soviet aid programme was terminated.

During much of this period of contention between the two systems, aid conditionality even under the IMF was mild. Further, during that period the non-socialist international economic system under the hegemony of the US worked in a way highly conducive to economic development. Between 1950 and 1973 — rightly called the Golden Age — not only were the advanced economies expanding at a rate twice their historical trend rates, but the international economic system recognized the special needs of developing countries.[5]

The principle of special and differential treatment for developing countries was accepted under GATT. They were, for instance, allowed to impose controls on imports of advanced country products while being free to sell their own manufactured products in industrial country markets.[6] Developing countries already had dispensation to impose controls on capital movements under the IMF Articles of Agreement. Importantly, in addition, these countries could at the same time use all the instruments of state industrial policy to assist their corporations in acquiring the capabilities required to be able to compete with the western firms. In sum, during most of the period 1950–80 developing countries benefited not only from the booming economic conditions in advanced countries for their exports, but also most significantly from the policy autonomy of the kind which they did not have in the pre-World War II period under colonialism.

This era, however, came to an end with the debt crisis in Latin America and sub-Saharan Africa in the 1980s. The crisis was brought about in large part by a fundamental change in US economic policy in the late 1970s, a decisive shift towards monetarism engineered by Paul Volcker, the then Chairman of the US Federal Reserve.[7] The change in US monetary policy led to a fourteen-fold increase in real international interest rates along with other unfavourable outcomes for developing countries (for example, a fall in the demand for their products and a huge terms-of-trade shock).

The debt crisis also changed the relative balance of power against developing countries. Whereas in the 1970s many of them were vociferously demanding a new international economic order, in the 1980s the debt crisis reduced them to being supplicants before the IMF. The upshot was a massive increase in conditionality being imposed on large parts of the developing world in terms of the Washington Consensus edicts. In return for balance of payments support, countries were asked to privatize, to

5. On the Golden Age of industrial economies, see Glyn et al. (1990), Maddison (1995) and Singh (1995).
6. Thus, for example, the highly successful East Asian countries such as Korea were export-oriented and were able to export a wide range of products while, in many sectors of the economy, maintaining strict controls on imports from advanced countries.
7. For an analysis of the debt crisis in the South in the 1980s and the reason why it affected Latin America much more severely than the Asian countries, see Singh (1993) and the literature cited therein.

deregulate and essentially follow neo-liberal economic policies. Conditionality increased further in the 1990s with the demise of the former Soviet
Union. Overt and blatant political conditionality (multi-party democracy,
human rights and good governance) was added to the onerous 'reform'
programme of the Washington Consensus. Conditionality was ratcheted up
still further in the wake of the Asian financial crisis of 1997. These hitherto
outstandingly successful economies were told that their economic and
political systems needed fundamental changes. Assistance from the IMF to
cope with the crisis was conditional on changing their labour laws, their
corporate governance, and the nature of the relationship between banks,
business and government towards an arms-length, Anglo-Saxon pattern.

Thus, developing countries today are overwhelmed by economic and
political conditionality attached to economic assistance from the North.
This is, therefore, a central issue for them as far as aid (whatever form it
takes) is concerned — a subject which unfortunately does not receive any
explicit consideration in Pronk's article. Yet, a very important consequence
of the greatly widening scope of conditionality, together with other changes
which had occurred under liberalization and globalization in the world economy, has been to deprive these countries of much of the policy autonomy
they had during the period 1950–80.

AID AND CONDITIONALITY: ANALYTICAL CONSIDERATIONS

Such far-reaching and intrusive conditionality raises the fundamental question of its economic and moral justification. Analysis and evidence suggest
that the economic argument is extremely weak, as is increasingly acknow-
ledged in aid-giving circles themselves (Pronk, 2001). The record of the wide-
ranging Washington Consensus conditionalities, involving political conditionalities as well as macroeconomic and microeconomic policy changes,
is, for example, uninspiring. Latin American countries which were the most
enthusiastic in adopting the Consensus policies, have not performed particularly well. Between the 1950s and 1980s those economies expanded at a
rate of 5.5 per cent to 6 per cent per annum. Their growth rate during the
last fifteen years is about half of that achieved in the 'bad old days' of rent-
seeking, corruption, pervasive role of the state and all the inefficiencies of
import substitution. The Washington Consensus reforms introduced under
conditionality may have brought stabilization, but certainly not growth of
output and employment at the socially required rates — to reduce poverty,
to meet the employment and basic needs of Latin America's fast growing
labour forces (see further, ECLA, 2001).

Similarly, more recently, the conditionality imposed on the crisis-affected
Asian countries by the IMF to change fundamentally their economic systems
towards the US/UK pattern also has no economic justification. There is
significant independent opinion to indicate that the crisis was primarily

caused not by crony capitalism but by precipitate financial liberalization implemented in countries such as Korea and Thailand prior to the crisis.[8]

Pronk, in his piece, more than once questions what is a 'good policy' and who determines it. Clearly, there is no agreement on this, not only between the international financial institutions and their critics, but also among these institutions themselves.[9] Martin Feldstein, the conservative US economist (former Chairman of President Nixon's Council of Economic Advisers), regards such IMF conditionality as not only unjustified in economic but also in moral terms. In the context of his discussion of the Asian crisis, he makes some very important points about this institution's conditionality which are worth quoting at some length:

> The fundamental issue is the appropriate role for an international agency and its technical staff in dealing with sovereign countries that come to it for assistance. The legitimate political institutions of the country should determine the nation's economic structure and the nature of its institutions. A nation's desperate need for short-term financial help does not give the IMF the moral right to substitute its technical judgements for the outcomes of the nation's political process...
>
> Imposing detailed economic prescriptions on legitimate governments would remain questionable even if economists were unanimous about the best way to reform the countries' economic policies. In practice, however there are substantial disagreements about what should be done. Even when there has been near unanimity about the appropriate economic policies, the consensus has changed radically. After all, the IMF was created to defend and manage a fixed exchange-rate system that is now regarded as economically inappropriate and practically unworkable.
>
> Today, there is nothing like unanimity about the appropriate policies for Korea or South East Asia. (Feldstein, 1998)

AID, CONDITIONALITY AND DEVELOPMENT IN THE 21ST CENTURY: AN INTERNATIONAL PERSPECTIVE

Jan Pronk seems to make the case for aid essentially on the basis that it can act as a catalyst for good things: good economic policies, good governance, etc. He is, with reason, agnostic about what constitutes good economic policy. He acknowledges the difficulties with the Washington Consensus policies, but is hesitant about suggesting alternatives — there is but a passing reference to heterodox policies. Pronk may be regarded as being on firmer ground in relation to governance since there is thought to be greater agreement on what constitutes good governance — democracy, account-ability, lack of corruption, etc. This is also arguable; but even if it were accepted, I think that (for the reasons given earlier) good governance is hardly helped by foreign interference whether it takes the form of carrots or

---

8. For a full discussion of this issue and for references to the relevant literature, see Singh and Weisse (1999).
9. The former chief economist of the World Bank, Joseph Stiglitz is a strident critic of the Washington Consensus; see for example Stiglitz (1998).

sticks — aid versus coercive intervention. Changes in governance must be left as far as possible to the internal processes of these countries, unless there are compelling reasons for the international community to be involved as in the case of genocide or widespread violation of human rights.

A related objection applies to Pronk's point about aid helping in 'managing conflicts' in situations of 'unsustainable development'. Unless the aid-giver is, and is perceived to be, a neutral entity by all parties to such conflicts, the use of aid as a catalyst could easily make the problem worse.

The concept of 'unsustainable development' in Pronk's conclusion raises further problems. A major issue here concerns the causes of 'unsustainability'. Sometimes, the latter may be due to domestic mismanagement, as suggested by Pronk. But, more often than not, it arises from international economic shocks over which developing countries have no control. Such shocks — for example the disastrous changes in the terms of trade and other relevant variables — have played a significant role in initiating and continuing a downward economic spiral in many developing countries. Further, as the Asian crises showed, even the most successful economies with strong fundamentals can become victims of external economic shocks. Indeed, unlike the Golden Age period, the present international economic system has made developing country economies more fragile, more prone to balance of payments and general economic and financial crises.[10] Aid is required to undo the collateral damage being done to developing countries by the present arrangements of the international economic system.[11]

Apart from these conceptual and practical difficulties with the notion of aid as a catalyst, another shortcoming of Pronk's analysis — as mentioned earlier — is that it looks at the question very much from the standpoint of the aid-giver. To complement this analysis, the previous sections have outlined some concerns of the developing countries in relation to aid conditionality in the context of their actual economic history in the twentieth century. The relevant lesson from the review of this experience is that developing countries' economic performance was much better during the period 1950–80 when they had greater policy autonomy, compared with their achievement under colonialism in the period 1900–50 and the post-1980 Washington Consensus period. It is significant not only that their performance was far superior in the middle period but also that this achievement occurred under very different initial conditions, and very different systems of governance and differing economic policies in the various countries.

---

10. See further UNCTAD (2000) which shows that the developing countries now become balance of payments constrained at a lower growth rate compared with earlier periods.

11. Reference here is to the lack of adequate co-operation among leading industrial countries on changes in exchange rates and other international monetary matters, resulting in the consequent supremacy of financial markets. This results in a lower rate of growth of real world demand than is required for the full utilization of resources. (See further Singh, 2000.)

In order to take the debate with Pronk further, it would be useful to consider, even if briefly, the issues of aid and conditionality explicitly from the perspective of developing countries. From their point of view aid should be based on need and be free of intrusive conditionalities, particularly with respect to policies and governance. Taking the second point first, normal technical and administrative conditionality, as with any financial assistance, is hardly objectionable. In relation to the nature of conditionality, it is useful to consider an analogy with the request of an individual economic agent for a house purchase loan or one for other family expenditures. The lender may ask the agent to provide guarantees or collateral and may fix payment terms considering the borrower's financial situation. This kind of conditionality is generally regarded as legitimate. But, if the lender were to insist on divorce of the borrower from the spouse, or even a laudable thing such as equal rights for all family members, this would be regarded as unacceptable interference. Similarly, developing countries feel that intrusive conditionalities beyond technical matters of the kind referred to above, particularly those relating to a country's economic and political institutions, are illegitimate.

Turning now to the question of need, there are two separate issues at stake. First is the question of total amount of aid and the second is that of its allocation. Taking the issue of allocation first, from a developing country perspective aid should be allocated on the basis of 'need', that is, countries with a greater level of poverty should receive more assistance. Of course, the problem of moral hazard has to be recognized and to the extent that it is feasible some attention has to be paid to performance, whether it is poverty reduction targets or other agreed concrete goals. However, the important point is that performance should not to be judged by apparent pursuit of one particular policy approach to development but, as far as possible, by clear evidence of progress in achieving mutually agreed stated goals, as for example increasing the proportion of children attending primary school.

With respect to the question of the total amount of aid, Pronk's conception of aid as a catalyst may be considered to be one rationale for providing aid by advanced country governments. However, this would not seem to be an adequate basis in a vastly unequal and closely inter-linked global economy and society in the twenty-first century.

In addition to the moral grounds for facilitating the reduction of abject poverty by means of development assistance and precipitating development, there are also powerful utilitarian grounds for developed countries to provide greater assistance to developing countries. The latter increasingly provide markets for advanced country products. To the extent that aid, whether tied or not, helps to enhance the productive capacities in developing countries, it also benefits advanced countries through a positive feedback loop of increased imports from these economies. This is particularly significant at a time of global economic recession and when enterprises in rich as well as poor countries are demand-rationed.

The minimum quantity of aid today should be clearly that which meets internationally agreed development and poverty reduction goals such as those set by the international community at the Millennium Assembly in 2000. The recently published report of the High Level Panel on Financing for Development (2001) (often referred to as the Zedillo Report after the Chairman of the Panel) estimates that merely to implement these international development targets would require a more than doubling of the current levels of ODA. The Panel notes that, in addition to this doubling of aid to meet these goals, international development co-operation requires funds to: (a) cope with humanitarian crises; (b) provide or preserve the supply of global public goods; and (c) confront and accelerate recovery from financial crises. The Panel therefore urges industrial countries to reaffirm and implement the aid target of 0.7 per cent of GNP, as part of efforts to meet these requirements.

However, further resources would be required in order to provide for all these tasks. Specifically, it would be necessary to institute schemes of international taxation, for example the taxation of international financial flows (Tobin-like tax), or charging a premium on international airline tickets, or ideally taxation of countries according to GDP per capita. In addition, in principle, from the developing countries' point of view it would be preferable that both bilateral and multilateral assistance be replaced by a single pool of resources for development assistance and public goods that is under the control of the whole international community (see South Centre, 1999).

The financing of international development co-operation primarily by means of international taxation, and its allocation by representative international organizations (as opposed to individual governments and donor dominated international institutions) according to countries' needs, is both a reasonable and feasible ambition for the twenty-first century.

REFERENCES

ECLAC (2001) *Rethinking the Development Agenda*. Santiago, Chile: CEPAL.
Feldstein, M. (1998) 'Refocusing the IMF', *Foreign Affairs* March: 20–33.
Glyn, A., A. Hughes, A. Lipietz and A. Singh (1990) 'The Rise and Fall of the Golden Age', in S. Marglin and J. Schor (eds) *The Golden Age of Capitalism: Reinterpreting the Post-War Experience*, pp. 39–125. Oxford: Clarendon Press.
High Level Panel on Financing for Development (2001) 'Recommendations of the High Level Panel on Financing for Development'. Report commissioned by the Secretary-General of the United Nations (June).
Levitt, K. P. (2000) 'The Right to Development'. The Fifth Sir Arthur Lewis Memorial Lecture, Castries, St. Lucia, Eastern Caribbean Central Bank, Bird Rock, Basseterre, St. Kitts.
Maddison, A. (1995) *Monitoring the World Economy*. Paris: OECD.
Patel, S. J. (1992) 'In Tribute to the Golden Age of the South's Development', *World Development* 20(5): 767–77.
Singh, A. (1993) 'Asian Economic Success and Latin American Failure in the 1980s: New Analysis and Future Policy Implications', *International Review of Applied Economics* 7(3): 267–89.

Singh, A. (1994) 'The Present State of Industry in the Third World: Analytical and Policy Issues', in G. K. Chadha (ed.) *Sectoral Issues in the Indian Economy: Policy and Perspectives*, pp. 104–55. New Delhi: Har-Anand Publications.

Singh, A. (1995) 'Institutional Requirements for Full Employment in Advanced Economies', *International Labour Review* 134(4–5): 471–96.

Singh, A. (2000) *Global Economic Trends and Social Development*. Occasional Paper 9. Geneva: United Nations Research Institute for Social Development.

Singh, A. and B. Weisse (1999) 'The Asian Model: A Crisis Foretold?', *International Social Science Journal* 16: 607–22.

South Centre (1999) *Financing Development — Key Issues for the South*. Geneva: South Centre.

Stiglitz, J. (1998) 'More Instruments and Broader Goals: Moving toward the Post Washington Consensus'. WIDER Annual Lecture, 7 January. Helsinki, Finland: WIDER.

UNCTAD (2000) *Trade and Development Report*. Geneva: UNCTAD.

World Bank (1998) *Assessing Aid: What Works, What Doesn't Work, and Why*. New York: Oxford University Press for the World Bank.

Chapter 8

The Effectiveness of Policy Conditionality: Eight Country Experiences

A. Geske Dijkstra

INTRODUCTION

The practice of donors setting conditions for policies in recipient countries in return for their aid has expanded over the last three decades. More and more donors make their aid conditional upon the implementation of certain policies. Furthermore, the number of policy areas within which conditions are formulated has expanded. The most recent expression of this is the set of conditions formulated for debt relief to Heavily Indebted Poor Countries (the HIPC initiative), which focus on government strategies to reduce poverty.

In his essay 'Aid as a Catalyst', Jan Pronk argues that 'well-focused aid conditionality is preferable to rigid selectivity' (this volume, p. 16). However, the emerging consensus in the literature is that 'buying reforms' (Collier et al., 1997) with aid is not very effective. It then becomes important to ask why policy conditionality is ineffective. What are the factors behind compliance or non-compliance ('slippage') on policy conditions? This article analyses the process of policy conditionality in eight countries: Bangladesh, Cape Verde, Mozambique, Nicaragua, Tanzania, Uganda, Vietnam and Zambia. Extensive empirical evidence on these countries has been gathered in the context of the Global Evaluation of Swedish Programme Aid.

In explaining what happened in these countries and why policy conditionality was often not effective, the article applies a principal–agent model (Killick, 1997; Killick et al., 1998). However, the analysis shows that this framework must be augmented in two ways: by including a more elaborated political-economy perspective, and by giving more attention to credibility aspects (see Mosley and Hudson, 1996). The final section returns to Pronk's normative question of whether donors should apply conditionality or

This chapter is based on a report written for the Department for Evaluation and Internal Audit of the Swedish International Development Cooperation Agency (Sida), Stockholm, in the context of the 'Global Evaluation of Swedish Programme Aid'. The author would like to thank Frank Dietz, Jan Kees van Donge, Howard White and two anonymous referees of *Development and Change* for helpful comments. The usual disclaimer applies.

'selectivity'. My argument boils down to reversing the quote from Pronk (above) to read: 'well-focused aid selectivity is better than rigid conditionality'.

POLICY CONDITIONALITY: THREE PARADOXES

Conditionality is the setting of policy conditions for aid. The receiving country is supposed to carry out certain policies in exchange for the aid (grants or loans) received. The International Monetary Fund (IMF) has always applied policy conditionality. It provided short-term balance of payments assistance in exchange for conditions set for macroeconomic policies; these conditions focused on fiscal and monetary policies. In the 1980s, and in response to the more structural balance of payments problems of many developing countries, new (and more concessional) lending instruments were created such as the Structural Adjustment Facility (SAF) and the Enhanced Structural Adjustment Facility (ESAF). The IMF increasingly included other aspects of the reform agenda amongst its conditions, such as trade liberalization, price liberalization and policies to increase tax income (Killick, 1995). In 1999, ESAF was changed into the Poverty Reduction and Growth Facility (PRGF). As the name already indicates, conditions for these loans focus on measures leading to poverty reduction, and the countries involved have to elaborate Poverty Reduction Strategy Papers (PRSP).

Until the early 1980s, the World Bank had mainly been involved in project lending. In the 1980s 'programme lending' increased rapidly in importance. The World Bank also began to disburse funds in exchange for the promise on the part of the recipient country that some specified macroeconomic policies would be implemented. More than the IMF, the Bank focused on *micro*economic reform measures, such as liberalization of prices, privatization, and public sector reforms, designed to increase production or supply. Structural Adjustment Loans (SAL) were extended, and later also Sectoral Adjustment Loans (SECAL). In the latter case, the money provided takes the form of freely-spendable balance of payments support, but the policy conditions attached to it refer to a specific sector, for example agriculture or banking. Parallel to the IMF's PRGF, the Bank is now elaborating Poverty Reduction Support Credits (PRSC), a form of budget support to facilitate the implementation of PRSPs.

In the course of the 1980s and 1990s, the number of conditions per loan increased, and conditions came to cover all possible sectors. At the same time, conditionality became tighter (Killick et al., 1998: 2–5). The World Bank specified an increasing number of 'preconditions' to be fulfilled before a loan could be approved, while the IMF had always required 'prior actions' to be taken before giving a loan. Furthermore, the money was often given in tranches. The agreements on policy conditions were written down in a 'Letter of Intent' (IMF) or a 'Letter of Development Policy' (World Bank). Formally, these documents were written by the recipient governments, but in practice IMF and World Bank staff wrote the major part. In the 1990s, the World Bank and IMF (the International Financial Institutions, or IFIs) began to work together in setting up a reform programme. The policy intentions of the governments were then documented in 'Policy Framework Papers'. Since 1999, the World Bank and IMF have worked jointly with governments in the elaboration of the Poverty Reduction Strategy Papers, which form the basis for new IMF and World Bank loans and for debt relief measures from the international donor community in the framework of the HIPC initiative.

The World Bank usually makes loans contingent upon the existence and implementation of an agreement with the IMF. This is called 'cross-conditionality'. Cross-conditionality is also applied by other donors, such as regional development banks, the EU and bilateral donors. These other donors make the disbursement of their aid and, in particular, their programme aid, dependent on the country being 'on track' with an IMF or IMF/World Bank programme.

In the 1990s, economic conditions were increasingly supplemented by political conditions. This is the so-called 'second generation' conditionality. Conditions regarding democracy, human rights and good governance mainly came from bilateral donors. The IFIs were initially reluctant to take this political conditionality on board — although the World Bank, in particular, was also afraid of losing its leading role if it did not include these demands from bilateral donors in its own programmes (Gibbon, 1993). In response, the Bank began to define the problems of 'governance' as referring to poor public management and public service delivery, and lack of accountability and transparency of government actions. 'Governance' in this more technical and depoliticized definition was then sometimes taken on board in the World Bank's policy conditions. In a few cases, the IFIs have integrated conditions regarding democracy and human rights. The more recent integration of policies to reduce poverty can be called a 'third generation' of policy conditionality.

Three Paradoxes

The giving of aid and loans against conditions on policies involves three fundamental contradictions or paradoxes. The first paradox is that donors attempt to 'buy' reforms with their aid, while the reforms are good for the country anyway (Streeten, 1987). If these policies enhance the welfare of the recipient country, why do the countries need to be induced with aid? And, if governments of recipient countries are convinced that these reforms are the good policies, why not get them to pay for the good advice, instead of being rewarded with loans?

Secondly, the giving of the aid money itself may reduce the incentive for recipient countries to carry out reforms. This is the risk of 'moral hazard' on the part of the recipient (de Vylder, 1994). For example, an important policy condition is usually the reduction of the budget deficit — yet if countries receive aid, they can finance excess expenditure, and no longer need to carry out tax reforms or to cut expenditure.

Thirdly, there is a contradiction between the setting of many conditions and the content of one of these conditions, namely the demands for more democratization and more accountability of government's actions. Conditions often involve 'parliaments' approving a law, for example, on the privatization of a state enterprise or on a tax reform. Obviously, some national sovereignty is needed in order to achieve democratic decision-making. This inconsistency raises the question of the *legitimacy* of policy conditionality, an issue taken up again in the conclusion.

THE EFFECTIVENESS OF POLICY CONDITIONALITY

Although the World Bank once concluded optimistically that, on average, 60 per cent of conditions are fulfilled (World Bank, 1988), several studies show that compliance is much more limited. The first major study of World Bank policy conditionality was carried out by Mosley, Harrigan and Toye: of the fourteen countries with World Bank adjustment programmes examined, only three proved to be successful. In most countries, extensive slippage occurred (Mosley et al., 1991). Another indication for limited compliance is that in 100 World Bank adjustment programmes, only 25 per cent of second or third tranch disbursements were paid according to schedule. Most were delayed, and 8 per cent were cancelled. (Killick et al., 1998: 30).

In spite of the longer tradition of IMF conditionality, IMF programmes do not appear to perform any better. Haggard, for example, looked at Extended Fund Facilities (EFFs) and found that twenty-four out of thirty programmes were 'renegotiated, had payments interrupted, or were quietly allowed to lapse' (Haggard, 1985: 505–6). Of twenty-five ESAF programmes, only five were concluded according to the schedule, fourteen were extended and two had been abandoned (Killick, 1995).

It must be borne in mind that formal compliance with stipulated conditions may imply that these policies would have been carried out anyway. In those cases, the implementation of policies cannot be taken as an indicator of the influence of the IFIs. In a recent econometric study, Dollar and Svensson concluded that domestic political variables on their own explain to a large extent whether reforms are carried out, while factors under control of the World Bank (such as the number of conditions, or efforts at preparation and supervision) proved not to play a role (Dollar and Svensson, 1998). In other cases, conditions may be fulfilled only cosmetically, or the effect of compliance is nullified by countervailing actions (Killick et al., 1998: 30–31).

The literature on the effectiveness of *political* conditionality is less extensive. Robinson (1993) concludes that the influence of aid and conditionality on the democratization processes that occurred in Africa in the early 1990s was limited. Other factors, such as the 'diffusion effect' from the changes in Eastern Europe and later from changes in neighbouring African countries, were more important. Crawford (1997) found that conditions improved in only thirteen out of twenty-nine countries where aid sanctions were applied for political reasons. In only nine of the thirteen could this improvement be partially attributed to donor pressure, and in only two cases was donor pressure significant in bringing about political change. Furthermore, the more specifically a political condition was formulated, the more often it proved to be implemented.

An Augmented Principal–Agent Framework

Theoretical models of policy conditionality provide insights in how conditionality works and why its effectiveness is limited.[1] These models usually start from the assumption that there is a conflict of interest between donor and recipient on policies, and that there is asymmetric information. They use a principal–agent framework (Killick, 1997; Killick et al., 1998; Murshed and Sen, 1995).

Principal–agent theory was originally designed to analyse the relationship between the shareholder (the principal) and the manager (the agent). The principal wants the agent to make decisions in her interest. The problem is, however, that there may be a conflict of interest between principal and agent so that the principal cannot always trust that the agent will act on her behalf. In addition, the principal cannot fully observe and monitor the agent's actions.

This model can be applied to the donor–recipient relationship, where the donor is the principal (P) and the recipient is the agent (A) (Killick, 1997; Killick et al., 1998). P wants certain actions to be done by A, and rewards A for this. P and A have different objective functions, which means that A does not have the same interest as P in complying with P's objectives. The asymmetric information means that A will always have more information on what he actually does than P. P can decide to incur costs in order to monitor A's compliance. However, monitoring can never be perfect since there is no one-to-one relationship between observable outcomes and A's actions, which are largely unobservable. P may also raise the rewards for compliance, but given imperfect information and the difficulties of monitoring, this may just increase the probability of moral hazard. The larger the difference in the objective functions between P and A, the more 'participation constraints' A will face. This leads to a first group of propositions for the relationship between donor and recipient; a second group of propositions refers to the kind of enforcement system that is in place, that

---

1. For a more extensive analysis of theoretical models see Dijkstra (1999a).

is, the system of rewards and punishments. In total, Killick et al. (1998) formulated fifteen propositions for the donor–recipient relationship. Most of these were confirmed in an empirical analysis of twenty-one countries.

Our empirical analysis of the effectiveness of policy conditionality in eight countries also confirmed many of the hypotheses of the principal–agent framework. However, in order to explain better the country experiences, Killick's framework needed to be expanded. In particular, a broader political economy framework proved to be necessary in which the balance of power within the government and within society as a whole was taken into account. A related issue was the power base of the negotiators on the government; if the IFIs only deal with a few technocrats in the Central Bank and the Ministry of Finance, this may reduce chances of implementation (see also Kahler, 1992). Furthermore, the *contents* of policy conditionality proved to influence the credibility of the conditions and thus the degree of acceptance by the recipient, as also postulated in Mosley and Hudson's bargaining model of the donor–recipient relationship (Mosley and Hudson, 1996). Similarly, donor credibility proved to play a role in whether or not sanctions on non-compliance were applied.

The eight country experiences can be described using the following eight points, which can be considered propositions of an *augmented* principal–agent framework.

The *probability of implementation* depends on:
1. Whether the negotiators on the government side either have the power to implement reforms, or have insight into the feasibility of implementing reforms;
2. Whether the objectives of the most powerful groups within government coincide with those of the donors, and the strength of domestic opposition to these objectives;
3. The extent to which the powerful actors in the government and in the opposition win or lose from reforms and from aid, and the likely result of a potential power struggle between these groups;
4. Whether the donors' advice is credible, and whether advice leads to economic growth;
5. The availability of aid: this may influence implementation positively, facilitating compliance with fiscal and other financial targets; or negatively, through the weakening of incentives for implementation (moral hazard).

The *threat of aid suspension* is not effective, because:
6. Donors have multiple, conflicting or unclear objectives. For example: a) in countries with large multilateral debts there is pressure for continued lending, b) there are political and bureaucratic pressures on the donor to continue lending, c) there is the 'adverse selection' problem — the allocation of aid tends to be determined also by need, which means that countries carrying out bad policies tend to get more aid;

7. 'Cross conditionality' does not work since different donors have different objectives and donor co-ordination is weak;
8. In countries with satisfactory or high economic growth, application of sanctions reduces donor credibility.

THE EXPERIENCES OF CONDITIONALITY IN EIGHT COUNTRIES

A first indication of the limited effectiveness of policy conditionality is that in six of the eight countries studied,[2] reforms were well under way when the IFIs came in with their structural adjustment programmes: Bangladesh, Cape Verde, Mozambique, Nicaragua, Tanzania and Vietnam. Only in Uganda and Zambia did structural adjustment programmes (initiated in 1987 and 1991 respectively) coincide with (attempts at) policy reforms; in both countries, there had been earlier SAPs, which had been aborted but had left debts. In Vietnam and Nicaragua the late appearance of the IFIs (in 1994 and 1991 respectively) was a consequence of an earlier US boycott against these countries. The fact that reform programmes were well under way before the IFIs interfered in most of these countries points to the primacy of domestic political factors in bringing about policy changes.

Another indication that the influence of the IFIs has often been overstated is that in only half of the eight countries were the IFI programmes a response to an internal or external crisis. Cape Verde and Vietnam did not have balance of payments problems, a large debt or high inflation. Uganda only had an inflation problem. Bangladesh was a kind of intermediate case: it faced soft macroeconomic disequilibria when the IFIs got involved. In spite of these different circumstances, all programmes attempted to 'buy' policy reform, and the contents of these reform conditions was similar. Given the different starting conditions, one might question the justification for, and the effectiveness of, standard IFI recipes for stabilization and structural adjustment.

Table 1 gives an overview of overall compliance with the programmes and the application of sanctions in the eight countries. In Bangladesh, the IMF did not conclude any new ESAFs after the first in 1990, because its fiscal and monetary targets generally were not met. The World Bank continued sectoral adjustment credits (SACs) in the 1990s, but with highly unsatisfactory outcomes and most credits were discontinued. In Vietnam, there was a failure to comply with the targets of both IMF and World Bank programmes of 1994 in the period 1996–97, and the programmes were interrupted. In Cape Verde the programme is recent and is still on track. In

---

2. Unless otherwise indicated, the information on the different countries is based on the eight country reports of the Sida evaluation (Ddumba-Ssentamu et al. 1999; Dijkstra, 1999b; Dijkstra and van Donge, 1999; van Donge and White, 1999; Leefmans and White, 1999; Ngia et al., 1999; White 1999a; White, 1999b).

Table 1. IFI Programmes in Eight Countries: Implemention and
Sanctions Applied

Country	Programme	Implementation	Sanction
Bangladesh	ESAF '90	Partial	No new ESAFs
	FSAC '90 (IDA)	Partial	Delays 2nd and 3rd
	2nd Ind SAC '92 (IDA)	No	tranch
	Jute SAC '94 (IDA)	No	Yes, no 2nd tranch
			Yes, no 2nd tranch
			(was largest amount)
Vietnam	ESAF '94	Yes until '97, then no	Yes
	SAC '94 (IDA)	No	Delay, and no new
			SAC in '97
Cape Verde	SAP '97	Yes	
	Standby '98	Yes	
Mozambique	ESAF '90	Yes	
	ERC '92 (IDA)	Yes	
	ERC 2 '94 (IDA)	Yes	
	ESAF 2 '96		
	ERC 3 '97 (IDA)		
Tanzania	AAC '90 (IDA)	Partial	No
	ESAF '91	No (Staff monitored	Yes, suspended, no
	FSAC '91 (IDA)	programmes '93–96)	ESAF in '94
	ESAF '96	Partial	No
	SAC '97 (IDA)	Yes	
		Yes	
Uganda	ESAF 1 '89	No	No
	ERC 2 '89 (IDA)	No	No
	ASAC '90 (IDA)	Yes, but delays	No
	SAC 1 '92 (IDA)	Yes, but delays	No
	FSAC '93 (IDA)	Yes, delays	No
	SAC 2 '94 (IDA)	Yes, delays	No
	ESAF 2 '94	Yes, one exception	One waiver
	ESAF 3 '97		
	SAC 3 '97 (IDA)		
Zambia	ERC 2 '91 (IDA)	Yes	
	RAP '91 (IMF)	Partial	No
	PIRC 1 '92 (IDA)	Partial	No
	PIRC 2 '93 (IDA)	Partial	No
	ESAC '94 (IDA)	Partial	No
	ERIP 1 '95 (IDA)	Partial	No
	ESAF '95	Partial	
Nicaragua	Standby '91	No	Yes, no 2nd tranch
	ERC 1 '91 (IDA)	Yes but reversal after	
		disbursement	
	ESAF '94	No	Yes, but ambiguous
	ERC 2 '94 (IDA)	No	Delay only
	ESAF 2 '98		
	FSAC '98 (IDA)		

Sources: Ddumba-Ssentamu et al. (1999); Dijkstra (1999b); Dijkstra and van Donge (1999); van Donge and White (1999); Leefmans and White (1999); Ngia et al. (1999); White (1999a, 1999b).

Mozambique, the IMF wanted to call its ongoing ESAF 'off-track' in 1995, but bilateral donors argued that targets had been too strict and that the programme should continue. This intervention was successful. Although there were some conflicts between the IFIs and the Mozambican government on reforms, the government has generally complied with the conditions, even going so far as to state publicly that unwanted policies were *their* policies.

In Uganda, targets were barely met in the first period of IFI involvement (1987–92), but overall compliance was good in the second period (1992–98). This coincided with the introduction of a cash budget. The number and coverage of IFI conditions regarding structural reforms in this country were far more limited than in, for example, Zambia. Even so, implementation of reforms that were agreed upon as conditions was often delayed, but no sanctions were applied. In Zambia and Tanzania, implementation of the IMF programme was limited until, respectively, 1991 and 1995, when these countries introduced cash budgets. In Zambia, fiscal targets were often not met after 1991 but the IMF quietly accommodated the targets. The non-compliance of IMF targets in Tanzania between 1993 and 1996 led to a staff-monitored programme, while financing was withheld. The World Bank programmes in these two countries included many conditions on structural reforms. Reforms were carried out during the 1990s but often with delays and sometimes less fully than agreed, but this did not lead to interruptions of finance from the Bank. In Nicaragua, the government did not meet with the IMF conditions in 1992–93 (this was partially after disbursements had been made), or in 1995–96. Conditions to World Bank credits were often not met or not met in time. Only once, in 1995, did this lead to a temporary suspension of financing by the Bank

It is fair to say, then, that most IMF programmes in the eight countries were not fully complied with. Of the eleven programmes that ran in these countries in the 1990s and that were closed by 1998, only three were successful: the 1990 ESAF in Mozambique, the 1994 ESAF in Uganda and the 1996 ESAF in Tanzania. In most cases where IMF targets were not met, new programmes were concluded soon after the break. The exceptions are Bangladesh and Vietnam. The policy conditions attached to World Bank structural adjustment credits were often implemented only partially, and with delays. In addition, as we will see below, reforms were sometimes carried out only cosmetically, countervailing actions were taken or policy reversals occurred. Yet, in most cases, new adjustment credits were given.

Explaining the Lack of Effectiveness

We can now examine the reasons for non-compliance of the programmes in the eight countries, following the framework elaborated above. The first five propositions deal with the probability of implementation.

(1) Whether the negotiators on the government side either have the power to implement reforms, or have insight into the feasibility of implementing reforms
This proposition can only be examined for the three countries in which fieldwork has been carried out, namely Nicaragua, Uganda and Vietnam. This issue proved particularly troublesome in Vietnam, where donors faced several problems in finding good actors for the policy dialogue. First, although at first sight Vietnam still has a centralized political system, in practice policy-making is a diffuse process. There is a large role for consensus building at all levels. Second, while organizations such as the Party, the Fatherland Front and the Army play important roles, this is not visible to donors. When talking to government officials, they do not know whether they are dealing with representatives of these organizations. Third, form often replaces substance in Vietnamese policy-making: laws may be approved but this does not have consequences for implementation. Fourth, it is often not clear what the 'current' government position is, since policies are seldom defined and policy changes tend to be reactive, made in response to crises. Fifth, sharp distinctions between categories, such as the public and private domain, or government vs. state-owned enterprises, are often not applicable. In sum, neither donors nor policy-makers know who has the power to implement reforms, nor what the outcome of the decision-making process will be. These factors also reduce the probability that any outcomes of the policy dialogue will actually be implemented.

In Nicaragua, the political situation after the elections of 1990 was delicate, with a large parliamentary and extra-parliamentary opposition. This implied that the elected government only had limited power to implement reforms. With hindsight, it is apparent that the government's negotiators often conceded reforms that were impossible to implement for domestic political reasons. However, it is difficult to conclude whether the negotiators were *unable* or *unwilling* to make a realistic assessment of the feasibility of reform implementation. Although the former is probably true to some extent, given the uncertainties in the political situation, the latter interpretation is also plausible. The government had an obvious interest in reaching an agreement, given the country's high aid dependence, heavy debts and the large extent of cross-conditionality — most bilateral aid and bilateral debt forgiveness was contingent upon the existence of an IMF programme. The 1998 agreement between IFIs and the government has been prepared mainly by technocrats, including an economist who was a former IMF staff member. This carries risks for the possibility of implementation.

In Uganda, donors stress the importance of the fact that the principal negotiator on the government side made a realistic assessment of the possibility of reform implementation. This holds, in particular, for the later period (after 1992). At the same time, and probably as a result of this perception, donors were willing to accept less far-reaching, but more realistic policy targets. In the earlier period (1987–92), Ugandan negotiators sometimes conceded to reforms that were not implemented. In this period, there was much less consensus among high government officials on the need for reform. The President and one or two others may have been convinced, but they were not able to carry through these reforms in the early period.

(2) Whether the objectives of the most powerful groups within government coincide with those of the donors, and the strength of domestic opposition to these objectives

In Uganda, there was a gradual process of increasing ownership on the side of the most important government officials, or increasing coincidence of donor and recipient's objectives between 1987 and 1992. Opposition, including that from ministers and from within parliament, gradually waned. This certainly facilitated the implementation of reforms. Since 1992, there have been virtually no differences over the contents of reforms, only over the speed of implementation (see below). There is no significant domestic opposition to reforms.

In Tanzania, Zambia and Bangladesh donors and government agree on the need for stabilization, but there are differences of opinion on issues like privatization of State Owned Enterprises (SOEs) and public sector reform. Implementation of these reforms was often delayed and was sometimes not carried out at all. In Mozambique, the government and the IMF disagreed on public spending limits, while the government and the World Bank disagreed on some liberalizations and privatizations. Not all of these were implemented. Given the diffuse policy-making process in Vietnam, it is impossible to determine who the most powerful actors are and what their objectives are.

In Nicaragua, objectives of donors and government officials coincided to some extent: on stabilization, on trade and financial liberalization in the economy, and on privatization of state enterprises. These were largely implemented. However, there was less agreement on privatization of public utility companies, public sector reform, tax reform and increases in fees for public utilities; there was also some disagreement on the speed of trade liberalization. There was also strong opposition to these issues within and outside parliament, which led to partial implementation, countervailing actions and policy reversals.

(3) The extent to which the powerful actors in the government and in the opposition win or lose from reforms and from aid, and the likely result of a potential power struggle between these groups

With respect to internal stabilization measures (fighting inflation through budgetary policies), non-compliance occurred in Mozambique, Nicaragua and Bangladesh, and, before the cash budget was introduced, also in Uganda, Zambia and Tanzania. The struggle for stabilization is not one between winners and losers since, in the end, everybody wins from stabilization. However, everybody may lose from particular stabilization measures, such as spending cuts or tax increases. Hence, stabilization is a 'collective action' problem (van Donge and White, 1999). Donor pressure may help to solve this problem and it has probably been influential to some extent in all countries where inflation was a problem. But the most important factor in reducing inflation has been aid money itself, which could be used for financing budget deficits. This was especially the case in Uganda, Tanzania, and Nicaragua, but also in Mozambique, Zambia and Bangladesh.

Reforms in Vietnam are now stalled around three issues: privatization of SOEs, banking reform, and further trade liberalization. The three are closely related. SOEs still benefit from high tariffs and from easy access to loans. Since the same group of people who hold high government, party and army positions also manage SOEs, this group benefits from the current situation and expects losses from reforms. However, many privatized SOEs also still benefit from protection and easy credits. Paradoxically, a large share of aid to Vietnam is project aid that is supporting the public sector and SOEs, thus helping to maintain them. Groups that would benefit from reforms include consumers, tax payers in general, farmers and managers of small enterprises, but they have much less power.

In Bangladesh, the situation with respect to reforms is similar to that in Vietnam. Donors want the privatization of SOEs and of the state banks, but these demands conflict with the interests of high government officials and with powerful unions of urban workers, and so meet with strong opposition.

In Uganda, implementation of some reforms was hampered because the government officials responsible for the implementation would lose from them. For example, privatization of SOEs was promised by the government in 1992,[3] but implementation only began in earnest in 1995, when a separate Privatization Monitoring Unit was created in the Ministry of Finance. Line ministries proved reluctant to privatize firms under their responsibility. Although many high-level government officials benefited from the existence of SOEs, privatization may also have been in their interest: in 1998, the donors claimed that the almost completed privatization process had benefited many persons closely related to the government. There had been little control of the process, and people could use their bureaucratic power to acquire some of the newly created market power. Workers of SOEs would be the losers of privatization, but this group is weakly organized in Uganda.

In Zambia, an undertaking to privatize was made after 1991, but it was not until 1995 that it really took off. In some cases, strong donor pressure was needed (for example, Zambia Airways and the state mining company)

---

3. Although, surprisingly, it was not a formal condition to adjustment credits at the time.

and even this was not successful for a long time. There were strong interests among government officials to retain these SOEs. One explanation for their eventual sale was that government officials had engaged in asset stripping first. In Mozambique, there were clear losers of certain liberalization and privatization measures. But donor pressure, in this case from the World Bank, was very strong. In the case of the cashew nut processing industries, the government was even forced to say that liberalization and privatization were *their own* measures, although the government did not agree with them.

Public sector reforms such as downsizing and decentralization are notoriously difficult to implement, since government officials are directly affected. In Uganda, downsizing of the public sector was relatively successful between 1993 and 1996, when aid was used for this retrenchment. But aid is by no means a sufficient condition: in Zambia and Tanzania much less was achieved in this area, probably due to strong labour unions in the public sector, which are absent in Uganda.

In Nicaragua, there were winners and losers from liberalization and privatization. Here — much more than in most African countries — there was a group of people with access to finance and to economic assets who were not dependent on protection or other favours from the government. These rich individuals, whose wealth was based on export agriculture, trade, and banking, had a strong interest in liberalization and privatization. The losers included workers of state enterprises and government employees; wage workers in general, who saw their wages reduced and taxes and government fees increased; and owners of small businesses and farms, whose access to finance was reduced. Most manufacturing firms also lost from the reforms, in particular from trade liberalization. Some firm owners were less affected, as they also owned other, more profitable assets, and some succeeded in negotiating specific favours from the government so that they remained protected. Aid often allowed the government to extend these favours. Some of the losers were well organized, in particular the labour unions and the Sandinista party in parliament. The government made an effort to weaken the opposition by ensuring that its leaders benefited from the reforms — again, programme aid was instrumental in this. This strategy was not entirely successful, however, as the opposition was able to partly reverse trade liberalization and to prevent the privatization of several public utility enterprises.

(4) The credibility of donors' advice, and whether advice leads to economic growth
In Vietnam, donors' advice would not easily gain credibility since economic growth was already high and inflation had been solved before the IFIs came with their programmes. A similar situation held for Bangladesh. In Nicaragua, the agreement with the IFIs helped stabilization, mainly by increasing the aid flow, but the economy continued to stagnate for three

years. This did not increase the credibility of the advice to reform, and in fact strengthened the opposition to reform.

In Uganda, donors gained some credibility as the beginning of the IFI programme in 1987 coincided with high rates of economic growth. Although this high growth rate cannot be attributed to reforms (which hardly came into force before 1992) and was due to other factors, such as the return of law and order in the country and the impact of aid itself, it certainly helped the acceptance and the implementation of reforms later on.[4] In Mozambique and Tanzania, economic growth during structural adjustment programmes was lower than in Uganda, but at least it was positive, on average, which may have given some credibility to the donors' advice. In Zambia the stagnant economy in the 1990s was probably one of the factors which hampered full implementation of the reform package. In Nicaragua, the zero growth rate until 1994 also limited the credibility of the IFIs. Although Vietnam and Bangladesh had high growth rates, this growth was not perceived as having any relationship with the involvement of the IFIs.

(5) The availability of aid, either facilitating compliance with fiscal and other financial targets, or weakening incentives for implementation (moral hazard)
The availability of aid has been important in many countries, and has often played a positive role in stabilization. Since aid helped to finance government expenditure, the reduction of inflation was made easier in Nicaragua, Mozambique, Uganda, Tanzania, and Zambia. In Bangladesh, a reduction in aid in the early 1990s did not lead to a larger deficit due to a concomitant increase in revenues, but in the late 1990s higher expenditure in combination with another aid shortfall did lead to higher inflation. In all these countries, the positive effects of aid on stabilization seem to have outweighed any potential moral hazard effect. However, in Nicaragua there is some evidence of moral hazard: in spite of large amounts of aid, expenditure targets were not always met. In fact, Nicaragua's public deficit did not decrease at all if aid is excluded. Some slippage also occurred in Tanzania, Zambia and Uganda, at least before these countries introduced cash budgets.

The availability of aid was sometimes important in financing retrenchment from SOEs or the public service, thus mitigating the social costs of these adjustments. However, in many countries aid led to postponing public sector reform and the privatization of SOEs and state banks, since, for example, it allowed governments to continue subsidizing state enterprises and to bail-out state banks for non-performing loans. In this sense, moral hazard has occurred in Vietnam, Bangladesh, Nicaragua, Tanzania, Zambia and Uganda.

The evidence relating to these five propositions on the probability of implementation suggests that all the propositions have played a role in one

---

4. See also Dijkstra and van Donge (2001).

or more countries (see Table 2 for a summary). In one case (Nicaragua), all five propositions were influential. The lack of power or lack of insight into the feasibility of implementation (1) was definitely important in those countries where this could be examined. The coincidence of objectives (2) proved to be much greater on stabilization than on structural reforms, and was probably an important reason why stabilization measures were more systematically implemented than reforms. However, the availability of aid itself (5a) also facilitated stabilization. The political economy perspective (3) proved to be important. In this area, it is interesting to observe that in several countries, perceptions on who wins from, especially, privatization, have changed. The credibility of donor advice through a high growth rate (4) played a positive role in Uganda, and to some extent also in Tanzania and Mozambique. In Zambia and (until 1994) Nicaragua, lack of growth was probably a negative factor in implementation. In Bangladesh and Vietnam, growth rates were high before, and independent of, IFI programmes, so could not enhance implementation of these programmes. Some moral hazard (5b) could be observed in most countries.

The Threat of Withholding Aid

In Nicaragua and Vietnam, programmes with the IFIs were interrupted due to non-compliance (Table 1). This also occurred in Tanzania between 1993 and 1995, and in Mozambique the IMF briefly called the programme off-track in 1995. In Zambia, IFI programmes were interrupted several times during the 1980s. In Bangladesh, several World Bank SACs were interrupted. In these countries, the sanction on non-compliance has been used. Nevertheless, in all countries except Bangladesh and Vietnam, negotiations began again soon after the interruptions, and new programmes came about. When the IMF did not disburse the third annual tranch on the 1994 ESAF to Vietnam in 1996, the World Bank stopped negotiating a new SAC. The World Bank itself had delayed disbursements on its first SAC (also 1994) due to non-compliance with the conditions set. In Bangladesh no new IMF programme came about after the ESAF of 1990. The World Bank still attempted two sectoral structural adjustment credits (SACs) in the 1990s, but neither of these was implemented as planned and second tranches were either not given or given with a delay. The last SAC (1994, see Table 1) was closed without disbursing the money, and no new programmes have been concluded. The hypotheses of the augmented principal–agent framework, in particular the sixth, may explain why this is so.

(6) Multiple, conflicting or unclear objectives of donors
Vietnam and Bangladesh both have very low multilateral debts, so the IFIs are not under financial pressure to continue lending. In addition, there is no need for an agreement with the IFIs to signal to other donors that the

Table 2. Evidence for Five Propositions on the Probability of Implementation of IFI Programmes in the 1990s

Country	Implementation (see Table 1)	(1) Power of negotiator and/or insight in feasibility of implementation	(2) Coincidence of objectives donor–recipient, strength of opposition	(3) Winners and losers of reforms	(4) Credibility of donor advice	(5a) Availability of aid	(5b) Aid leads to moral hazard
Nicaragua	Weak	Technocrats, no power or no realistic estimates	Coincidence on stabilization and on some reforms, not on all	Powerful winners from privatization and liberalization, losers less powerful but could delay	Low, given low growth rate	Important for stabilization and for 'bribing' opposition	Some in fiscal policy; also in postponing reforms
Vietnam	Weak	Diffuse power structure	Difficult to tell what government objectives were	Government officials lose from privatization, financial and trade liberalization	Limited, given high growth and low inflation before advice	Not important	Some, in postponing reforms
Bangladesh	Weak		Coincidence on stabilization, not on reforms	Government officials and strong unions lose from privatization, financial and trade liberalization	Limited, given that high growth was not perceived as result of IFI programme	Not important (early 1990s); lack of aid affected stabilization (late 1990s)	Some, in postponing reforms
Uganda '87–'92	Weak		Gradually increasing coincidence, also within government		Increasing, given high growth rate	Important for stabilization	
Uganda after '92	Good, some delays	Good insight in feasibility	Some differences on speed of implementation	Perception of government officials on interest in privatization gradually changed	High, high growth rate		Some, in postponing reforms

Tanzania '90–'96	Weak			Some, given moderate growth	Important for stabilization	Some, in postponing reforms
Tanzania after '96	Good	Coincidence on stabilization (since 1996), not always on other reforms	Officials lose from civil service reform	Some, given moderate growth	Important for stabilization	
Zambia	Good, but not on all issues and with delays	Coincidence on stabilization, not always on other reforms	Perception of government officials gradually changed; officials lose from civil service reform	No credibility, given stagnant economy	Important for stabilization	Some, in postponing reforms
Mozambique	Good			Some, given moderate growth	Important for stabilization	

country should get (freely spendable) programme aid — the kind of aid that can be used to pay the debts to multilaterals. In Vietnam, most bilateral donors reduced programme aid in reaction to the discontinuation of the IMF programme. In Bangladesh, bilateral donors stopped giving programme aid in the early 1990s — formally because balance of payments support had proven inefficient and was no longer necessary after the liberalization of foreign exchange, while budget support was not considered appropriate given government spending priorities. One could add to this, that there was no need for debt relief.

Zambia and Tanzania have a history of interrupted IFI programmes, but negotiations on new programmes have always re-started soon after the break. This was especially true for Zambia before 1991. The donors' multiple, conflicting and unclear objectives probably played a role here: these countries had large debts to the multilateral institutions, and consequently there was a need for large amounts of programme aid.

(7) 'Cross conditionality' and the lack of donor co-ordination
Nicaragua represents a clear case of a lack of donor co-operation. The second tranch on the 1991 IMF programme was not disbursed because of the non-achievement of targets. However, this non-achievement was partly due to a suspension of already promised aid in that period. The US suspended aid for political reasons that had nothing to do with IMF or World Bank conditions. The different objectives of different donors endangered the very success of the stabilization and adjustment programme in 1992.

In 1995, during SAC 2 and the first ESAF (1994–96), donor objectives again proved to be inconsistent. The ESAF was discontinued because the monetary targets were not met. However, the IMF representative in the country convinced the other donors that they should continue giving aid, arguing that stabilization would be at risk if all programme aid were to stop. In the meantime, the IMF tried to come to some agreement with the government on new monetary and fiscal targets. This testifies to conflicting objectives within the IMF itself. On the one hand, it wanted to maintain its credibility by not disbursing a second tranch since the targets had not been achieved; on the other, it did not want to apply a 'real' (effective) sanction to Nicaragua,[5] because this would endanger the stabilization that had been achieved. This argument comes very close to the adverse selection hypothesis (the need for aid is bigger with larger deficits, and thus in countries that do not meet the targets). However, since the IMF was asking for *programme aid*, not aid in general, the 'need for aid' was probably defined in relation to the large multilateral debt that needed to be serviced.

---

5. The size of the IMF loan was limited compared to programme aid funds from other donors.

While cross-conditionality thus broke down at the instigation of the IMF itself, other donors suspended aid at about the same period, but they did so for other reasons. The World Bank postponed the second tranche of SAC 2 because of delays in the privatization of public utility enterprises, and many bilateral donors suspended programme aid in early 1995 because of a constitutional crisis between Parliament and the Executive (see below). As a result of these suspensions, it became more difficult for the government to comply with the new targets of the IMF 'bridging programme'.

In Mozambique, the IMF wanted to call the programme off-track in 1995, because of non-compliance with spending limits. However, bilateral donors convinced the IMF to continue disbursing, arguing that limits had been too tight. The IMF gave in and the programme remained on track. Thus, in this case sanctions were not applied, as a result of intervention from bilateral donors. Zambia after 1996 also illustrates a lack of donor co-ordination: bilateral donors stopped programme aid (see below), while multilaterals continued.

(8) In countries with high economic growth, sanctions reduce donor credibility
During the first period (1987–92) in Uganda, disbursements of the IFIs continued in spite of limited implementation of the programmes. The two World Bank structural adjustment credits of this period were rated as 'unsatisfactory' and 'marginally unsatisfactory', respectively. In 1992 there was a brief suspension of aid from both bilaterals and multilaterals. Government and donors disagreed over the exchange rate used in the auctions of foreign exchange. The result of this conflict was that the government went beyond donor demands, and fully liberalized the foreign exchange market. After 1992, Uganda kept to the IMF targets and implemented most of the agreed structural reforms, although often with delays; aid was not suspended again. The continuation of aid in spite of unsatisfactory policies in the first period, and slow reforms in the second can be explained by the fact that economic growth was high. In the Ugandan case, the IFIs assessed the *outcome* of the programme, not the *process* (the policy reforms). The IFIs would have lost credibility if they had not supported this 'showcase' of adjustment.

Table 3 gives a summary of the reasons why the threat of withholding aid is not effective. It seems that the existence of a large multilateral debt (6a) is the most important factor in determining whether new IFI programmes will be concluded. This fact reduces the effectiveness of the threat of punishment. The 'adverse selection' argument (6c) seems to be subordinated to the existence of a multilateral debt, since Bangladesh undoubtedly also has a large 'need for aid', while this does not seem to be a reason for IFIs to conclude structural adjustment programmes. Political and bureaucratic pressures to continue lending (6b) will always be present, but their effects do not discriminate between the countries reviewed here. Some countries (Nicaragua and Zambia) suffered from a lack of donor co-ordination (7), often meaning that bilateral donors did not disburse while multilaterals continued. This made it

Table 3. Evidence for Propositions on Why the Threat of Withholding Aid is not Effective

Country	Sanctions by IFIs (see Table 1)	(6a) Large multilateral debt	(6b) Political and bureaucratic pressures	(6c) Adverse selection	(7) Lack of donor co-ordination in sanctions (between multi- and bilateral donors)	(8) Donor credibility
Nicaragua	Yes, but new programmes	Yes		Yes	Yes	
Vietnam	Yes	No			No	
Bangladesh	Yes	No			No	
Uganda '87–'92	No	Yes				Yes
Uganda after '92	No	Yes				Yes
Tanzania '90–'96	Yes, but new programmes	Yes		Yes		
Tanzania after '96	No	Yes				
Zambia	No	Yes		Yes	Yes	
Mozambique	No	Yes		Yes		

more difficult for these countries to meet the monetary and fiscal targets of the IMF. Continuation of programmes without any sanctions in Uganda can be explained by the high growth rate in that country (8).

The Effectiveness of Political Conditionality

Since bilateral donors are the driving force behind political and governance conditions, influence on policies is often carried out through channels other than the structural adjustment programmes of the IFIs. One of these may be the Consultative Group (CG) meetings in which all donors meet and discuss their support to a particular country. Governance issues may also be attached to sectoral adjustment loans of the World Bank and of regional development banks, and to (sectoral) budget support provided by bilateral donors.

Democracy and Human Rights

In Uganda, Vietnam, Bangladesh, Mozambique and Cape Verde no political conditionality — in a strict sense, so excluding governance issues — has been applied (see Table 4, second line). In Uganda, it seems that donors have been convinced that a no-party democracy is a good system (probably because it is conducive to the continuation of stabilization and adjustment). In Vietnam donors appear to realize that their influence is limited: the country is not aid-dependent and certainly not likely to change its political system in response to aid reductions. The (formal) political system in

Table 4. Overview of Political and Governance Conditionality, Instruments and Effectiveness

Topic	Applied in	Specific issue	Aid suspension	Effective
Civil service reform	Nicaragua	No	No	No
	Tanzania	No	No	
	Uganda	No	No	
	Zambia	No	No	
Transparency Corruption	Nicaragua	No	No	No
	Uganda	Yes ('98)	No	Yes
	Zambia	Yes ('93)	Yes	Yes
	Mozambique	No	No	No
Democracy, political system	Nicaragua	Yes ('95)	Yes	Yes
	Zambia	Yes ('96)	Yes	No
	Tanzania	Yes	Yes	No
Human rights	Bangladesh	No	No	No
	Vietnam	No	No	No

Sources: See Table 1.

Bangladesh, Mozambique and Cape Verde does not give rise to complaints:
donors have expressed concern for the human rights situation in Bangladesh, but this has not stopped them from giving project aid.

Political conditionality was applied in Nicaragua in 1995 on a very
specific issue: the Constitutional crisis. Bilateral donors wanted to put
pressure on the government to solve the conflict between Executive and
Parliament on the reforms to the Constitution. Sweden, in particular, played
an important role, being the first to suspend its programme aid and publicly
announcing this decision. Other bilateral donors followed but without
making their decision publicly known. Apparently, the suspension was
successful: the crisis was solved. But this solution was also due to active
mediation undertaken by several bilateral donors in the 'Support Group for
Nicaragua'. The fact that a specific issue was involved enhanced the chances
of success of these interventions by donors.

In Zambia, programme aid was withdrawn because of political conditions. Bilateral donors demanded that former President Kaunda should
stand in the 1995 elections. Since this did not happen, the bilaterals reduced
programme aid in 1996, but multilateral donors continued disbursing. This
weakened the effectiveness of the sanction. The Zambian government did
not make any concession in the political arena. Programme aid from
bilateral donors continued to be at low levels in 1997 and 1998, mainly due
to dissatisfaction with the political situation. However, the slow implementation of the privatization of the state copper mine and of public sector
reforms also played a role, as did governance issues. In Tanzania, bilateral
donors have complained about the unfairness of the elections in Zanzibar,
and aid to this island was reduced, but these criticisms had no consequences
for the aid relationship with the mainland.

Governance

In most countries examined, an increase in donors' attention to governance issues can be observed. In Nicaragua, Tanzania, Uganda and
Zambia, donors have demanded more transparency and accountability of
government revenues and expenditure, with a view to enhancing a correct use of government funds and to limiting corruption. In Nicaragua, donors tried to protect and strengthen the position of the Inspector
General of the Republic, who had revealed financial misdemeanours
among high government officials and who had been threatened by the
government.[6] In Tanzania, the tax system, with its many exemptions,
received much attention from donors. The number of tax exemptions was

---

6. He was put in jail in October 1999, but was released before the end of the year after heavy
    donor pressure.

reduced in the months before a CG meeting in 1995, but then increased again. This shows that governments can easily give an appearance of compliance but then do otherwise. In Zambia, two ministers were accused of drugs trafficking in 1993. They resigned after a CG meeting. In 1995, donors demanded the establishment of a drug enforcement agency and an anti-corruption commission. The suspension of bilateral programme aid that followed in later years, however, was more related to political demands than to these issues of governance.

In Uganda, government accounts are more transparent than in many other countries, but improvements are still possible, especially with respect to the incipient decentralization. Donors are also concerned about corruption. More and more cases of corruption have been publicly revealed and all politicians seem to be concerned about it, but sanctions are rarely applied. While donors had been complaining about this for a long time, they did not put hard pressure on the government until the December 1998 CG meeting. By then, there were signs that the privatization process had been accompanied by corruption on a large scale. The donors forced President Museveni to take charge of privatization, which he did. In addition to the high level of aid dependence and the general willingness on the part of high government officials to comply with donor demands, this demand was also sufficiently specific to be honoured by the government.

A problem with demands for 'good governance' is the complex relationship between earlier reforms, such as privatization and liberalization, and these demands for transparency and accountability (White, 1999b). In Zambia, Nicaragua, Uganda and probably also in ongoing privatization in Tanzania, many high government officials benefited from liberalization and privatization. Bringing these processes into the open would undermine the power base of the government that has promoted these reforms.

In Mozambique, donors are increasingly dissatisfied with the misuse of funds, including aid funds. However, this has not yet led to suspension of aid, and if anything, corruption seems to be on the increase. In Vietnam and Bangladesh, donor complaints about governance mainly concern alleged malpractice of SOEs and state banks, and the close relations between these organizations and government officials. The privatization of SOEs and banks, and more liberalizations, are still among the demands from the IFIs. So far, they have had little success, and given the experiences of other countries one might wonder whether these reforms will solve the governance issues. In Cape Verde, governance does not seem to be an issue at all: donors are satisfied with the relative efficiency of the government.

CONCLUSIONS

A number of conclusions can be drawn from this review of the experiences of these eight countries. First, domestic factors were most important in explaining policy reforms. The role of donors in general, and of the IFIs in particular, has often been overstated. The hypotheses of an augmented principal–agent framework help to explain what happened in the different countries, why compliance was often weak and why the threat of with-holding aid was not effective in most cases.

Conditionality as the 'buying of reform' involves three steps: the making of the agreement, the implementation and monitoring phase, and the phase of rewards or punishments. The first step proved to be important for the extent of compliance. Given their dire financial and economic situation and heavy indebtedness, some recipient countries were under strong pressure to reach an agreement (Nicaragua, Mozambique, Zambia, Tanzania and to some extent Uganda). In such circumstances, governments may give in to demands that they do not agree with or that are politically unfeasible. In the Vietnamese context, the problems began with the diffuse decision-making process in the country, and the lack of clearly defined government objectives and policies. Agreements are worth little in this context.

Second, the country experiences suggest that a broad political economy perspective is necessary to understand whether stabilization and reform measures will be carried out. It is important to recognize who the winners and losers of the reforms will be, and to judge their strength. For internal stabilization, for instance, a strong, but not necessarily authoritarian, central government seems to be necessary. Programme aid funds play an important role in compliance. On the one hand, they allow many countries to more easily meet IMF targets for stabilization; on the other hand, some countries (and sometimes the same ones) were induced to slippage. Programme aid may facilitate structural reforms as well, but only indirectly, by allowing a compensation to powerful losers, as happened to some extent in Nicaragua. On the negative side, programme aid induces moral hazard by allowing continuation of subsidies to SOEs or state banks.

Third, sanctions will be less effective if donors have different objectives, and if one donor has multiple objectives, as proved to be the case with the IMF in Nicaragua. If countries have a large debt, and in particular large debts to multilateral institutions, donors are under strong pressure to continue lending or to reach new agreements. Programmes may be inter-rupted but new programmes will soon be concluded. Vietnam and Bangla-desh are the exceptions that prove this rule: no new programmes have been concluded, but these countries do not have a multilateral debt problem, so there is no need for the IFIs to continue lending, or to stimulate bilaterals to give programme aid. In Uganda before 1992, continuation of the pro-grammes can be explained by successful outcomes, in spite of very limited implementation of reforms.

Another important factor, as demonstrated by the eight countries, is the credibility of both donor and recipient. If economic growth is high, donor credibility will improve since the advice has apparently been good. Recipient credibility will also improve, since policies appear to have been good. In Uganda, the policy dialogue works relatively smoothly due to high growth in the past twelve years. This example shows that exogenous factors may play a role. However, there are other sides to the credibility coin. If the recipient does not believe that recommended policy measures will enhance economic growth, this may not only affect compliance, but the recipient may also be right: if implemented, these measures may not enhance growth, thus seriously affecting mutual confidence in the donor–recipient relationship. In the eight countries studied, there are some examples of 'incredible' policy advice, such as the IMF spending limits in Mozambique, and to some extent also in Nicaragua and Uganda, the liberalization of cashew nut processing in Mozambique, and the liberalization of the capital account in Zambia before stabilization was achieved, which runs counter to accepted consensus in the literature (see, for example, McKinnon, 1993).

The analysis of the eight countries shows that donors' political and governance demands can be effective in some cases, especially if demands are specific, and thus of less significance. Recipient countries will tend to give in on these specific issues, but will renege on others. Demands with respect to the political system were not honoured in any country, and whilst donors may have some influence in the fight against corruption, this happens only if corruption is also seen as a domestic issue.

The limited effectiveness of policy conditionality has also been found in other studies. In spite of this consensus, however, the conditions for debt relief to HIPCs (Heavily Indebted Poor Countries) are more extensive than ever.[7] Apart from its limited effectiveness, this conditionality may also be questioned from an ethical perspective. How can we be sure that the recommendations are correct or that they are the *only* way to success? The country experiences analysed here revealed some inadequate conditions. Although it is beyond the scope of this article to review the extensive literature on 'pro-poor growth', it is clear that we still know very little about this topic. Another problem related to this issue of legitimacy is the inconsistency between donors pushing certain conditions and the content of one of these conditions, namely the requirement for democratic decision making in the recipient country.

In view of the limited effectiveness of setting conditions, several authors have suggested that donors should not attempt to buy reform (*ex ante*), but should reward good performance (*ex post*) (Collier et al., 1997; Killick et al., 1998; White and Morrissey, 1997; World Bank, 1998). This means that greater selectivity be applied in choosing countries that receive aid. In his essay, Pronk argues against this greater selectivity. In his view, conditionality

---

7. For example, the IMF document on the Enhanced HIPC initiative (Andrews et al., 1999: 9) speaks about fostering 'greater ownership by debtor governments of policy targets ...', but at the same time seeks 'a more participatory and transparent process in designing development strategies, increasing the poverty focus of economic and social programs, and ensuring that the savings from debt relief are used exclusively for poverty alleviation'.

is preferrable to selectivity, since countries need help to implement policies that they themselves want to carry out, but for some reason are unable to achieve. However, if it can be established that countries want to carry out certain policies preferred by the donors, these countries would probably not be harmed by selectivity: they would be selected as aid recipients, and donors could play the role Pronk would like to give them. If conditionality would mean 'helping countries which are themselves trying to meet certain criteria', as Pronk (p. 16) suggests, there would be nothing against it. Unfortunately, however, the practice of conditionality is rather different. The country experiences analysed above show that conditionality often means donors attempting to force certain policies onto unwilling governments — policies which may not be the only option, or even the most appropriate, for the particular country. Of course, donors will always be selective since no donor can give aid to all countries. In my view, donors can base their selection either on good intentions (especially if there is a new government) and/or on some simple outcome indicators. Donors should not attempt to use aid to buy policies, nor should selectivity be based on policies. The first is not effective, and in both cases, this practice denies the country the right to design its own policies and find its own ways. Instead of trying to buy reform, donors should give advice and promote debate on policies, rather than prescribe the one and only recipe.

REFERENCES

Andrews, David, Anthony R. Boote, Syed S. Rizavi and Sukhwinder Singh (1999) *Debt Relief for Low-Income Countries: The Enhanced HIPC Initiative.* IMF Pamphlet Series No. 51. Washington, DC: IMF.

Collier, Paul, Patrick Guillaumont, Sylviane Guillaumont and Jan Willem Gunning (1997) 'Redesigning Conditionality', *World Development* 25(9): 1399–407.

Crawford, Gordon (1997) 'Foreign Aid and Political Conditionality: Issues of Effectiveness and Consistency', *Democratization* 4(3) 69–108.

Ddumba-Ssentamu, John, Geske Dijkstra and Jan Kees van Donge (1999) 'What Does the Showcase Show? Programme Aid to Uganda'. Sida Evaluation Report 1999/17:6. Stockholm: Sida (www.sida.se/programaidevaluation).

Dijkstra, Geske (1999a) 'Programme Aid, Policies and Politics: Programme Aid and Conditionality'. Sida Evaluation Report 1999/17:10. Stockholm, Sida (www.sida.se/programaidevaluation).

Dijkstra, Geske (1999b) 'Debt, Dependence, and Fragile Development: Programme Aid to Nicaragua'. Sida Evaluation Report 1999/17:4. Stockholm: Sida (www.sida.se/programaid evaluation).

Dijkstra, Geske and Jan Kees van Donge (1999) 'Development by Default: Programme Aid to Bangladesh'. Sida Evaluation Report 1999/17:1. Stockholm: Sida (www.sida.se/programaid evaluation).

Dijkstra, A. Geske and Jan Kees van Donge (2001) 'What does the "Show Case" Show? Evidence of, and Lessons from Adjustment in Uganda', *World Development* 29(5): 841–63.

Dollar, David and Jakob Svensson (1998) 'What Explains the Success or Failure of Structural Adjustment Programs?' World Bank Policy Research Working Paper no 1998. Washington, DC: The World Bank.

van Donge, Jan Kees and Howard White (1999) 'Counting the Donors' Blessings: Programme Aid to Tanzania'. Sida Evaluation Report 1999/17:5. Stockholm: Sida (www.sida.se/programaidevaluation).

Gibbon, Peter (1993) 'The World Bank and the New Politics of Aid', in Georg Sorensen (ed.) *Political Conditionality*, pp. 35–62. London: Frank Cass/EADI.

Haggard, Stephan (1985) 'The Politics of Adjustment', *International Organization* 39(3): 505–34.

Hutchful, Eboe (1996) 'Ghana', in Poul Engberg-Pedersen, Peter Gibbon, Phil Raikes and Lars Udholt (eds) *Limits of Adjustment in Africa,* pp. 141–214. Oxford: James Currey; Portsmouth, NJ: Heinemann.

Kahler, Miles (1992) 'External Influence, Conditionality and the Politics of Adjustment', in Stephan Haggard and Robert R. Kaufman (eds) *The Politics of Economic Adjustment,* pp. 89–136. Princeton, NJ: Princeton University Press.

Killick, Tony (1995) *IMF Programmes in Developing Countries: Design and Impact.* London: Routledge.

Killick, Tony (1997) 'Principals and Agents and the Failings of Conditionality', *Journal of International Development* 9(4): 483–95.

Killick, Tony, Ramani Gunatilaka and Ana Mar (1998) *Aid and the Political Economy of Policy Change.* London and New York: Routledge.

Leefmans, Naomi and Howard White (1999) 'Supporting Success: Programme Aid to Cape Verde'. Sida Evaluation Report 1999/17:2. Stockholm: Sida (www.sida.se/programaid evaluation).

McKinnon, Ronald I. (1993) *The Order of Economic Liberalization: Financial Control in the Transition Economy.* Baltimore, MD, and London: Johns Hopkins University Press.

Mosley, Paul, Jane Harrigan and John Toye (1991) *Aid and Power: The World Bank and Policy-Based Lending.* London: Routledge.

Mosley, Paul and John Hudson (1996) 'Aid, Conditionality and Moral Hazard' (mimeo).

Murshed, S. Mansoob and Somnath Sen (1995) 'Aid Conditionality and Military Expenditure Reduction in Developing Countries: Models of Asymmetric Information', *The Economic Journal* 105(429): 498–509.

Ngia, Le Xuan, Jan Kees van Donge and Howard White (1999) 'Fostering High Growth in a Low Income Country: Programme Aid to Vietnam'. Sida Evaluation Report 1999/17:7. Stockholm: Sida (www.sida.se/programaidevaluation).

Robinson, Mark (1993) 'Aid, Democracy and Political Conditionality in Sub-Saharan Africa', in Georg Sorensen (ed.) *Political Conditionality*, pp. 85–99. London: Frank Cass/EADI.

Streeten, Paul (1987) 'Structural Adjustment: A Survey of the Issues and Options', *World Development* 15(12): 1469–82.

de Vylder, Stefan (1994) 'Why Deficits Grow: A Critical Discussion of the Impact of Structural Adjustment Lending on the External Account in Low-income Countries'. Conference paper. Stockholm.

White, Howard (1999a) 'Reform, Rehabilitation and Recovery: Programme Aid to Mozambique'. Sida Evaluation Report 1999/17:3. Stockholm: Sida (www.sida.se/program aidevaluation).

White, Howard (1999b) 'A Black Sheep Among the Reformers: Programme Aid to Zambia'. Sida Evaluation Report 1999/17:8. Stockholm: Sida (www.sida.se/programaidevaluation).

White, Howard and Oliver Morrissey (1997) 'Conditionality when Donor and Recipient Preferences Vary', *Journal of International Development* 9(4): 497–505.

World Bank (1988) *Adjustment Lending: Ten Years of Experience.* Washington, DC: The World Bank.

World Bank (1998) *Assessing Aid: What Works, What Doesn't, and Why.* Oxford and New York: Oxford University Press for the World Bank.

Chapter 9

Aid and the Geopolitics of the Post-Colonial: Critical Reflections on New Labour's Overseas Development Strategy

David Slater and Morag Bell

INTRODUCTION

The accentuation of international inequalities across the North–South divide (UNDP, 1999: 3; World Bank, 2000: 3) has become an issue of increasing global significance. This is not only reflected in the social science literature on development but also in public debates and controversy concerning the role of institutions such as the World Bank and the World Trade Organization. In the post Cold War era, combined questions of inequality, poverty and social exclusion have become central to many of the key discussions of international relations and development aid. In the case of poverty, strategies to eliminate or reduce its presence in the world have been directly linked to security concerns (Blair, 2000: 6; Klare, 2000: 10; OECD, 1996; Sachs, 2001: 52), but they can also be related to the ethics of development policy and the overarching ethos of constructing a more just and equal world. Within this context we aim to analyse the nature and specificity of the overseas development strategy of New Labour, in Britain, as it has emerged from 1997 onwards. Our reflections will focus on the relations between New Labour politics and the British government's specific treatment of overseas development. In the setting of the literatures on post-colonialism, aid and development, we intend to examine the specific concepts and approaches that help to frame such a strategy and its unfolding dynamic in the years following the General Election of 1997.

In examining Britain's overseas development strategy under New Labour, we shall seek to account for the distinctiveness and novelty of this strategy in the context of the contemporary discussion on aid and development. The perspective we deploy connects ideas and issues from domains of knowledge which tend to remain independent of each other — namely, aid and development studies, and post-colonial theory (for a recent exception, see Sylvester, 1999). In the setting of aid and development, our purpose is to raise certain questions concerning power, knowledge and geopolitics and to do so in a way that we hope might generate a broader conceptual and policy-oriented debate.

CONTEXTUALIZING CONTINUITY AND CHANGE

Examining North–South relations in terms of some of the main conceptual and thematic landmarks of development thinking, a number of important continuities can be discerned for the post Second World War era. Hence, a concern from the 1960s and 1970s with marginality and the informal sector is reflected in contemporary discussions of poverty and social exclusion, whilst the modernization theory of the 1950s and 1960s, with its emphasis on the importance of the Western diffusion of capital, technology and institutional innovations, is reflected in the contemporary prioritization of the spread of Western forms of democratic governance and modernity (Alexander, 1995). Conversely, change and discontinuity are manifested in the post Cold War period; for example, ostensibly new dangers to world order and development have been linked to, *inter alia*, drug-trafficking, ethno-regional strife, environmental degradation and the generalized spread of violent conflicts (Huntington, 1998; Kaplan, 1997).

The geopolitical watershed of 1989 has been particularly significant for changes in the global picture on development aid. With the end of the Cold War and the demise of the Soviet bloc there has been a 'double squeeze' on development aid. Thus, on the one hand countries of the former USSR and Eastern Europe are much less capable of supplying aid funds, with detrimental results for former Soviet allies such as Cuba, Afghanistan and Vietnam. On the other hand, many countries of the former Soviet bloc have become aid recipients in competition with countries of the South. More crucially, the end of the Cold War and the evaporation of the 'Soviet communist threat' have eliminated a key rationale for allocating aid, whilst the countries of the South have far less manoeuvrability in a world devoid of superpower rivalry.

In this sense, it is not surprising that, in contrast to the 1970s and 1980s, the flows of foreign aid to developing countries fell noticeably in the 1990s. Net ODA (Official Development Assistance) flows from the DAC (Development Assistance Committee) countries to developing countries and multilateral organizations dropped markedly from US\$ 60.8 bn in 1992 to US\$ 48.3 bn in 1997, a fall of 20 per cent in real terms. This represented a decline in ODA as a percentage of the combined GNP of the OECD countries from 0.33 per cent in 1992 to 0.22 per cent in 1997, less than a third of the agreed target of 0.7 per cent (Rasheed, 1999: 25). Recent World Bank data confirm this trend, showing that official aid from the wealthy states of the OECD fell from US\$ 32 a head in 1990 to US\$ 19 a head in 1998 (*The Guardian* 16 February 2001: 18). Specifically for the United Kingdom, the ODA/GNP ratio fell from 0.29 in 1995 to 0.27 in 1996

(Randel and German, 1999: 235) and by 1999, two years into the New Labour government, the ratio had fallen to 0.23.[1]

In contrast to this decline in the 'aid flow', private financial flows to the third world have witnessed a strong increase, so that between 1988 and 1997 private flows to the developing countries rose from US\$ 36 bn to US\$ 252.1 bn, while their share of total North–South transfers grew from 38 per cent to 78 per cent (Thérien and Lloyd, 2000: 27). Moreover, even for the world's forty-four poorest countries, foreign investment, according to UNCTAD, has risen steadily over the past decade, from an annual average of under US\$ 1 bn in 1987–92 to nearly US\$ 3 bn in 1998 (*The Economist* 20 May 2000: 127).

Although development aid decreased during the 1990s, it is certainly not in a state of terminal decline. According to van de Walle (1999: 337), in 1997 sub-Saharan Africa for example still received over US\$ 16 bn in official development assistance. It should also be noted here that for Africa as a whole aid dependency, roughly measured with a cutoff point of 10 per cent of GNP, has seen a notable increase: while in 1975–79, seventeen African countries showed a mean annual ODA of more than 10 per cent of GNP, by 1980–89 the number had risen to twenty-five, and for the 1990–97 period there were thirty-one African aid recipients (representing an estimated total population of 365 million people) whose ODA averaged more than 10 per cent of GNP (Goldsmith, 2001: 125). The association of aid with dependence raises issues concerning the desirability, effectiveness and long-term value of aid for the societies of the South. Can aid be a catalyst for development, as Pronk (this volume, Ch. 1) suggests?

Certainly, in its evaluation of aid, the World Bank (1998) has taken a generally positive view, which is further reflected in the World Development Report for 2000, where it is noted that 'aid can be highly effective in promoting growth and reducing poverty' (World Bank, 2000: 73).[2] In a similar vein, Cassen (1994: 9), in his comprehensive review of aid, stresses the point that 'the great majority of aid succeeds in its developmental objectives'. New Labour has also underscored the key place of aid in the development process (Labour Party, 1999). Overall, there is an official view that development assistance has, amongst other things, contributed to a fall in child mortality, improved access to clean water, helped in the control of disease, brought better educational provision and generated a more efficient network of infrastructure and utilities. This positive, if at times guarded,

---

1. This figure was accessed from the DFID web site on 29 June 2000. It is noted by the Department of International Development that the 0.23 figure was anomalous due to 'the different time frame of our financial year and the DAC's use of the calendar year and is largely the consequence of the timing of the deposit of promissory notes in respect of the International Development Association (IDA) and the African Development Fund; lower than predicted spending by the EC; and the timing of bringing to book expenditure on Kosovo' (see http://www.dfid.gov.uk).

2. For a useful critique of the World Bank's (1998) report on aid, see, for example, Lensink and White (2000), as well as the discussion in Pronk (this volume, Ch. 1).

approach stands in sharp contradiction to the proponents of 'post-development' perspectives, who tend to equate 'development', or 'progress' or 'modernization', with a whole range of negative characteristics, seeing these conceptual markers as rooted in the history of Western imperialism (see, for example, Rahnema and Bawtree, 1997; and for a recent appraisal, Nederveen Pieterse, 2000).[3]

Here is one example of a salient divergence of interpretation which affects a broad range of discussion surrounding themes of development, aid and the impacts of globalization. Along one connected and potentially enabling pathway we encounter an emphasis on the post-colonial that is not only about periodization but also and more specifically connected to questions of theoretical, methodological and ethico-political positionality (Ashcroft et al., 1998; Bell, 1998; Rattansi, 1997; Slater, 1998). Research on post-colonial themes has received most attention in the fields of comparative literature and cultural studies (Bhabha, 1994; Said, 1978, 1993; Spivak, 1999), but problems raised in this domain are pertinent to a critical consideration of the relation between aid and development, just as issues of poverty, inequality and development policy can be relevant to a treatment of post-coloniality.

PROFILING A POST-COLONIAL PERSPECTIVE

With respect to our own argument, a post-colonial perspective can be delineated in relation to the following three elements:

- First, as a mode of enquiry, the post-colonial can be associated with the post-structural and the post-modern in the sense that it foregrounds issues of difference, agency, subjectivity, hybridity and resistance. It does so, however, in a way which aims to destabilize Western discourses of modernity, progress and development, always making connections with the continual salience of colonial and imperial imaginations.
- Second, the post-colonial can be deployed to bring into play the mutually constitutive role played by colonizer and colonized, centre and periphery, or globalizers and the globalized. In other words, rather than remain within a frame that only sees a one-way power relation between the dominant and the dominated, the post-colonial turn recognizes that in these dynamic interactions both entities in the relation are inevitably affected, albeit in quite different ways.

---

3. As one rather symptomatic example from the post-development perspective, we might quote from Teodor Shanin, who writes of progress thus: 'those who first adopted the notion of progress presented their own understanding as the highest achievement of progress to date, and consequently projected the shape of the coming future to the rest of mankind — as an example to all, a natural leader of all. This lent the idea its immense arrogance' (Shanin, 1997: 68).

- Third, the post-colonial as a critical mode of enquiry can be used to pose a series of questions concerning key policy documents as 'sites of enunciation'. For example, who are the agents of knowledge, where are they located, for whom do they speak, how do they conceptualize, where are the analytical silences, who is being empowered and who is being marginalized?

This kind of perspective leads us to pursue a number of analytical openings in this article. The first is to focus on the significance of power and representation in the context of the content, orientation, thematic prioritization and conceptual architecture of a given overseas development strategy (Baumann, 1999; Sutton, 1999), where issues of poverty and inequality, globalization and partnership, and rights and responsibilities are paramount. Secondly, it leads us to examine the nature of the donor–recipient nexus in development assistance (Crewe and Harrison, 1998; Edwards and Sen, 2000; Mosley et al., 1991), taking into account the ways rights and responsibilities are specified in the context of the geopolitics of North-South relations. Thirdly, we raise the issues of sites and agents of knowledge and their differential recognition (Said, 1983) within the official documents on development, being cognisant of uneven access in the overall framing of long-term strategy (Gasper and Apthorpe, 1996). Fourthly, we assess the conceptual and thematic configuration of the official development documentation to identify and evaluate the existence of newness, especially linked to New Labour notions of 'Third Way' politics; and finally, we evaluate to what extent two Labour government White Papers (DFID, 1997 and DFID, 2000) transcend erstwhile ethnocentric orientations in the analysis of and policy prescription for the 'developing world'. Is the partnership model, for example, free from what an influential OECD document referred to as 'paternalistic approaches' to development (OECD, 1996: 13)?

These analytical openings represent one way of giving substance to a critical post-colonial perspective. The key focus of our discussion will be the two New Labour White Papers of 1997 and 2000. In examining these documents, we intend to prioritize questions of voice, agency, representation, knowledge and power. The distinctiveness of our approach is best understood in terms of the way we explore the border zones between development issues and post-colonial enquiry.

NEW LABOUR AND DEVELOPMENT: SO WHAT'S NEW?

Since 1997, the British Labour government under Prime Minister Tony Blair has formulated an overseas development strategy which has given priority to tackling poverty in a global era. This was reflected in an initial White Paper, *Eliminating World Poverty: A Challenge for the 21st Century* published in November 1997 (DFID, 1997), and its successor published in December 2000 and entitled *Eliminating World Poverty: Making Globalisation Work for the Poor* (DFID, 2000). The suggestion that Labour's strategy represents a new beginning in the diagnosis and treatment of development problems can be linked to four elements of a New Labour Agenda, namely:

- the existence of a firm belief in the importance of aid and development, as institutionally reflected in the establishment of a new and independent Department for International Development (DFID) which was assigned a Cabinet seat and a wide development co-operation mandate;
- an emphasis on the close connections linking ethics, human rights and overseas development strategy;
- a primary focus on efforts to eliminate world poverty and promote sustainable economic growth that benefits the poor, and
- a distinctive application of 'Third Way' politics (Blair, 1998; Giddens, 1998, 2000) to questions of development strategy, with, for instance, particular attention being given to new forms of partnership with the private sector, the NGO community and 'partner governments' from the developing world, the identification of 'stakeholders' and the specification of rights and responsibilities in the development process.

Clearly, with such a combination of elements there will be connections with past policies and predispositions, and whilst such a combination is surely distinctive it might be argued that it is just that — distinctive, and not actually 'new'. Moreover, some may well argue that much of the apparent novelty is little more than effective state of the art 'spin'.[4] What we want to propose here, as a first approximation, is that the mobile combination of these elements and the way they help mould the Labour government's discourse of development does reflect an important sense of novelty.

One example of the interweaving of continuity and discontinuity concerns the way world poverty itself has been highlighted and framed. Already in the mid-1970s, in the White Paper entitled *The Changing Emphasis in British Aid Policies: More Help to the Poorest* (Ministry of Overseas Development, 1975), it was stated that the Government intended to ensure that a higher proportion of British aid should directly benefit not only the poorest countries, but the poorest people in those countries; this was to be done through an emphasis on a 'basic needs' approach to development coupled with the introduction of integrated rural development projects — in fact a precursor of today's pro-poor growth strategy for rural areas. As a positive effect of the White Paper of 1975, aid as a percentage of GNP grew in the period of the Wilson and Callaghan governments, from 0.37 per cent in

---

4. In relation to foreign policy for example, Douglas Hurd commented that what was most annoying about New Labour was the pretence 'that a shift of two or three degrees is a shift of 180 degrees and that all [New Labour's] predecessors were immoral rogues', from Hurd (1997), quoted in Abrahamsen and Williams (2001: 260).

1974 to 0.52 per cent in 1979 (White, 1998: 155). Internationally of course, poverty has received recurrent attention in a wide range of development documents, such as the *World Development Reports* of 1990 and 2000/1 (World Bank, 1990, 2000), where poverty was assigned the keynote focus.

We would thus argue, as regards poverty elimination as well as other issues of the development problematic, that it is the dynamic combination of meanings, conceptualizations, and ethical justifications that needs to be considered. It is this changing combination which provides the basis for understanding the distinctiveness and novelty of New Labour's development strategy. To elaborate this idea we will now examine chronologically the 1997 and 2000 White Papers; this will be followed by a succinct critical analysis that will endeavour to show the commonalities and divergences between the two statements of strategy.

A TALE OF TWO WHITE PAPERS

The 1997 White Paper

In terms of aid and development, the incoming Labour government of May 1997 inherited a situation in which no new White Paper had been produced during eighteen years of Conservative government; furthermore, during the 1980s aid as a percentage of GNP had fallen to 0.28 per cent in 1986 and to 0.27 per cent by 1990 (White, 1998: 156). Even so, in terms of priorities, there were some longer-term facets of continuity, certainly with reference to the problems of world poverty. For example, in the mid-1990s, the then UK Minister for Overseas Development, Linda Chalker, concluded an address on Britain's approach to multilateral aid by stressing the importance of 'poverty reduction' and 'sustainable development', combined with the pronounced aim of ensuring that what was done in the field of aid 'represents value for money' (Chalker, 1994: 250).

Whilst the Labour government set about distinguishing itself from its predecessor in a number of areas, as we shall see below, there were nonetheless certain links with Thatcherite discourse. Tony Blair, for instance, in his Fabian pamphlet on *The Third Way: New Politics for the New Century* (Blair, 1998: 5) reminded the Labour Party that in retrospect some of the reforms of the Thatcher Government were 'necessary acts of modernisation, particularly the exposure of much of the state industrial sector to reform and competition'. His advocacy of economic liberalism was also captured in the statement that 'free trade has proved itself a motor for economic development, political cooperation and cultural exchange' (ibid.: 18), a view that could be effectively encapsulated within a Thatcherite discourse.

However, there was much that was novel and distinctive. In the specific domain of overseas development strategy the new Secretary of State for International Development, Clare Short, in her foreword to the 1997 White Paper, boldly stated that 'it is our duty to care about other people, in particular those less well off than ourselves', and 'we have a *moral* duty to reach out to the poor and needy' (Short, 1997: 5) — words that find an echo in Tony Blair's preface to the 2000 White Paper, where he defines the elimination of world poverty as the 'greatest *moral* challenge facing our generation' (Blair, 2000: 6, emphasis added in both cases). This strong sense of moral duty was closely linked to the prioritization of human rights and a more ethical foreign policy (DFID, 1997: 16), previously underlined in the first days of New Labour's term of office by the then Foreign Secretary Robin Cook, who referred to the significance of an 'ethical dimension' to foreign policy (quoted in Abrahamsen and Williams, 2001: 250). At the same time, the stress on moral duty, the ethical dimension in foreign affairs and the welcoming of 'ethical investment movements' (DFID, 1997: 46) were associated with a belief in the uniqueness of Britain's position in the world. The White Paper notes that, 'no other country combines membership of the Group of Seven industrialised countries, membership of the European Union, a permanent seat on the Security Council of the United Nations (UN) and membership of the Commonwealth... [o]ur particular history places us on the fulcrum of global influence', and, finally, 'helping to lead the world in a commitment to poverty elimination and sustainable development is an international role in which all the people of Britain could take pride' (DFID, 1997: 20).[5]

The 1997 White Paper constituted a clear statement of moral purpose in respect of the elimination of world poverty (DFID, 1997: 8), but also and rather crucially it was an exercise in codifying the '*differentia specifica*' of New Labour's aid and development strategy. Its geopolitical import (and we use the term geopolitical here because politics can never be realistically viewed as being a-spatial), was to chart a *break* from the past and to signal the advent of a new design and a new practical reason, which would be relevant globally *and* nationally.

The 1997 document had four essential components: development and poverty as challenge; the building of partnerships; policy consistency; and finally the support for development. Of these four, partnerships and policy consistency received the most detailed consideration and in subsequent discussion of the document, the place of partnership has aroused the most attention. We would argue here that the framing and orientation of the 1997 White Paper was influenced by a combination of official development discourse, most evidently represented by the World Bank, and ideas stemming from 'Third Way politics'. In this appraisal we shall concentrate on the latter influence since this relates more closely to the issue of distinctiveness, and the need to mark a new beginning. We shall re-align our focus when we consider the 2000 White Paper.

---

5. The invocation of 'uniqueness' is repeated in Blair's *Third Way*, where he notes that 'we are uniquely placed, with strong partnerships with the EU, the US and in Asia, to create a distinctive global role' (Blair, 1998: 18).

The 'Third Way' influence was most clearly visible in the way models of development were interpreted. These models were characterized as having two flaws: either prioritizing state interventionism, with its attendant pitfalls of corruption and inefficiency; or maintaining a belief in a 'minimalist State and unregulated market forces', which had failed to guarantee economic growth and had generated increases in inequality. The alternative was to chart a path between these two opposites, to 'create a new synthesis which builds on the role of the State in facilitating economic growth and benefiting the poor' (DFID, 1997: 12). This new synthesis or 'Third Way' — the attempt, as Giddens (1998: 26) puts it, to transcend both old-style social democracy and neo-liberalism — talks of a 'virtuous State' playing a key role in 'supporting economic arrangements which encourage human development, stimulate enterprise and saving and create the environment necessary to mobilise domestic resources and to attract foreign investment' (DFID, 1997: 12). It is only governments, provided they are 'virtuous', that can provide the 'right political and economic framework' for the elimination of world poverty — in the words of Blair (1998: 15), the time of 'big government means better government is over'. The motor is provided by economic growth and the framework is closely linked to the priority given to partnerships in development, a point we will return to below.

The notion of a virtuous, effective State which is part of the New Labour discourse is also of course mirrored in the World Bank's *World Development Report* of 1997, where a very similar role is assigned to the State in its relation to the private sector (World Bank, 1997), with the well-discussed shift in conceptual emphasis from the idea of a minimal to an effective State being a key dimension. Here, then, is a coalescence of the two influences of World Bank strategy and 'Third Way politics'.

We have already referred to the place of a moral imperative in New Labour discourse, and this connects to a stress on 'rights and responsibilities'. Whilst responsibilities and duty were once seen as the preserve of the Right, in Blair's view New Labour must give these values a renewed weight, since for too long the demand for rights from the state was divorced from the responsibilities of the citizen. According to Blair, rights require the reciprocity of responsiblity and duty, or 'the rights we enjoy reflect the duties we owe: rights and opportunity without responsibility are engines of selfishness and greed' (Blair, 1998: 4). A vibrant civil society which enshrines rights and responsibilities, and where the government is a partner to strong communities, has become a key policy objective of the Third Way (ibid.: 7).[6]

---

6. This viewpoint is repeated in Giddens' book on the Third Way, where he writes that a prime motto for the new politics might well be 'no rights without responsibilities'. With the gowth of individualism, the claiming of rights should be coupled with obligations to society. As an ethical principle, Giddens states, 'no rights without responsibilities' must apply to everyone (Giddens, 1998: 65–66).

In the 1997 White Paper, rights and responsibilities are mentioned in the opening section on the challenge of development where human rights are situated in a framework of State responsibility. States, for example, have a responsibility to ensure that human rights are respected (DFID, 1997: 16). We should strive for a global society in which people everywhere can enjoy their full civil and political rights, and where economic endeavour is joined together with accountable government, or, in other words, with government that assumes its responsibilities (ibid.: 10). In the later section on partnerships the same message is repeated in terms of the need for 'political commitment to poverty elimination on both sides' — that is, the developing countries should also assume their responsibility in the common effort with the donor countries to work towards the elimination of poverty (ibid.: 37). It is in fact the rights/responsibilities couplet that acts as a setting for the discussion of partnership, which forms a crucial part of the 1997 document.

Clearly, in the world of development, the concept of partnership has a history, stretching back at least, for example, to the 1969 Pearson Report on *Partners in Development* (Jolly, 1999: 40). More recently, the OECD (1996) report on development co-operation included an annex on 'development partnerships in the new global context' and the report's overall title of *Shaping the 21st Century* finds an echo in the 1997 White Paper sub-title of world poverty as 'a challenge for the 21st century'. Thus the idea of partnership was obviously not created *ab initio* by New Labour,[7] but its meaning and deployment do tell us something about the distinctiveness of New Labour's development strategy.

The 1997 document declares that building partnerships will involve:

- working closely with other donors and development agencies to establish partnerships with developing countries in order to strengthen the commitment to eliminate poverty and to help mobilize the political will be necessary to achieve the international development targets,
- pursuing these targets in partnership with poorer countries who are also committed to them, and
- putting into place new ways of working with the UK private and voluntary sectors, and the research community, so that there will be progress towards meeting international development targets, including the measurement of the effectiveness of our efforts (DFID, 1997: 22).

The partnership aspect of the 1997 White Paper can be briefly assessed around the following points. First, it was clear that one innovative feature of New Labour's perspective involved partnerships with developing countries,

---

7. In the mid-1990s, for instance, Linda Chalker, the Conservative Government's Minister for Overseas Development, underscored the importance of partnership in development co-operation (Chalker, 1994: 250).

where a genuine attempt would be made to identify governments who would be committed to the same development aims as those of the UK government. Second, the main focus for the discussion of partnerships in Britain was with the private sector, and in a section entitled 'Working with British Business', it was argued that since the developing countries contain a majority of the population in the faster growing markets, there ought to be a shared interest between Government and business in supporting sustainable development. In the same section, a critical comment was included to the effect that the 'pursuit of short-term commercial objectives, such as the previous Government's support for the Pergau project or Westland helicopters', should be avoided (ibid.: 41). This was clearly an attempt by the Government to distinguish itself from the previous administration. At the same time it underlined the importance of business in the New Labour perspective on development, for example, through the establishment of a new awards scheme to recognize private sector companies who have developed partnerships for sustainable development (ibid.: 46). As Blair (1998: 8) expressed it in a national context: 'New Labour's partnership with business is critical to national prosperity'. The prioritization of business and the private sector reflected one strand of Third Way politics but was also closely linked into the main lines of World Bank development strategy.

Third, although an attempt was being made to move away from previous formulations of the donor–recipient relation with its associated hierarchy, there was little evidence that a previous dialogue had been held with the governments of developing countries, through which the notion of partnership could have grown out of a dialogical encounter. Maxwell and Riddell (1998: 264) express this point rather well, noting that potential partners might interpret the UK's take on partnership to mean the following: 'we know how best to achieve development ... we know how you should alleviate poverty ... either you accept the approaches which we think are right for you or you will not qualify for a long-term partnership with us ... if you do not accept our view of development, then we will not provide you with aid'. It is therefore legitimate to ask how far, if at all, the 1997 document moved away from the unequal relations of power and representation that characterize political conditionality (Sørensen, 1993). Equally, one could ask, how much had been done to change the intrinsically one-sided nature of the aid relationship, and to what extent was there any cognizance of the inter-relations between cultural differentiations and political rules and obligations (Kayizzi-Mugerwa, 1998)?

It is in this arena of debate that we connect back to the uses of a post-colonial perspective. Rather than developing a critical assessment of the 1997 document at this point, however, we will first examine the 2000 White Paper and then raise a series of joint questions and critical points that will bring together an overall evaluation of New Labour's overseas development strategy, seen as a continuing enterprise.

The 2000 White Paper

Why were there two White Papers on the elimination of world poverty in the space of three years? For Hewitt (2001) in his review of the 2000 document, there are two basic reasons. First, the 2000 White Paper was a response to the 'post-Seattle' anti-globalization movement, and second it was needed as a way of making connections between the national and the global, by joining up strategies to confront poverty inside the UK with poverty worldwide. This 'joining up' may also be linked to the political personae involved, where Gordon Brown as Chancellor of the Exchequer and Clare Short as International Development Secretary at the time shared a keen interest in tackling poverty and in confronting what they considered to be the misguided views of those who were taking to the streets to protest globalization, or what is more appropriately regarded as a specific neo-liberal form of globalization. This personal connection was also expressed in a jointly authored newspaper article entitled, 'Our answer to the protestors', published in *The Guardian* (4 July 2001: 15). The authors wrote that 'it is our task to show the demonstrators against globalization that the way to attack poverty is not to retreat from global cooperation — to the free-for-all or protectionism of the 1930s — but to strengthen it', and 'to achieve this we must assemble a new *global partnership*' (emphasis added).

On global partnership, the second White Paper contains far more treatment of globalization than of partnership, and in this sense at least contrasts quite markedly with the 1997 document which in a context of partnership gave more emphasis to social questions of health, education, gender and environmental change. The 2000 White Paper is much more a treatise on globalization, ostensibly written by economists who take a positive position on the merits of economic liberalization in world trade and investment. Key sections are devoted to markets, investment, trade, skills and knowledge, private finance, environmental problems and development assistance.

As in the 1997 White Paper, the task of eliminating world poverty is defined as a 'moral challenge' (Blair, 2000: 6) and this is repeated in the first chapter on the challenge of globalization which states that 'making globalisation work more effectively for the world's poor is a moral imperative' (DFID, 2000: 14). Also as previously, a link is made to issues of security and national interest; we read that many of the problems which affect the UK — war, crime and the trade in illegal drugs — are caused by poverty, and at the same time, the commitment to help eliminate world poverty reflects the government's 'determination to tackle poverty and social exclusion in the UK' (Blair, 2000: 6). These interpretive ties are underscored in the first chapter where, after a passage concerning the future potential for growing conflicts over scarce resources and new social tensions that could easily cross national borders, a geopolitical warning is given that 'there can be no secure future for any of us — wherever we live — unless we promote greater global social justice' (DFID, 2000: 14). This bringing together of the national and the global which we referred to in our discussion of the 1997 White Paper is given more space in the 2000 document. For example, in the context of globalization it is suggested that the 'distinction between domestic and international policy is increasingly blurred', with 'domestic policies such as taxation having international aspects and most "international" policies such as trade having domestic dimensions' (ibid.: 19). This sense of the blurring of boundaries between the national and the global is a clear reflection of the significance attached to the increasing impact of globalization. In fact, before publication of the 2000 White Paper, Blair clearly linked globalization to 'Third Way politics', stating that, 'the driving force behind the ideas associated with the Third Way is globalisation because no country is immune from the massive change that globalisation brings' (Blair [1999], quoted in Fairclough, 2000: 27).

Let us now consider the way globalization is conceptually interpreted in the 2000 document (DFID, 2000: 14–15). Globalization, as a process, is defined in terms of the growing interdependence and interconnectedness of the modern world. This is specified in relation to the increased ease of movement of goods, services, capital, people and information across national borders. It is argued that the process is driven by advances in technology and reductions in the costs of international transactions, which diffuse ideas, raise the share of trade in world production and increase capital mobility. In addition, globalization is reflected in the spread of global norms and values, the diffusion of democracy, the proliferation of global agreements and treaties and the worldwide growth of transnational companies. The 2000 White Paper endorses this benign view and contrasts it with a counterposed position which ostensibly defines globalization in terms of the unleashing of market forces, a minimal role for the state and an explosion of inequality. This latter standpoint is depicted as regarding the move towards a more open and integrated global economy as tantamount to laying the foundations for more exploitation, poverty and inequality. From the DFID perspective this is the anti-globalization stance which has received far more public attention, post-Seattle,[8] and which risks undermining all the benefits of globalization, leading, for example, to a situation where poor countries become marginalized from the world economy.

What many of the NGOs involved in the process of contesting the neo-liberal discourse of globalization are arguing, together with many critical social scientists, is that it is not globalization *per se* that is at stake but rather questions such as the *conditions* under which it takes place, the *terms* of engagement it requires between the countries of the North and the South,

---

8. There is already a burgeoning literature on the Seattle events and their aftermath; see, for example, the overview text of Cockburn et al. (2000), and a series of short articles in the journal of international studies *Millennium* 29(1): 105–40 (2000) where Mary Kaldor, Fred Halliday, Stephen Gill and Jan Aart Scholte discuss some of the key issues.

the *identification* of winners and losers in the process, the *politics* of decision-making within key institutions such as the IMF, the WTO and the World Bank, and the recognition of *asymmetrical power relations* in the conduct of international development.

There is in the manner of DFID's treatment of globalization an apparent failure to recognize the conflict of interest and priorities between the operation of transnational corporations and the welfare of third world populations. Moreover there is a rather uncritical projection of globalization as being equivalent to a beneficial spread of all things Western, as with the modernization theory of the 1950s and 1960s. Elsewhere, for example in a short article in *The New Statesman* (18 September 2000: 22), Clare Short declares that globalization is not just about increased trade and mobility of capital, but also about the 'growing internationalisation of *our* culture and values' (emphasis added) and therefore 'globalisation is here to stay'. Is this the real agenda then: globalization = Westernization?   ·

A response might be that in the 2000 White Paper, much importance is given to the role of developing countries so that development strategies must be adapted to local circumstances and 'must be nationally owned and nationally led by developing and transition countries' (DFID, 2000: 13). This point is repeated in relation to poverty reduction strategies in a later part of the document (ibid.: 91), and can be seen as a follow-up to key recommendations in the OECD (1996) report on future development strategy.[9] However, given the lack of consensus over what types of policies might achieve patterns of equitable economic growth, a more creative initiative would be a participatory process involving developing country governments and civil societies, in which the differing needs of developing countries are recognized, and wherein their right to democratically decide their own development path is respected (WDM, 2001). So, where the document refers to sustainable development strategies in the global economy, and the need for developed and developing countries to have more 'joined-up and coherent policies' (DFID, 2000: 19), the voices and political priorities of developing countries require more recognition — especially if being 'joined-up' is to avoid the pitfalls of old-fashioned political conditionality in the aid encounter. This suggestion takes us back to key aspects of the 1997 White Paper, and forward to a combined evaluation of the two White Papers.

---

9. For example, in a section on effective partnerships, the OECD document stressed the point that 'as a basic principle, locally-owned country development strategies and targets should emerge from an open and collaborative dialogue by local authorities with civil society and with external partners, about their shared objectives and their respective contributions to the common enterprise... each donor's programmes and activities should then operate within the framework of that locally-owned strategy in ways that respect and encourage strong local commitment, participation, capacity development and ownership' (OECD, 1996: 14).

QUESTIONING NEW LABOUR'S DEVELOPMENT STRATEGY

For the developed and developing countries to have policies which are more effectively 'joined-up' raises a number of questions concerning partnership and the donor–recipient relation, and clearly connects to the theme of power and representation mentioned in our outline of a post-colonial perspective. It is clear that New Labour gives considerable weight to the idea of *genuine* partnership, where there is a political *commitment* to tackle poverty elimination on *both* sides, so that the old conditionalities of development assistance can be transcended (DFID, 1997: 37, emphasis added). This point is again repeated in the 2000 White Paper, which states that, 'over-prescriptive aid conditionality has a poor track record in persuading governments to reform their policies' (DFID, 2000: 92).

In the hoped-for political commitment to tackle poverty elimination, the expectation is that the developing countries will be disciplined enough to take the responsibility of making explicit their strategies to achieve agreed-upon targets and share their plans internally and externally. In the 2000 document, it is argued that the process of formulating poverty reduction strategies is 'putting developing countries in the lead, devising and driving forward their own development strategies, ... but international support is *conditional* on economic, social and environmental policies which will systematically reduce poverty' (DFID, 2000: 91, emphasis added). At the same time, it is emphasized that the donor community must play its part and multilateral development institutions such as the World Bank are singled out as crucial players because of their 'political neutrality and technical expertise' which enable them to take both a leadership and co-ordination role on global issues such as human rights and refugees, debt reduction, gender equality, the environment and AIDS (DFID, 1997: 34). This leadership role is expressed in the 2000 document in terms of the need for global political institutions to 'better manage and counterbalance global markets, and to help promote global social justice' (DFID, 2000: 99).

These statements and other related passages carry a double supposition — namely that the multilateral development institutions are politically neutral, although being political institutions, and that the donor community should be seen as a unified actor offering leadership on a whole series of issues. Correspondingly, the developing countries are encouraged to assume a dependent leadership function under the auspices of the international donor community, which is invested with a directing and conditioning power. The leadership role assigned to the international donor community has not infrequently been couched in terms of educational metaphors. In the 1997 document for instance, when reference is made to development banks, we read that the better-off countries will be encouraged to graduate from low-interest loans and eventually 'they should graduate entirely from such borrowing...' (DFID, 1997: 36). The notion of developing countries being seen as potential graduates was used previously by the World Bank (1992:

68), when referring to the deployment of structural adjustment policies, and the use of such a metaphor emanates from earlier colonial visions of tutelage and trusteeship.

Furthermore, the positing of political neutrality can be viewed as necessary to the construction of a benevolent image of partnership where both developed and developing, donor and recipient are set to gain, provided both parties accept the rules of the partnership game. But in fact, as Fowler (2000) reminds us, partnership in the aid encounter might well be a conduit for new forms of foreign penetration as countries of the South are induced and persuaded into accepting a specific Northern-driven agenda which displaces alternative visions, for example strategies to confront global inequalities, and generates new forms of 'developmental assimilation'. In this scenario other internal agendas and priorities, as well as accountability to domestic social actors, can be side-tracked through the power effects of donorship such as disciplining, monitoring and subordinating inclusion.

In a donor–recipient relation where the beneficial effects of a mutually sustaining dialogue are implicitly pre-empted, one tends to encounter a one-way flow of organizing conduct and direction. For example, both White Papers, and especially the more recent, share a notion of diffusion that is essentially one-way, from West to non-West or from North to South. In a discussion of the spreading of educational opportunity, the 2000 White Paper states that, 'one of the ways in which globalisation could help eliminate poverty is by speeding up the diffusion of knowledge and technology to developing countries' (DFID, 2000: 36), just as we read of a 'diffusion of global norms and values' (ibid.: 15). The significance given to diffusion, which is also evident in Clare Short's definition of globalization as the 'internationalization of our culture and values', mentioned earlier, is further mirrored in the way poor countries are described as being in need of 'greater access to knowledge, ideas and new information and communication technologies' (ibid.: 20), with access to new technologies having the potential to 'help poor people leapfrog some of the traditional barriers to development' (ibid.: 39). These statements reflect a belief in the relevance of a one-way flow; that the poor have to wait for the benefits of access to Western knowledge and technology, as if (a) this is an immanently positive process, and (b) the developing countries have no independent sources of knowledge and ideas relevant not only to their own societies but to the world as a whole. Such a universalist vision replicates one of the key facets of the modernization theory of the 1950s and 1960s which rendered the third world other as a passive recipient of dynamic innovations emanating from the West. On such a basis contemporary partnership can be seen as the continuation of tutelage under a globalizing guise.

A similar problem emerges with regard to the actual discussion of globalization. Here, a primary emphasis falls on the prudent management of the process. For example, according to the 2000 White Paper, 'managed wisely, the new wealth being created by globalisation creates the opportunity to lift millions of the world's poorest people out of their poverty' (ibid.: 15), and the crucial task is making globalization work better for the poor, a task for which the private sector is deemed to have a key role (ibid.: 59). Global-ization is assumed to be a process which is underway in a form that needs to be managed wisely for the benefit of developing countries; but their potential role in challenging this process, or in seeking its reform to give greater weight to their own social, economic and political concerns is absent from the contextualization of the debate on global change. Furthermore, the analysis of globalization is de-politicized in the sense that the conflicts, antagonisms and differential benefits that it presupposes and entails are omitted from the analytical account and the pivotal dimension becomes management. But management by whom, for whom and for what purposes?

The politics of management connects to the issue of surveillance. In the fourth chapter of the 2000 White Paper, which deals with harnessing private finance, the word surveillance receives considerable attention, being used four times in just two pages. In the context of financial stability, it is contended that 'we need improved surveillance — better monitoring of the performance of developed and developing country economies'; moreover, 'the codes and standards of financial supervision will only work if there is an effective surveillance mechanism to monitor their implementation' (ibid.: 53). For this to happen, 'we believe that an enhanced IMF surveillance process ... which draws on the work and expertise of others, provides the best framework' (ibid). But where is the awareness that IMF 'surveillance' of economies of the South over the last two decades has been a highly controversial subject? Flowing from the controversy have been questions such as: who has the power to monitor the agents of financial surveillance and where is the democratic accountability in these global institutions? (see, for example, Woods, 2000).

In all three examples — *diffusion, management* and *surveillance* — there is clear evidence of an approach which situates developing countries in the position of being passive recipients, of being managed and monitored according to an agenda which appears to have gone beyond the sound and fury of controversy and conflict. Let us take another example which relates to both White Papers, and which concerns the question of 'political neutrality', and the traditional discourse of international development.

Under the influence of the official discourse of international development, and specifically the role therein of the World Bank, the IMF and the OECD, both White Papers endorse the prevailing view concerning the centrality of economic growth and foreign investment in the elimination of world poverty. For example, in the 1997 document it is suggested that the combination of a sound fiscal balance and more open domestic and foreign trade will provide the right framework for encouraging the private sector to act as the main engine of economic growth. Specifically, it is asserted that 'establishing the conditions that allow economic growth to accelerate in the poorer countries is ... a critical prerequisite for sustainable poverty elimination' (DFID, 1997:

15–16). This is coupled with an acceptance of the IMF's contributions to the establishment of 'sound macro-economic and financial policies to encourage pro-poor growth' (ibid.: 34), and a firm belief that it is in the interests of developing and developed countries alike to generate the right conditions for attracting 'beneficial private investment to developing countries' (ibid.: 61).

In the 2000 document these arguments are generally reiterated with the difference that some intermittent emphasis is given to the need for reform at the international level. Thus, in a passage on the World Trade Organization, it is suggested that there should be more transparency and openness, whilst the WTO should be retained, strengthened and reformed so that 'it works for poor countries' (DFID, 2000: 69). Moreover, in another passage on private enterprise, the need to promote corporate social responsibility is underscored, with the example being given that the UK government provides support to programmes such as the Ethical Trading Initiative which helps to improve working conditions in the international supply chains of its members (ibid.: 59). There are a number of other related passages on reform and accountability which may not be particularly stringent but do contrast with the 1997 document, and reflect the importance of the growing debate on globalization and development, post-Seattle. Nevertheless, the imprint of economic liberalism remains clear, with continual emphasis being given to the driving idea that bringing together economic growth, free trade, private investment, effective government and open economies will provide the most appropriate strategy for reducing poverty. In one pithy phrase, it is called 'making markets work for the poor' (ibid.: 31). Four critical comments are relevant at this juncture.

First, the DFID representation of the relations between growth, development and poverty assumes a series of beneficial links between private and especially foreign investment, economic growth and development and a reduction of poverty. However, whether or not economic growth will lead to development — characterized, for example, by reductions in unemployment, inequality and poverty (discussed some thirty years ago by Seers, 1972) — will depend on a range of socio-political variables relating, for instance, to the distribution of wealth and income, the nature of State power and the existence of the political will to effect policies of redistribution and social reform. In the DFID perspective, these complex relationships tend to be de-politicized and redrawn as matters of rationality, calculation and responsibility.

Second, there is a twin assumption, present in both documents, that there is no fundamental contradiction between neo-liberal economic policies and the reduction of inequality and poverty, and that there are no development problems that cannot eventually be solved through effective reform and the necessary political management. However, the negative social and economic effects of structural adjustment programmes, which have been a primary element of neo-liberalism, are well known (see, for example, Chossudovsky,

1997; George and Sabelli, 1994; González-Casanova, 1999), and the deployment of neo-liberal policies has been accompanied by the intensification of inequality (Sutcliffe, 2001; Wade, 2001). Both DFID documents avoid serious examination of these interconnected trends.

Third, as Abrahamsen and Williams (2001) point out, how free trade is viewed is likely to vary considerably between developed and developing country partners, as was evident during the Commonwealth Summit in Edinburgh in 1997, where a number of Commonwealth delegates expressed strong reservations about free-market principles. The Commonwealth Secretary General, Chief Emeka Anyaoku, for instance, warned that the benefits of globalization had been unequally distributed and for many developing countries, globalization entailed marginalization. Similarly, at the G-77 Summit in Havana, where the political leaders of 122 developing nations came together in April 2000, the final declaration strongly criticized neo-liberal globalization and demanded debt cancellation for the countries of the South (reported in *El País* 15 April 2000: 8; also see Khor, 2000). Thus, a genuine dialogue which entails the 'developed' listening to the 'developing' would in this context be likely to lead to a different framing of the issues of free trade, development, inequality and poverty reduction. Genuine dialogue clearly implies, if it is to be effective, a recognition that there are other sites of enunciation and other agents of knowledge, located in the South, whose vision and conceptual and political priorities might be quite different from those of the donor community, as we suggested earlier. The recognition of other voices requires political will, but it is also crucially linked to the presence or absence of a genuine belief in partnership and reciprocity.

Finally, it is important to mention the way both White Papers interpret the determinants of economic growth in East Asia. For example, in the 2000 White Paper, it is written that the 'initially poor countries that have been most successful in catching up in recent decades — the newly industrialising east Asian countries and China — seized the opportunity offered by more open world markets to build strong export sectors and to attract inward investment', and together with massive investment in education this opening up contributed to marked reductions in poverty (DFID, 2000: 17). What this scenario occludes is the crucial role played by the State in all the East Asian success stories, a point that has been amply documented in such well-known works as Amsden (1985), Gore (1996), Henderson (1993) and Wade (1990). Again the DFID narrative follows the orthodox neo-liberal interpretation, which has been shown to be somewhat misleading. Furthermore, the reference to 'catching up' is another illustration of the linear view of development, first outlined in modernization theory, in which the more developed countries would offer the less developed a mirror for their own future development.

New Labour's failure to critique neo-liberal thought, notwithstanding a wariness of its excesses, does not of itself define its newness. Such a newness

is more appropriately located in the way New Labour contextualizes the link
between the process of globalization and the elimination of world poverty.
Globalization is interpreted as a process which, whilst being inevitable and
irreversible, is also enabling and positive, even though its 'darker side',
exemplified by drug-trafficking, child labour, prostitution and pornography
is also mentioned (DFID, 2000: 29). Globalization is seen as a process which
can help to bring about the elimination of world poverty. But for this to
happen it has to be made to work for the poor; it has to be managed wisely
and sensibly and the wealth generated by its effects harnessed in a rational
and responsible way, so as to ensure the reduction and eventual elimination
of poverty in a world which does not need any fundamental political change,
nor any transformation of the existing relations of geopolitical power.
Instead of arguing that the present form of globalization — neo-liberal
globalization — and the reduction of world poverty are in conflict or
irreconcilable, or at least posing difficult dilemmas for development
strategy, New Labour makes these two phenomena appear compatible.
The conditioning assumption is that globalization and poverty reduction
can go together, provided that there is sound management, effective
monitoring, sensible co-ordination, and the acceptance that a respect for
rights must be accompanied by the fulfilment of responsibilities. New
Labour's discourse is new in the sense that instead of recognizing the existence of contrary aims or counterposed tendencies, as with neo-liberal globalization and poverty reduction, it proposes a going beyond, a transcendence
of these conflicting themes. Globalization and poverty reduction can be
'joined-up' for everyone's benefit in a world without political antagonism.
More generally, as Mouffe (2000: 108–28) has argued in her critique of
'Third Way politics', a world of conflict and struggles between political
adversaries gives way to a new form of consensual politics and acceptance of
the established order.

Under the neo-liberal form of globalization, the established order for
developing countries has been characterized by privatization, minimizing
state economic regulation, rolling back welfare, reducing expenditures on
public goods, tightening fiscal discipline, tax reductions, favouring freer
flows of capital, stricter controls on organized labour, increased dollariza-
tion of the economy, and currency repatriation. The detrimental effects of
these associated tendencies on the developing world are not discussed in the
DFID documents, although at one point it is recognized that 'there are
substantial inequities in the existing international trading system' (DFID,
2000: 69). Rather, the increased opening up of economies and the blurring of
national and international policies under globalization are portrayed as
essentially positive for the world as a whole, an 'economics without enemies'
as Rose (1999: 483) puts it. The diffusion and globalization of 'our values'
and the increased socio-economic and spatial integration of the world
through the greater spread of transport and communications infrastructure
(DFID, 2000: 73–74), are depicted as uncontroversial and beneficial to all.

CONCLUDING COMMENTS

Deploying a post-colonial perspective to interpret New Labour's aid and development strategy, we have foregrounded issues of power and representation, the sites and agents of knowledge and the geopolitics of the donor–recipient relation, as particularly reflected in the contextualization of partnership. We have examined the two key influences on the DFID approach to poverty and development questions — namely 'Third Way politics' and official thinking on development strategy as originating, for example, in OECD and World Bank documentation. We have traced certain important elements of the 1997 and 2000 White Papers, such as the significance of partnership, moral injunctions, expressed, for example, in the notion of a 'virtuous state', and the New Labour treatment of globalization. At the same time, we have endeavoured to identify the shifts of emphasis between the two documents, especially visible in the greater stress given by the 2000 document to economic and financial themes, and the debate over globalization, post-Seattle.

Our problematization of New Labour's development strategy would not be complete without a signalling of the positive features contained in the DFID White Papers, features which from a post-colonial viewpoint can be envisaged as examples of a constructive engagement with the issues. These features can be identified as follows.

- The 2000 White Paper fully commits the UK government to the multilateral untying of aid; tied aid is rightly seen as a damaging carry-over of outdated policies from the past.
- The UK government is prepared to take a leading role in emphasizing the international importance of poverty reduction, including a willingness to openly criticize the European Union for the decline in the proportion of EC development aid going to low income countries (DFID, 2000: 95); it is also prepared to urge the WTO to commit itself to achieving the International Development Targets for poverty reduction (ibid.: 69).
- The declared intention to introduce a new International Development Bill to ensure that the development programme continues to be focused on the reduction of poverty is to be welcomed, as is the intention to ensure that UK development assistance as a proportion of GNP rises to 0.33 per cent by 2003/04. However, this will be still less than half of the UN target and considerably below the 1999 figures on aid for Denmark, Norway, the Netherlands, Sweden and Luxembourg (aid as a percentage of GNP) (Sachs, 2001: 53).
- The strong stance taken in favour of anti-corruption strategies and the willingness to 'put our own house in order', through legislation aimed at giving UK courts jurisdiction over UK nationals who commit offences of corruption abroad, is clearly a positive step (DFID, 2000:

26). Rather than assume, as is often the case, that corruption is essentially a third world phenomenon, there is an attempt to broaden the debate to take seriously the existence of corrupt practices (such as money laundering) within Western countries.

- Although the point is not given extended treatment, land reform in developing countries, whereby secure access to land and other productive assets is guaranteed for poor people, is mentioned as an essential requirement for making a market economy 'work for the poor' (DFID, 2000: 32).
- Significant attention is given to the need to struggle continually against gender discrimination, as 'the most widespread form of social exclusion and discrimination' (ibid.: 27). The 2000 White Paper justly declares that 'there can be no equitable globalisation without greater equality and empowerment for women' (ibid.). Equally, it is argued that the UN Convention on the Rights of the Child needs to be implemented as part of the strategy against abject child poverty and the violation of so many children's basic human rights. Both these objectives reflect the White Paper's stress on global social justice. One can add here that what is missing in this laudable approach (and missing in both White Papers) is any reference to the global need to confront all forms of racial discrimination. Indeed, the complex connections between race and development are absent in so many related discussions

This absence might be considered as symptomatic of something deeper — of a paradox at the heart of New Labour's approach to globalization. For example, with the notion that national and international boundaries are becoming more blurred, and that we are living in an increasingly borderless world, where is the awareness of the increased fortification of Western frontiers, of the reinforcement of borders? Taking a post-colonial perspective, how does New Labour's 1999 Asylum and Immigration Act capture the blurring of boundaries? In fact, the Act has introduced a series of deterrent measures for asylum-seekers which are harsher than in the past. Asylum-seekers are to be dispersed around the country, and they will no longer be eligible for social security benefits. They are to be supported at 70 per cent of the income support benefit allotted to citizens, and the support will be distributed in the form of vouchers, which are only to be spent at designated stores, making them instantly identifiable as asylum-seekers. In a final twist, as Dummett (2001: 127) informs us, if they offer vouchers higher in value than the goods they are buying, the store will be required by the Goverment to keep the change.

These measures have gone hand in hand with: 1) the imposition of visa requirements on people coming from countries from which many were likely to flee, in search of asylum elsewhere; 2) the imposition of penalties on operators of any means of transport, such as lorry drivers, who may be carrying a passenger without papers fully in order, even if the individual concerned is subsequently granted asylum; 3) the increased use of detention as a measure to discourage asylum-seekers; and 4) a generalized atmosphere of hostility towards asylum-seekers, including the continuous use of the description 'bogus' asylum seekers, which New Labour has done little to challenge. In fact, as has recently been revealed, a ministerial order dated 23 April 2001 actually authorizes immigration officers, who are exempted from the Race Relations (Amendment) Act of 2000, to subject people of certain ethnic backgrounds 'to a more rigorous examination than other persons in the same circumstances'.[10]

Surely, if part of a 'joined-up' global imagination includes an awareness of why some peoples have little choice but to become either asylum-seekers or the new migrants of an unstable and turbulent world, then if people of 'moral conscience' are to 'join together to achieve a more decent and sustainable future for *us all*' (Short, 2000: 7, emphasis added), this must include a greater capacity for *self-critique*, or critique not only of one's own society but of the history and geopolitics of occidental power and privilege. Without this willingness and capacity, we may be more susceptible to an approach, which, in the words of Rose (1999: 490), 'appeals to an imaginary universal moral consensus, in order to justify a banal and stultifying vision of a future much like the present, only without its downsides'.

REFERENCES

Abrahamsen, R. and P. Williams (2001) 'Ethics and Foreign Policy: The Antinomies of New Labour's "Third Way" in Sub-Saharan Africa', *Political Studies* 49(2): 249–64.
Alexander, J. C. (1995) *Fin-de-Siècle Social Theory*. London: Verso Books.
Amsden, A. H. (1985) 'The State and Taiwan's Economic Development', in P. Evans, D. Rueschemeyer and T. Skocpol (eds) *Bringing the State Back In*, pp. 78–106. Cambridge: Cambridge University Press.
Ashcroft, B., G. Griffiths and H. Tiffin (1998) (eds) *Key Concepts in Post-Colonial Studies*. London and New York: Routledge.
Baumann, P. (1999) 'Information and Power: Implications for Process Monitoring — A Review of the Literature'. Working Paper 120. London: Overseas Development Institute.
Bell, M. (1998) 'Reshaping Boundaries: International Ethics and Environmental Consciousness in the Early Twentieth Century', *Transactions of the Institute of British Geographers* 23(2): 151–75.
Bhabha, H. (1994) *The Location of Culture*. London and New York: Routledge.
Blair, T. (1998) *The Third Way: New Politics for the New Century*. London: The Fabian Society.
Blair, T. (2000) 'Foreword by the Prime Minister', in DFID *Eliminating World Poverty: Making Globalisation Work for the Poor*, p. 6. Government White Paper on International Development, Cm 5006. London: Department for International Development.
Cassen, R. (1994) *Does Aid Work?* Oxford: Clarendon Press.
Chalker, L. (1994) 'Britain's Approach to Multilateral Aid', *Development Policy Review* 12(3): 243–50.

10. The 'ethnics' in question are listed as: Kurd, Roma, Albanian, Tamil, Pontic Greek, Somali and Afghan (see *The Guardian* 8 May 2001: 14).

Chossudovsky, M. (1997) *The Globalization of Poverty: Impacts of IMF and World Bank Reforms*. London: Zed Books.

Cockburn, A., J. St. Clair and A. Sekula (2000) *5 Days That Shook the World: Seattle and Beyond*. London: Verso Books.

Crewe, E. and E. Harrison (1998) *Whose Development? An Ethnography of Aid*. London: Zed Books.

DFID (1997) *Eliminating World Poverty: A Challenge for the 21st Century*. Government White Paper on International Development, Cm 3789. London: Department for International Development.

DFID (2000) *Eliminating World Poverty: Making Globalisation Work for the Poor*. Government White Paper on International Development, Cm 5006. London: Department for International Development.

Dummett, M. (2001) *On Immigration and Refugees*. London and New York: Routledge.

Edwards, M. and G. Sen (2000) 'NGOs , Social Change and the Transformation of Human Relationships: A 21st-Century Civic Agenda', *Third World Quarterly* 21(4): 605–16.

Fairclough, N. (2000) *New Labour, New Language?* London and New York: Routledge.

Fowler, A. (2000) 'Beyond Partnership: Getting Real about NGO Relationships in the Aid System', *IDS Bulletin* 30(3): 1–13.

Gasper, D. and R. Apthorpe (1996) 'Introduction: Discourse Analysis and Policy Discourse', *The European Journal of Development Research* 8(1): 1–15.

George, S. and F. Sabelli (1994) *Faith and Credit*. London: Penguin Books.

Giddens, A. (1998) *The Third Way*. Cambridge: Polity Press.

Giddens, A. (2000) *The Third Way and its Critics*. Cambridge: Polity Press.

Goldsmith, A. A. (2001) 'Foreign Aid and Statehood in Africa', *International Organisation* 55(1): 123–48.

González-Casanova, P. (1999) 'La Explotación Global', in R. Valero (coord.) *Globalidad: Una Mirada Alternativa*, pp. 69–95. Mexico City: CELAG.

Gore, C. (1996) 'Methodological Nationalism and the Misunderstanding of East Asian Industrialisation', *The European Journal of Development Research* 8(1): 77–122.

Henderson, J. (1993) 'Against the Economic Orthodoxy: On the Making of the East Asian Miracle', *Economy and Society* 22(2): 200–17.

Hewitt, A. (2001) 'Beyond Poverty? The New UK Policy on International Development and Globalisation', *Third World Quarterly* 22(2): 291–6.

Huntington, S. P. (1998) *The Clash of Civilisations and the Remaking of the World Order*. London and New York: Touchstone Books.

Hurd, D. (1997) 'Foreign Policy and Human Rights'. Foreign Affairs Committee, minutes of evidence HC 369-ii, 16 December.

Jolly, R. (1999) 'New Composite Indices for Development Co-operation', *Development* 42(3): 36–42.

Kaplan, R. D. (1997) *The Ends of the Earth*. London: Papermac.

Kayizzi-Mugerwa, S. (1998) 'Africa and the Donor Community: From Conditionality to Partnership', *Journal of International Development* 10(2): 219–26.

Khor, M. (2000) 'Havana Summit critiques Globalisation', *Third World Resurgence*, G-77 Havana Summit Special Issue (May) 117: 5–8.

Klare, M. T. (2000) 'Permanent Preeminence: US Strategic Policy for the 21st Century', *NACLA Report on the Americas* XXXIV(3): 8–15.

Labour Party (1999) 'Britain in the World'. Consultation paper. London: The Labour Party.

Lensink, R. and H. White (2000) 'Aid Allocation, Poverty Reduction and the *Assessing Aid* Report', *Journal of International Development* 12(3): 399–412.

Maxwell, S. and R. Riddell (1998) 'Conditionality or Contract: Perspectives on Partnership for Development', *Journal of International Development* 10(2): 257–68.

Ministry of Overseas Development (1975) *Overseas Development, The Changing Emphasis in British Aid Policies, More Help for the Poorest*. Command Number 6270. London: Her Majesty's Stationery Office.

Mosley, P., J. Harrigan and J. Toye (1991) *Aid and Power — The World Bank and Policy-Based Lending. Vol. 1*. London and New York: Routledge.

Mouffe, C. (2000) *The Democratic Paradox*. London: Verso Books.

Nederveen Pieterse, J. (2000) 'After Post-Development', *Third World Quarterly* 21(2): 175–91.

OECD (1996) *Shaping the 21st Century: The Contribution of Development Co-operation*. Paris: OECD

Rahnema, M. and V. Bawtree (1997) (eds) *The Post-Development Reader*. London: Zed Books.

Randel, J. and T. German (1999) 'United Kingdom', in I. Smillie and H. Helmich (eds) *Stakeholders: Government–NGO Partnerships for International Development*, pp. 235–46. London: Earthscan.

Rasheed, S. (1999) 'Poorest Nations and Development Co-operation: In Search of an Elusive Ethic', *Development* 42(3): 25–30.

Rattansi, A. (1997) 'Postcolonialism and its Discontents', *Economy and Society* 26(4): 480–500.

Rose, N. (1999) 'Inventiveness in Politics', *Economy and Society* 28(3): 467–93.

Sachs, J. (2001) 'American Foreign Aid', *The Economist* 14 July: 52–3 (London).

Said, E. W. (1978) *Orientalism*. London: Routledge and Kegan Paul.

Said, E. W. (1983) 'Travelling Theory', in E. W. Said *The World, the Text and the Critic*, pp. 227–47. Cambridge, MA: Harvard University Press.

Said, E. W. (1993) *Culture and Imperialism*. London: Chatto and Windus.

Seers, D. (1972) 'What Are We Trying to Measure?', *Journal of Development Studies* 8(3): 21–36.

Shanin, T. (1997) 'The Idea of Progress', in M. Rahnema and V. Bawtree (eds) *The Post-Development Reader*, pp. 65–71. London: Zed Books.

Short, C. (1997) 'Foreword', in DFID *Eliminating World Poverty: A Challenge for the 21st Century*. Government White Paper on International Development, Cm 3789. London: Department for International Development

Short, C. (2000) 'Foreword', in DFID *Eliminating World Poverty: Making Globalization Work for the Poor*. Government White Paper on International Development, Cm 5006. London: Department for International Development.

Slater, D. (1998) 'Post-Colonial Questions for Global Times', *Review of International Political Economy* 16(4): 647–78.

Sørensen, G. (ed.) (1993) *Political Conditionality*. London: Frank Cass.

Spivak, G. (1999) *A Critique of Postcolonial Reason*. Cambridge, MA, and London: Harvard University Press.

Sutcliffe, B. (2001) *100 Ways of Seeing an Unequal World*. London: Zed Books.

Sutton, R. (1999) 'The Policy Process: An Overview'. Working Paper No 118. London: Overseas Development Institute.

Sylvester, C. (1999) 'Development Studies and Postcolonial Studies: Disparate Tales of the "Third World"', *Third World Quarterly* 20(4): 703–21.

Thérien, J-P. and C. Lloyd (2000) 'Development Assistance on the Brink', *Third World Quarterly* 21(1): 21–38.

UNDP (1999) *The Human Development Report 1999*. Oxford and New York: Oxford University Press.

Wade, R. (1990) *Governing the Market: Economic Theory and the Role of Government in East Asian Industrialisation*. Princeton, NJ: Princeton University Press.

Wade, R. (2001) 'Global Inequality: Winners and Losers', *The Economist* 28 April: 93–7 (London).

van de Walle, N. (1999) 'Aid's Crisis of Legitimacy: Current Proposals and Future Prospects', *African Affairs* 98: 337–52.

WDM (World Development Movement) (2001) 'Parliamentary Submissions — International Development Committee Inquiry on the Government White Paper' (January): www.wdm.org.uk, accessed on 7 February 2001.

White, H. (1998) 'British Aid and the White Paper on International Development: Dressing a Wolf in Sheep's Clothing in the Emperor's New Clothes?', *Journal of International Development* 10(2): 151–66.

Woods, N. (2000) 'The Challenge of Good Governance for the IMF and the World Bank Themselves', *World Development* 28(5): 823–41.

World Bank (1990) *World Development Report 1990*. Oxford and New York: Oxford University Press.

World Bank (1992) *The World Bank Annual Report 1992*. Washington, DC: The World Bank.

World Bank (1997) *World Development Report 1997*. Oxford and New York: Oxford University Press.

World Bank (1998) *Assessing Aid: What Works, What Doesn't and Why*. Washington, DC: The World Bank.

World Bank (2000) *World Development Report 2000/2001: Attacking Poverty*. Oxford and New York: Oxford University Press.

Chapter 10

Good Governance and Aid: Selectivity Criteria in Development Assistance

Wil Hout

INTRODUCTION

Over the past decade, the governance discourse has come to dominate the discussion on development assistance. Previous concerns, focusing on the lack of resources needed for development, such as capital or knowledge, or on the unfavourable international structure, have partly or wholly given way to considerations related to the purported quality of governance and policies. As many scholars have pointed out in the recent past, the World Bank's reports on the effectiveness of aid (in particular, Burnside and Dollar, 1997, and World Bank, 1998) have epitomized the *volte-face* in policy circles on the prerequisites of development assistance.

Recently, several authors have questioned the suitability of good governance as an *ex ante* criterion for development assistance policies (see, for example, the different contributions in Hermes and Lensink, 2001). In his analysis of the concept, Martin Doornbos (2001: 102–3) argued that the emphasis on good governance in development assistance has resulted in a change from 'conditionalities' to 'selectivity'. In the opening essay of this volume, Jan Pronk has manifested himself as one of the prime critics of the use of good governance as a criterion for the selection of countries as recipients of development assistance: 'Policy improvement and better governance should not be seen as pre-conditions for development and for development aid, but also as development objectives themselves' (p. 16). Pronk's essay is directed against the tendency among dominant policy-makers — among whom his successor as Dutch Minister for Development Co-operation, Eveline Herfkens — to transform the good governance requirement into a *sine qua non*. According to this criterion, only countries that meet minimum quality standards of governance are eligible for aid. The pernicious consequence of such a requirement is that there is no incentive built into assistance policies for countries to improve the level of governance, nor can assistance policies be used to help countries improve the quality of governance.

Pronk (p. 16) advocates a return to conditionality instead of selectivity: 'Conditionality means helping countries which are themselves trying to meet certain criteria. It means helping to meet the conditions for good governance and good policy-making'. In this respect, Pronk's position is similar to that of the Dutch Scientific Council for Government Policy (WRR). In a report published in early 2001, the WRR argued that:

> The policy aimed at reducing poverty in developing countries should have more attention than at present for improving law and governance, particularly because poorer countries are less capable of making sufficient progress by themselves. As a complement to multilateral policies aimed at poverty reduction, the council argues that bilateral policy should place more emphasis on the priority of good governance. (Scientific Council for Government Policy, 2001: 8)[1]

After decades of zealous commitment to development assistance on a project basis, which led to an involvement with almost 120 developing countries, the Netherlands' government in 1998 decided to reduce the number of aid-receiving countries. The primary criteria for the revamped Dutch development assistance would be the average level of income and the quality of governance in potential recipient countries (Minister for Development Co-operation, 1998: 3). The selection process resulted in an initial choice of nineteen structural and three temporary partner countries (Minister for Development Co-operation, 1999: 5).

This chapter will assess the good governance criterion as applied in Dutch development assistance policy by performing a quantitative analysis (logistic regression) on data concerning the quality of governance in developing countries. First, a brief characterization is presented of the main elements of the new policy on development assistance of the Dutch government since August 1998; this is followed by a description of the research design and of the data that were used. The next section then discusses the main results of the logistic regressions that were performed, before a brief conclusion is offered.

THE CHANGE TOWARD GOOD GOVERNANCE

The formation of the second Dutch government to be headed by Labour Party leader Wim Kok was concluded in August 1998 with two major changes in the domain of development policy. The first change was the replacement of Jan Pronk, who had been Minister for Development Co-operation from 1973 to 1977 and from 1989 to 1998, by Eveline Herfkens, a former World Bank director. The second change concerned the policy orientation of the Netherlands on development co-operation. The second so-called 'purple' coalition of the labour party (PvdA), the right-wing liberals

---

1. This and further quotes from documents in Dutch were translated by the author.

(VVD) and the social liberals (D66) agreed to concentrate the allocation of structural Dutch development assistance on countries that would meet the criteria of 'good policy, including economic policy, and good governance, on the basis of international standards' (Regeerakkoord, 1998: 93).

In his second and third terms in office (1989–98), Pronk's policy orientation was dominated by what may be termed a post-Cold War agenda. The two White Papers that were put out by Pronk (Minister for Development Co-operation, 1990, 1993) contained an outline of policy priorities, which focused on traditional and new issues of concern. Among traditional Dutch concerns were poverty alleviation and the assistance of marginalized groups in developing countries, as well as attention for structural (national and international) issues related to the development potential of countries in the South. New additions included a focus on freedoms and human rights, a concern with violent conflicts and attention to environmental issues. On the basis of these criteria, Pronk had already envisaged a reduction of the number of 'regular co-operation countries' from fifty-eight in 1989 to thirty-four in the mid-1990s.

The change of development policy in the second Kok government reflected the increasing dominance of the aid debate by the multilateral financial agencies, most notably the World Bank. As alluded to in Hoebink's overview of the use of criteria in European development assistance (2001: 178–9, 188), the Dutch position on good governance bears considerable resemblance to the 'technocratic' approach. This approach has been brought forward by multilateral donor agencies and focuses on the functioning of state institutions and the implementation of policies aimed at low inflation, a balanced budget and openness to trade (the so-called 'Washington consensus'). In comparison with the policies of other European governments, recent Dutch development co-operation is much less influenced by other interpretations of the good governance concept, which focus on the promotion of human rights (in the case of the Scandinavian countries) or see good governance primarily as a means for reducing poverty (as in the British position on development co-operation).

Towards the end of 1998, Minister Herfkens sent a letter to Parliament which contained an outline of the policy that has been implemented in subsequent years. According to her letter (Minister for Development Co-operation, 1998: 3), the restructuring of structural development assistance (the part of official development aid that is channelled through Dutch embassies in developing countries) would mean a reduction of the group of seventy-eight major recipient countries (the countries that received more than 1 million Dutch guilders in 1997). The primary criteria for the reduction of the number would be the recipients' socio-economic policy and the 'situation in the realm of good governance'. In addition, the extent of poverty and the need for aid, operationalized as a maximum per capita GNP of US$ 925, would be applied as a third principle: 'An important part of the existing international consensus is that the limited availability of concessionary funds requires the concentration of aid on poorer countries' (ibid.)

According to Herfkens' letter to Parliament of November 1998, the Dutch government would base its judgement of developing countries' socio-economic and macroeconomic policies on the reporting of 'relevant multilateral organizations'. Its judgement of the quality of governance would involve the assessment of the countries' financial management, the state of human rights protection and the level of democratization of society (ibid.: 3–4). From a later communication of the Minister to Parliament one may conclude that the prime instrument for judging the quality of governance and policy appears to be the so-called 'IDA performance'. This is a measure calculated by the International Development Association (IDA) on the basis of twenty indicators, ten of which concern policies aimed at sustainable growth and poverty alleviation, four relate to policies targeted at the reduction of poverty, and six measure the quality of governance and management of the public sector (Minister for Development Co-operation, 1999b: 2–3).

The initial selection of countries that resulted from the application of these criteria was subject to 'a series of additional considerations', such as the quality of the existing development assistance programme in the recipient country, the efforts of the potential recipient to strengthen the regional legal order, the relative importance of Dutch aid in the light of the presence of other bilateral and multilateral donors, and the recipient country's socio-economic or cultural relations with the Netherlands. Finally, the Minister indicated that attracting investment from the Dutch private sector in 'growth industries' would be an important task for the embassies in their implementation of the development assistance policy (Minister for Development Co-operation, 1998: 4–5).

The original selection of countries was put before Parliament in February 1999 and included a list of nineteen plus three potential recipients: Bangladesh, Bolivia, Burkina Faso, Eritrea, Ethiopia, Ghana, India, Macedonia, Mali, Mozambique, Nicaragua, Pakistan, Sri Lanka, Tanzania, Uganda, Vietnam, Yemen, Zambia, Zimbabwe, South Africa, Egypt and the Palestinian Territories (Westbank and Gaza). Pakistan and Zimbabwe were subsequently removed from the list because of the internal political situation. South Africa, Egypt and the Palestinian Territories were included for a variety of (mainly political) reasons, such as the transition to a new political regime, the elimination of pockets of poverty and support for the Middle East peace process. It was envisaged that these countries would receive Dutch development assistance for a limited period of time, with a maximum of five years (Minister for Development Co-operation, 1999a: 5). The Palestinian Territories were later removed from the list of temporary partner countries, while Indonesia was added.

In addition to the '17 + 3' countries that were judged as eligible for structural assistance, a total of twenty-eight countries have been selected for support of environmental policies or for human rights, peace-building and good governance programmes. The relative importance of structural development co-operation *vis-à-vis* the thematically oriented programmes is underlined by the amount of money that is allocated to these two parts of the Dutch development assistance budget: in the budget for 2000, 959.4 million guilders were earmarked for the 17 + 3 countries, while 475.6 million guilders were assigned for spending in the twenty-eight 'theme countries'. The remaining twenty-four countries which had previously received aid, but which were not included in any of the above mentioned categories, are considered as 'exit countries' — 'where it is, on the whole, possible to end existing projects and programmes within a period of two to three years without capital destruction' (Minister for Development Co-operation, 1999c: 6).

DATA AND RESEARCH DESIGN

Data

There is fairly general acknowledgement that it is difficult to measure the level of good governance. In the first place, it is hard to capture such a complex subject matter as the quality of a country's governance in one or even a few indicators. In the second place, the reliability of measurements of governance in over one hundred developing countries is likely to be small.

Over the past decades, many researchers who were interested in the quality of governance in developing countries have used the indices that were developed by Raymond Gastil. Since the mid-1970s, Gastil and others have collected data on political rights and civil liberties in a large number of countries for Freedom House. The Freedom House data have acquired a great deal of popularity because of the time span for which they are available (1973 to the present) and the wide coverage of countries (167 in Gastil, 1990). Various analyses of the data (Burkhart and Lewis-Beck, 1994; Inkeles, 1990) have concluded that the indices can be accepted as valid indicators of the quality of the political regime.

The Freedom House data are used in this article as an indicator of the nature of the political system, defined as the extent to which civil liberties and political freedoms are respected in the system.[2] The yearly values of the civil liberties and political freedoms indices that are published by Freedom House lie between a maximum score of 1 and a minimum score of 7. On the basis of the yearly values I have calculated the average score for both indices over the ten-year period between 1991 and 2000.

---

2. These data were downloaded from http://www.freedomhouse.org.

Parallel to the Freedom House data, a second set of data was used for the analysis of good governance. This data-set was compiled by Kaufmann, Kraay and Zoido-Lobatón (1999), all researchers at the World Bank Institute.[3] The disadvantage of these data is that the indicators are based on observations made in 1997 and 1998. The clear advantage of the data, however, is that they encompass many or most dimensions of the good governance concept as it is generally used. Kaufmann et al. have applied a so-called 'unobserved-components model' to a large group of variables, deriving from fifteen data sources. The World Bank researchers have extracted six clusters from these variables and each of these clusters represents an aspect of good governance. The six indicators defined by Kaufmann et al. (1999: 7–8) are the following:

- *voice and accountability:* the extent to which citizens of a country are able to participate in the selection of governments;[4]
- *political stability/lack of violence:* the likelihood that the government in power will be destabilized or overthrown by possibly unconstitutional and/or violent means;
- *government effectiveness:* the quality of public service provision, the quality of the bureaucracy, the competence of civil servants, the independence of the civil service from political pressures and the credibility of the government's commitment to policies;
- *regulatory burden:* the incidence of market-unfriendly policies such as price controls or inadequate bank supervision, and the burdens imposed by excessive regulation in areas such as foreign trade and business development;
- *rule of law:* the extent to which agents have confidence in and abide by the rules of society;
- *graft:* the extent to which public power is used for private gain (corruption).

Each of these six indicators was measured using a scale running from a minimum of -2.5 to a maximum of $+2.5$, with higher values corresponding to better governance outcomes.

In addition to the governance indicators, the developing countries' income per capita will be introduced as a control variable. As became clear from the preceding section, the Dutch Minister for Development Co-operation based the decision to include some countries as partners, and reject others, partly on the basis of a needs indicator. Data on Gross National Product per capita were collected from World Bank sources as an indicator of income per capita (World Bank, 1999: 190–2). Because of the

---

3. These data were downloaded from http://www.worldbank.org/wbi/governance.
4. This variable also contains the indicators political rights and civil liberties from the Freedom House data-set.

skewed distribution of the variable, the logarithm of GNP per capita has been used instead of the absolute value.

Research Design

The Freedom House and World Bank data-sets were used to determine the differences in eight governance indicators between the countries that had been selected by the Dutch government as structural partners and those countries that had been rejected. Three groups of 'non-partners' are considered consecutively:

- the twenty-four countries that were rejected as partners in 1999 (hereafter referred to as the 'group of 24');
- all developing countries (including the group of 24);
- the thirty-four developing countries that meet the poverty criterion (a per capita income lower than US$ 925: World Bank, 1999) but were not included among the partner countries by the Dutch government. This group is analysed both including and excluding the group of 24 because both groups (consisting of, respectively, twenty-four and fifty-eight countries) are interesting 'control groups' against the 17 and 17 + 3 partner countries.

The approach that is taken here means that all units of analysis (developing countries) are assigned one of two scores (0 or 1) on the basis of whether or not they were selected as partner countries for a structural development relationship by the Dutch government. This means that the dependent variable is binary. The independent variables (the scores on the eight governance indicators and the income variable) are either measured at the interval level (as in the case of the two Freedom House indicators) or at the ratio level (the six World Bank indicators).

The data characteristics coupled with the substantive question (to what extent can the list of Dutch partner countries be reproduced on the basis of governance indicators?) lead to a choice for logistic regression as technique of analysis (Hosmer and Lemeshow, 1989). Logistic regression follows regular linear regression in that the technique attempts to find the best fitting model to represent the relationship between a dependent and a set of independent variables. It differs from linear regression in that the dependent variable is not continuous but dichotomous. Logistic regression analysis results in an estimate, on the basis of the maximum likelihood method, of the overall fit of the specified model and of the relative importance of each of the independent variables.

RESULTS OF THE ANALYSES

The results of the logistic regression analyses that were performed on the Freedom House and World Bank data are summarized in Tables 1

Table 1. Logistic Regression Analyses on Freedom House Data

	(1) 17 vs. 24 countries	(2) 17+3 vs. 24 countries	(3) 17 vs. all developing countries	(4) 17+3 vs. all developing countries	(5) 17 vs. poor (incl. G-24)	(6) 17+3 vs. poor (incl. G-24)	(7) 17 vs. poor (excl. G-24)	(8) 17+3 vs. poor (excl. G-24)
Political rights	.36	.16	.35	.18	.31	.17	.42	.21
Civil liberties	.43	.31	−.09	−.06	.17	.09	−.10	−.09
Log GNP/capita	4.06**	2.14*	4.00**	2.66**	3.32**	1.81*	3.23**	1.52
Constant	−13.98**	−7.79*	−10.15**	−6.24*	−9.65**	−4.97	−9.15*	−4.04
Chi square	13.99**	6.67	26.21**	17.50**	13.61**	6.00	10.33*	3.77
R_L^2	.26	.11	.26	.16	.17	.07	.16	.05
No. of observations	40	43	129	132	76	79	53	56
Per cent of 17/17+3 correctly classified	70.6	70.0	11.8	10.0	23.5	5.0	23.5	20.0
Per cent of other correctly classified	82.6	73.9	96.4	99.1	91.5	98.3	86.1	94.4
Lambda	.47	.40	0.0	.05	0.0	0.0	0.0	.10

Note: * = significant at .05 level; ** = significant at .01 level

and 2.[5] In both cases, analyses were made for eight sub-samples, comprising the countries that are mentioned in the top rows of the two tables. Because of missing data, fewer observations were included in the analyses than would have been theoretically possible.

The fifth line of Table 1 indicates that five of the eight logistic regression analyses of the Freedom House data resulted in a significant fit of the models specified.[6] In these cases, the chi-square value is significantly different from zero at the 5 or 1 per cent significance level, which implies that a meaningful distinction can be made between the two groups on statistical grounds. In the case of the analyses of the 17 + 3 vs. the group of 24 (column 2) and the 17 + 3 vs. the poor countries (column 6), the value of chi-square was nearly significant (p = .08 and p = .11, respectively).

The coefficient of determination for logistic regression,[7] which is given in the sixth line of Table 1, is relatively low in most cases. Only in the analyses of the 17 vs. the group of 24 (column 1) and of the 17 vs. all developing countries (column 3), is the R_L^2 value slightly higher, but also in this case the association between the independent and the dependent variables is rather weak.

Interestingly, the two governance variables included in the analyses of the Freedom House data (political rights and civil liberties) do not help to discriminate between the countries which were selected for Dutch structural development assistance and those which were not. In all except one of the analyses, the income variable (log GNP/capita) is a relatively powerful explanatory factor, contributing to the distinction between partner and non-partner countries. The positive and significant value of the coefficient for the income variable indicates that countries with lower incomes have greater probability to be in the group of selected countries than higher income countries. The low and non-significant value of the coefficient for the two governance variables provides an indication that these variables have little or no predictive value as to which countries are and which are not included among the recipients of Dutch development assistance.

These results are also reflected in the partial correlation coefficients (not reported in Table 1), which express the relationship of a selected independent variable with the dependent variable while removing the effect of all other independent variables on the first two variables. In all cases, the partial

---

5. Tables 1 and 2 present the results with respect to the full models. Handbooks on logistic regression (Hosmer and Lemeshow, 1989; Menard, 1995) advise repeating the regressions without irrelevant variables. I have chosen not to present the results without the non-significant variables in this essay because (a) the presented analyses serve to *test* models that include governance indicators, and (b) the analyses without irrelevant variables invariably produce conclusions identical to the ones presented here.

6. When the control variable (log GNP per capita) was omitted, none of the eight analyses produced a significant fit.

7. The R_L^2 that is reported here is analogous to the coefficient of determination (R^2) in linear regression. It is calculated as the ratio between the model's chi-square and the log-likelihood of the model without the independent variables (Menard, 1995: 20).

correlation coefficients of the two governance indicators are equal or close to zero, while the value of these coefficients for the income variable ranges between .12 and .37.

The eighth and ninth rows of Table 1 indicate the percentage of correctly classified cases for the two categories of the dependent variable. In addition to this, the bottom row presents the value of lambda, which is a measure of predictive efficiency and expresses the proportion of reduction of error. In a way, lambda provides a summary of the percentages of rows eight and nine. The value of lambda ranges between moderately strong and very low, which indicates that the predictive value of the independent variables, on the whole, is fairly limited. As can be seen in the eighth row of Table 1, a relatively good classification is obtained only when the 17 or 17 + 3 countries are compared with the group of 24. In all other analyses, the percentage of correctly classified countries falls to 23.5 or less, with a particularly bad result in the case of the comparison between the 17 + 3 and all poorest developing countries (including the group of 24).

Interestingly, things are different where the quality of classification of the non-selected countries is concerned. The percentages in the ninth row show that at least three-quarters of the non-selected countries were correctly classified. The percentage is lowest when the 17 or 17 + 3 countries are compared with the group of 24 (columns 1 and 2), but increases to almost 100 per cent in the case of the comparison between the 17 + 3 countries and all developing countries (column 4). These results show that, on the basis of the governance indicators in the Freedom House data-set and, in particular, the income variable, one can predict rather well which of the group of 41 (column 1) or 44 (column 2) previous recipients of Dutch development assistance were *not* selected for inclusion in the list of 17 or 17 + 3 countries. When the group is expanded to include all developing countries (columns 3 and 4) or the poorest developing countries (columns 5–8), the predictive value of the independent variables becomes even better.

Logistic regression analysis also offers the opportunity to identify the outliers among all analysed cases. Notable outliers in the analyses on the Freedom House data were Macedonia (in four analyses) and Sri Lanka (in three analyses). Countries that were deviants in two cases were: Bolivia, Vietnam, South Africa, Egypt and Indonesia. The causes for the misclassification of these countries appear to be high income in the case of Macedonia and a combination of income level and a relatively bad score on the political rights and civil liberties indices in the case of Sri Lanka. In addition to these countries, Bolivia and South Africa appear as outliers most probably because they had an income per capita of more than US$ 925 in 1997, whereas Vietnam, Egypt and Indonesia scored badly on the two governance indices.

Table 2 contains the results of the logistic regression analyses of World Bank data. Different measures indicate that the overall fit of the models specified in Table 2 is much better than in the case of the Freedom House indicators. All eight logistic regression analyses have a chi-square value that is significantly different from zero, with seven of these significant at the 1 per cent level.[8] The value of R_L^2 is reasonably high, and exceeds .30 in most cases, which suggests a moderate to relatively strong association between the independent and dependent variables.

As was the case with the Freedom House data, only very few variables of the World Bank data-set appear to play an important role in discriminating between the countries which were selected for Dutch structural development assistance and those which were not. The weight of the income variable (log GNP/capita) in the analyses of the World Bank data mirrors the role it played in the previously described analyses. The positive sign of the income variable indicates that countries with higher income have a greater probability of being in the group of non-selected countries than lower income countries. In addition to this, the variable regulatory burden appears to play an important role with respect to predicting the group membership of developing countries. The consistently negative sign of the coefficient shows that developing countries with more market-friendly policies stand a much better chance of being selected for a structural aid relationship by the Dutch government. The signs of the other variables are mostly too weak (voice and accountability, political stability) or too inconsistent (government effectiveness) to warrant interpretation. The sign of the variable rule of law is almost always negative. Although this variable is not significant, its coefficients indicate that, on the whole, countries that were selected are characterized by more respect for the law. The findings with respect to the last variable (graft) reflects an unexpected outcome: countries that were selected for Dutch development assistance tend, on the whole, to have more corruption than the countries that are not included among the 17 or 17 + 3. Upon closer inspection of the World Bank data-set, it appeared that *all* countries in the groups of 17 and 17 + 3, except South Africa, had a score lower than zero on the graft indicator, meaning that they scored lower than average with respect to the control of corruption.

As was the case with the Freedom House data-set, the results that were summarized in the previous paragraph are mirrored in the values of the partial correlation coefficients of the six independent variables (not reported in Table 2). With the exception of two analyses where government effectiveness appeared to have a small influence, the only partial correlations that did not equal zero related to the variables regulatory burden and log GNP/capita. In the former case, the partial correlations ranged between − .09 and − .30, while the correlation of the latter variable usually fell in the .23 to .40 range.

The three bottom lines of Table 2 indicate that the regression model that was specified on the basis of World Bank data produced much better classification results than the model analysed above with the Freedom House data-set. The lambda values presented in the bottom row of Table 2 show a moderate to high association between the observed and predicted grouping

---

8. When the control variable (log GNP per capita) was omitted, only two of the eight analyses produced a significant fit.

Table 2. Logistic Regression Analyses on World Bank Data

	(1) 17 vs. 24 countries	(2) 17+3 vs. 24 countries	(3) 17 vs. all developing countries	(4) 17+3 vs. all developing countries	(5) 17 vs. poor (incl. G-24)	(6) 17+3 vs. poor (incl. G-24)	(7) 17 vs. poor (excl. G-24)	(8) 17+3 vs. poor (excl. G-24)
Voice and accountability	.35	.31	.16	.19	.21	.32	.16	.14
Political stability/lack of violence	.60	.70	.44	.56	.17	.32	−.46	.06
Government effectiveness	−3.12	−3.53	−.13	−.42	.06	−.33	3.24	1.72
Regulatory burden	−2.72	−2.21	−3.48**	−2.64**	−3.77**	−3.29**	−4.96*	−4.11**
Rule of law	−.77	.31	−1.32	−.70	−1.22	−.49	−1.55	−.15
Graft	2.08	1.81	.52	.18	.78	.56	1.11	−.86
Log GNP/capita	5.54**	3.20*	7.41**	4.91**	5.77**	3.11*	8.01*	2.43
Constant	−15.43*	−9.24*	−19.01**	−12.54**	−14.77**	−7.85*	−20.43*	−6.70
Chi square	21.21**	16.66*	43.07**	33.07**	27.73**	21.08**	25.86**	19.91**
R_L^2	.44	.32	.49	.33	.40	.27	.47	.33
No. of observations	35	38	101	104	60	63	41	44
Per cent of 17/17+3 correctly classified	81.3	79.0	50.0	47.4	68.8	52.6	81.3	73.7
Per cent of other correctly classified	84.2	73.7	97.7	98.8	95.5	93.2	92.0	76.0
Lambda	.63	.53	.38	.42	.56	.37	.69	.42

Note: * = significant at .05 level; ** = significant at .01 level

of selected and non-selected countries. Generally speaking, the specified regression model is better at predicting the non-selected countries than the selected ones. The lowest percentage of correctly classified non-selected countries is 73.7 (row 13, column 2), while the prediction of selected countries reaches a low of 47.4 when the 17 + 3 countries are compared to all developing countries. In the case of comparisons between the 17 or 17 + 3 countries with the group of 24 (columns 1 and 2) and the poorest developing countries (columns 7 and 8) the percentage of correctly classified cases is well over 70.

The analyses of the World Bank data show some convergence with those of the Freedom House data-set where the identification of deviant cases is concerned. Notable outliers in the analyses on the World Bank data were Macedonia, which was an outlier in seven analyses, Vietnam (in five analyses) and South Africa (in four analyses). The causes for the misclassification of these countries are rather clear. In the case of Macedonia and, particularly, South Africa, the misclassification was the result of the relatively high income of the country. In addition to having a relatively high per capita income, Macedonia also ranked among the lower half of the countries on five out of six governance indicators in the World Bank data-set. In the case of Vietnam, the remarkable feature was the bad score that the country received on five out of six governance indicators.

By way of summary, the reported research findings indicate that Dutch policy choices on the selection of partner countries for structural development assistance can only to a very limited extent be reproduced with the help of governance indicators. To the degree that the selection can be reproduced, it appeared that a poverty or income variable (GNP per capita) was a much better predictor. The two macropolitical indicators of the Freedom House data-set proved to be particularly bad predictors of Dutch policy choices. Of the six indicators that are contained in the World Bank data-set (which was developed as part of the Governance Matters project of the World Bank Institute's Governance Group), it was only the variable that measures regulatory burden in developing countries which made a notable difference in the various tests. This indicator, which is basically a reflection of the extent to which developing countries pursue market-friendly policies, helped differentiate between the countries that were and those that were not selected for a structural assistance relationship with the Netherlands. Although this cannot be proven on the basis of the analyses included in this study, it looks as if the attitude towards the market in developing countries was an important element for Dutch policy-makers in deciding whether to include or exclude countries as the major recipients of Dutch development assistance.

CONCLUSIONS

In this chapter, the use of selectivity criteria on the basis of governance has been criticized from different angles. First, it was argued that good governance is a controversial selection criterion *per se*. Secondly, it was demonstrated that, even if good governance is accepted and adopted as a condition for development assistance, the implementation of this condition in the Dutch case is far from perfect. As Dutch development policy is one of the best current examples of the application of selectivity criteria related to the quality of governance — reflected in the reduction of partner countries for structural development assistance — the finding that it is almost impossible to replicate the choice of the 17 or 17 + 3 countries with the help of reputable governance data-sets is disconcerting in at least three ways.

First and most obviously, the results of the analyses are unsettling because the choice of partner countries does not meet the minimum requirement of transparency. When important decisions concerning the question of which group of developing countries is no longer to receive development assistance cannot be replicated on the basis of independent sources of information, considerations of political expediency may become more influential. It is exactly this aspect which has spurred a lot of criticism since the announcement was made to reduce the number of partner countries on the basis of governance criteria. In particular, the relatively non-transparent selection procedure led some commentators (such as van Hulten, 1999) to suspect that the choice of countries was not immune to opportunism.

In the second place, the research findings are disconcerting because of the apparent bias of the Dutch selection of aid-receiving countries in the direction of the 'Washington Consensus'. The orientation of developing countries towards the market proved to be the most influential variable in the analyses reported above. This means, most probably, that support will be given mainly to countries that emphasize orthodox policies — aimed, for instance, at the reduction of inflation and balancing the budget — and that 'heterodox' policies, such as those aimed at reducing inequality, supporting agriculture with subsidies or social policy measures (Pronk, this volume, p. 15), will be rewarded much less.

In the third place, the findings reported here are worrying because the choices that are made by policy-makers simply may not correspond with the criteria which they themselves wish to apply. The apparent limited ability to reproduce the selection of 17 and 17 + 3 countries when governance data are used *in addition to* a variable reflecting average income in developing countries is particularly disappointing because it means, most likely, that money is spent on countries which, according to the intended criteria, do not deserve it, while deserving countries are excluded.

The inclusion of badly-governed, and the exclusion of relatively well-governed developing countries from the group of Dutch partner countries may have more profound implications. As Pronk (pp. 17–18) has indicated, the primary importance of aid is its role as a catalyst, 'sometimes to help generate other resources or gain access to them, sometimes to help create domestic capacity or manage conflicts resulting from various forms of unsustainable development'. Poor countries that, in the words of Emanuel de Kadt (2001: 266), would need enhancement of their governing capacity may be exactly the ones that are punished by the application of an *ex ante* governance criterion. The catalytic effect that aid could have on the quality of governance in some developing countries might be threatened by the selectivity principle. The governance criterion in development assistance policies may thus easily turn out to be its own worst enemy.

APPENDIX: LIST OF DEVELOPING COUNTRIES IN THE ANALYSES

F = Countries included in the Freedom House data-set
W = Countries included in the World Bank data-set
P = Countries with a GNP/capita under US$ 925 in 1997 (source: World Bank, 2000)
N = No GNP data available in the World Development Report 1999–2000 (World Bank, 2000)

Structural partner countries
Bangladesh FWP
Bolivia FW
Burkina Faso FWP
Eritrea FWP
Ethiopia FWP
Ghana FWP
India FWP
Macedonia FW
Mali FWP
Mozambique FWP
Nicaragua FWP
Sri Lanka FWP
Tanzania FWP
Uganda FWP
Vietnam FWP
Yemen FWP
Zambia FWP

Temporary partner countries
Egypt FW
Indonesia FW
South Africa FW

Countries removed from the list
Algeria FW
Angola FWP
Botswana FW
Burundi FWP
Cameroon FWP
Chile FW
Haiti FWP
Jamaica FW
Kazakhstan FW
Kyrgyz Republic FWP
Laos FWP
Lesotho FWP
Liberia FWN
Madagascar FWP
Malawi FWP

Mauritania FWP
Morocco FW
Niger FWP
Nigeria FWP
Papua New Guinea FW
Seychelles F
Sudan FWP
Suriname FW
Thailand FW

Other developing countries
Afghanistan FWN
Albania FWP
Antigua and Barbuda F
Argentina FW
Armenia FWP
Azerbaijan FWP
Belarus FW
Belize FW
Benin FWP
Bhutan FWP
Bosnia and Herzegovina FWN
Brazil FW
Bulgaria FW
Cambodia FWP
Cape Verde FW
Central African Republic FWP
Chad FWP
China FWP
Colombia FW
Comoros FWP
Congo, Republic of FWP
Congo, Dem. Republic of FWP
Costa Rica FW
Côte d'Ivoire FWP
Croatia FW
Cuba FWN
Cyprus W

Cyprus (Greek part) F
Cyprus (Turkish part) FN
Djibouti FWN
Dominica F
Dominican Rep. FW
Ecuador FW
El Salvador FW
Equatorial Guinea FW
Estonia FW
Fiji FW
Gabon FW
The Gambia FWP
Georgia FWP
Grenada F
Guatemala FW
Guinea FWP
Guinea-Bissau FWP
Guyana FWP
Honduras FWP
Iran FW
Iraq FWN
Jordan FW
Kenya FWP
Kiribati FP
Latvia FW
Lebanon FW
Lithuania FW
Malaysia FW
Maldives FW
Marshall Islands F
Mauritius FW
Mexico FW
Micronesia F
Moldova FWP
Mongolia FWP
Myanmar FWN
Namibia FW
Nauru FN
Nepal FWP
Pakistan FWP
Palau FN

Palestinian Territories WN	Samoa F	Trinidad and Tobago FW
Panama FW	São Tomé and Principe FWP	Tunisia FW
Paraguay FW	Senegal FWP	Turkey FW
Peru FW	Sierra Leone FP	Turkmenistan FWP
Philippines FW	Slovak Republic FW	Tuvalu FN
Puerto Rico W	Slovenia FW	Ukraine FW
Qatar W	Solomon Islands FWP	Uruguay FW
Romania FW	Somalia FWN	Uzbekistan FW
Rwanda FWP	Swaziland FW	Vanuatu F
St. Kitts and Nevis F	Syria FW	Venezuela FW
St. Lucia F	Tajikistan FWP	Yugoslavia WN
St. Vincent and the	Togo FWP	Zimbabwe FWP
Grenadines F	Tonga F	

REFERENCES

Burkhart, Ross E., and Michael S. Lewis-Beck (1994) 'Comparative Democracy: The Economic Development Thesis', *American Political Science Review* 88(4): 903–10.

Burnside, Craig and David Dollar (1997) 'Aid, Policies and Growth'. World Bank Working Paper 1777. Washington, DC: The World Bank.

Doornbos, Martin (2001) 'Good Governance: The Rise and Decline of a Policy Metaphor', *Journal of Development Studies* 37(6): 93–108.

Gastil, Raymond Duncan (1990) 'The Comparative Survey of Freedom: Experiences and Suggestions', *Studies in Comparative International Development* 25(1): 25–50.

Hermes, Niels and Robert Lensink (eds) (2001) 'Changing the Conditions for Development Aid: A New Paradigm?', Special Issue of *Journal of Development Issues* 37(6).

Hoebink, Paul (2001) 'Good governance als voorwaarde en doel bij enkele Europese donoren' [Good Governance as Condition and Objective for Some European Donors], in: Scientific Council for Government Policy (2001) *Ontwikkelingsbeleid en goed bestuur* [Development Assistance Policy and Good Governance], pp. 163–204. Reports to the Government 58. The Hague: Sdu Publishers.

Hosmer, David W. and Stanley Lemeshow (1989) *Applied Logistic Regression*. New York: John Wiley.

van Hulten, Michel (1999) 'De 19 van Herfkens' [Herfkens' 'Group of 19'], *Internationale Spectator* 53(7/8): 430–5.

Inkeles, Alex (1990) 'Introduction: On Measuring Democracy', *Studies in Comparative International Development* 25(1): 3–6.

de Kadt, Emanuel (2001) 'Goed bestuur in Africa: De realiteit in het licht van traditie en geschiedenis' [Good Governance in Africa: Reality in the Light of Tradition and History], in Scientific Council for Government Policy (2001) *Ontwikkelingsbeleid en goed bestuur* [Development Assistance Policy and Good Governance], pp. 241–76. Reports to the Government 58. The Hague: Sdu Publishers.

Kaufmann, Daniel, Aart Kraay and Pablo Zoido-Lobatón (1999) 'Governance Matters'. Policy Research Working Paper 2196. Washington, DC: The World Bank.

Menard, Scott (1995) *Applied Logistic Regression Analysis*. Quantitative Applications in the Social Sciences Series 07-106. Thousand Oaks, CA: Sage.

Minister for Development Co operation (1990) 'Een wereld van verschil: Nieuwe kaders voor ontwikkelingssamenwerking in de jaren negentig' [A World of Difference: New Framework for Development Co-operation in the 1990s]. Second Chamber, 1990–1991 Session, 21813, No 2.

Minister for Development Co-operation (1993) 'Een wereld in geschil: De grenzen van de ontwikkelingssamenwerking verkend' [A World in Conflict: Assessing the Boundaries of Development Co-operation]. The Hague: Information Service Development Co-operation.

Minister for Development Co-operation (1998) 'Letter to Parliament on Policy Intentions Regarding the Application of Criteria for Structural Bilateral Development Assistance'. Second Chamber, 1998–1999 Session, 26200 V, No 8.

Minister for Development Co-operation (1999a) 'Letter to Parliament on Country Policy for Structural Bilateral Assistance'. Second Chamber, 1998–1999 Session, 26433, No 1.

Minister for Development Co-operation (1999b) 'Letter to Parliament on Country Policy for Structural Bilateral Assistance'. Second Chamber, 1998–1999 Session, 26433, No 2.

Minister for Development Co-operation (1999c) 'Letter to Parliament on Country Policy for Structural Bilateral Assistance'. Second Chamber, 1999–2000 Session, 26433, No 18.

Regeerakkoord [Coalition Agreement] (1998) Second Chamber, 1997–1998 Session, 26024, No 10.

Scientific Council for Government Policy (2001) *Ontwikkelingsbeleid en goed bestuur* [Development Assistance Policy and Good Governance]. Reports to the Government 58. The Hague: Sdu Publishers.

World Bank (1998) *Assessing Aid: What Works, What Doesn't and Why*. New York: Oxford University Press.

World Bank (1999) *World Development Report 1998/99*. New York: Oxford University Press.

World Bank (2000) *World Development Report 1999/2000*. New York: Oxford University Press.

Chapter 11

International Development Targets and Official Development Assistance

Santosh Mehrotra[1]

INTRODUCTION

It is difficult to disagree with the sensible conclusions of Pronk (Chapter 1), or with his appropriate questioning of the arguments made by Burnside and Dollar (1997) and World Bank (1998) for reallocating aid on the basis of 'good policy'. Coming from someone who has spent fifteen years as the Minister of Co-operation of a donor country, donors should take these arguments more seriously than they have taken the World Bank's policy conclusions based on its own research. The World Bank's work had already been subjected to serious methodological challenges by Hansen and Tarp (2000), Lensink and White (2000) and Beynon (1999). Unfortunately, as Pronk effectively agrees, the Bank study became an ex-post rationalization of what was already a fact — a dramatic reduction in Official Development Assistance (ODA) in the 1990s. The Bank's study struck at the roots of the case for higher ODA since it argued (and donors accepted) that re-allocations of aid to countries with 'good policies' (defined by the Bank in terms of orthodox Fund policies) could achieve as much reduction in poverty as a tripling of current aid budgets. Worse still, donor governments paid little heed to the argument, also emerging from the same model, that reallocating according to poverty indicators produces bigger benefits (in terms of numbers lifted out of poverty) than reallocating on the basis of policy indicators (Beynon, 1999).

This said, the question one still needs to ask after reading Pronk is: what can be done to increase total ODA, and especially to ensure that the international development targets (IDTs) for 2015 do not remain a wish-list, like the targets of so many world summits of the 1990s?[2] The gap between the

1. The views expressed in this paper are those of the author, and should not be associated with those of UNICEF or UNDP.
2. The IDTs are mostly a re-statement of goals set in 1990, at the World Summit for Children (New York), and re-affirmed (with some alterations) by the World Summit for Social Development (Copenhagen, March 1995). These were meant to be achieved by the year 2000. The IDTs agreed in 1996 by the donors (OECD, 1996), extended the dates on the goals of the WSSD, which were later adopted at the Millennium Summit at the UN in late 2000.

rhetoric of international development targets and the reality of official development assistance is the subject of this paper.

In 1996, OECD's Development Assistance Committee (DAC) committed itself to the development goals outlined at earlier United Nations conferences. These goals are: halving of the proportion of people living in extreme poverty by 2015; universal primary education in all countries by 2015; elimination of gender disparities in primary and secondary education by 2005; reduction in under-five mortality by two-thirds of the 1990 level by 2015; reduction of maternal mortality by three-fourths during the same period; access through the primary health care (PHC) system to reproductive health services by 2015; national strategies to reverse current trends in the loss of environmental resources by 2005 and a reversal of these trends by 2015. Clearly all of these IDTs (with the exception of the first and last) relate to the provision of basic social services — basic health, reproductive health, drinking water and sanitation, and basic education. In the following, we will examine the donor record in respect of total ODA as well as ODA for basic services.

First, however, it is necessary to indicate why ODA might be necessary for the achievement of IDTs. The bulk of the resources for achieving the IDTs will come from the national budgets of developing countries. However, in low-income countries, the budgetary situation is unlikely to permit the achievement of these goals without additional external resources. This is true of the forty-one Heavily Indebted Poor Countries (HIPC), but not only for HIPCs. We have estimated elsewhere, that to achieve basic services for all, a further US$ 70–80 billion annually are needed (in addition to the roughly US$ 136 billion currently spent annually on these services, including US$ 5 billion annually by donors), at a conservative estimate (Mehrotra and Delamonica, forthcoming). In other words, additional domestic resources should be found to finance basic social services, but new international sources of funding also need to be identified.

As far as new domestic sources are concerned, it is well known that the repeated stabilization and adjustment episodes since the early 1980s have concentrated their efforts on public expenditure cuts, rather than revenue mobilization, as a means of budget deficit reduction. This situation needs to change, and the international community (G-7, Development Committee, Interim Committee) should encourage the IMF to place greater emphasis on expanding the tax base and raising tax revenues as a means of budget deficit reduction.

ODA FOR BASIC SOCIAL SERVICES

For most low-income countries external resources will be critical to the achievement of the IDTs. However, the record on total ODA, especially since the announcement of the IDTs in 1996, is not encouraging. It has fallen from a high of 0.61 per cent of GNP in 1961 to 0.37 in 1980, dropping further to 0.31 over 1988–89 and to a low of 0.24 in 1999. Only a small number of countries have ever exceeded the UN target of 0.7 of GNP for aid (set in 1970). Denmark, the Netherlands, Sweden and Luxembourg are the only European Union member states that meet the ODA standard (which is accepted by all UN members, except the USA). Norway, a non-EU member, also meets the target. Luxembourg, the newest member of this group, has proved that it is possible to raise ODA to 0.7 per cent of GNP in a short time. None of the G-7 countries are members of this group; on average, they allocated 0.21 of their GNP to ODA in 1999. These same five countries also have the highest grant equivalent of total ODA as a percentage of GNP, and provide the highest ODA per capita of donor country — in the range of US\$ 184 to US\$ 326, compared to a range of between US\$ 33 (USA) and US\$ 98 (France) for the G-7 countries (in the period 1998–9) (OECD, 2001).[3]

The IDTs are unlikely to be achieved without universal access to basic services. However, less than 10 per cent of the bilateral ODA is allocated to basic health, basic education and water and sanitation. Moreover, the category 'water and sanitation' — which accounts for 5 per cent of ODA — includes more than drinking water and sanitation.[4] The ODA for basic social services showed almost no change in the period since 1996 on aggregate (Mehrotra, 2001).

The sectoral composition of ODA for the social sectors shows the same disappointing trend as overall ODA. For each of the major social services relevant for the achievement of the IDTs, we examine the allocations of ODA before and after the announcement of the IDTs.

Given the commitments made to Education for All at the Jomtien Conference in 1990, one would expect that ODA earmarked for education — not just basic education, but overall — would have increased. However, between 1990 and 1995 it rose only very slightly, from US\$ 5.5 billion to US\$ 6 billion, and has tended to decline since. Since the announcement of IDTs, it has averaged US\$ 5.6 billion. As a share of total commitments, ODA for education hovered around 10 per cent throughout the 1990s. ODA to basic education — most relevant for universalizing primary education and eliminating gender disparities in schooling — has not risen much overall (although it has increased from some donors). Despite the fact that more and more donors have been reporting their ODA to basic education, the absolute value of DAC bilateral assistance to basic education fell from US\$ 644 million over 1995–6, on an average annual basis, to \$592 million

---

3. These five were called the G-0.7 by the ministers of development co-operation of the five countries (*Financial Times*, 19 November 2001).

4. OECD DAC's Creditor Reporting System includes the following categories under water and sanitation: water resources; rural and urban water and sanitation (including drinking water); water resources protection; and emergency distress relief. In other words, the share of basic services in total ODA is an overestimate.

over 1997–9 — in other words, it was lower after the IDTs were announced. At the same time, schooling indicators in developing countries barely changed over the 1990s. In the regions with the lowest net enrolment rates at primary level there was only a marginal increase over the decade: in sub-Saharan Africa (SSA) from 56 to 60, in South Asia from 65 to 71, and in the Middle East from 77 to 81 (UNICEF, 2001), when both the World Summit for Children and the Jomtien Conference had been calling for NERs of 100 by the year 2000. Similarly, the gender gap remained a concern in the same regions, with the NER in SSA at 63 for boys and 57 for girls, in South Asia at 74 versus 68, and in the Middle East at 84 versus 77.[5]

The value of donor assistance to the health sector as a whole (as opposed to basic health) grew from US$ 2 billion in 1990 to US$ 3.1 billion in 1996. It fell in 1997 and 1998, and rose in 1999 to US$ 4 billion. The average annual ODA for health over the seven-year period 1990–96 was US$ 2.3 billion, while over 1997–9 it was US$ 2.9 billion. By 1995–6 most DAC donors were reporting their ODA to basic health: over 1995–6 ODA to basic health averaged about US$ 990 million; over 1997–9 it averaged US$ 856 million. Overall, just 2 per cent of total ODA was allocated to basic health over the 1990s.

The ODA allocated to health, basic health and water/sanitation is naturally of some concern since health outcome indicators barely improved over the 1990s. The smallest improvement has been in under-five mortality (U5MR, an IDT goal) over 1990–2000 in the region with the highest rate — sub-Saharan Africa. In SSA the U5MR fell from 181 in 1990 to 175 in 2000. In South Asia, the rate declined from 128 to 100. Children can die from many causes, and deciding which is the primary cause can be difficult. Malnutrition is associated with half of all deaths. In developing countries as a whole, the percentage of under-fives who were malnourished declined only slightly, from 32 to 28 per cent, between 1990 and 2000.[6]

Assistance to population/reproductive health services tended to increase slightly in the 1990s — it averaged US$ 572 million annually over 1990–96, and US$ 644 million over 1997–8 — but here too the outcomes relevant to the IDTs remain dismal. The proportion of births attended by skilled health personnel has been recommended as a measure of progress for maternal mortality, the reduction of which is an IDT. In SSA, where maternal mortality is highest, delivery care hardly improved over the 1990s, with barely 42 per cent of mothers covered during delivery by the end of that decade, as against 40 per cent in 1990. There has been some progress in South Asia, but from a very low base (26 per cent in 1990 to 36 per cent in 2000). At the same time, there remain huge unmet needs with respect to contraceptive use. While the

---

5. Between 1990 and 1999, the gender gap globally was halved, falling from 6 per cent to 3 per cent. However, in the three most backward regions the gap still remained at 6 per cent in 1999. All outcome indicator data in the paper are drawn from UNICEF (2001).
6. The share of children underweight declined in South Asia from 54 per cent to 48 per cent; and that in SSA continued to hover around 31 per cent over the decade.

developing country average for contraceptive use increased from 53 per cent in 1990 to 65 in 2000, in SSA it only grew from 15 to 23 per cent, in South Asia from 39 to 48 per cent, and in the Middle East/North Africa from 38 to 54 per cent. The result is that these three regions have a fertility rate much higher (5.7, 3.5 and 3.7 respectively) than the developing country average of 3.0 in 2000, just as it had been higher in 1990.

ODA for water and sanitation accounts for the largest share of all basic social service related ODA. It amounted to US$ 1.8 billion in 1990, rising to US$ 3.1 billion in 1996 (averaging US$ 2.45 billion over 1990–96). The average over 1997–9 rose slightly, to US$ 2.6 billion per annum. However, OECD DAC does not disaggregate the data for drinking water and for other uses. In fact, if water supply is excluded from the calculation of ODA for basic social services, the share of DAC bilateral ODA allocated to basic social services falls from around 10 per cent of ODA to 5 per cent.

The water challenge is greatest of all the basic social services, since many more people are without improved water sources than without access to schooling or basic health services.[7] In 1990 some 1.2 billion people lacked access to safe drinking water; 1.1 billion still lacked it in 2000. Despite all the commitments about reducing child deaths in the World Summit for Children (1990), repeated in the World Summit for Social Development (1995), the improvement over the decade with respect to access to safe drinking water was an increase from 53 to 57 per cent in SSA, from 71 to 76 per cent in East Asia, and from 72 to 85 per cent in South Asia. Even more people lack access to sanitary means of excreta disposal than those without safe water. In 1990, 2.6 billion people lacked such access; in 2000 the figure was still 2.4 billion. Half of those lacking access are in Asia, with two-thirds of the South Asian population and half of East Asia without access in 2000 — although here there has been major progress in both sub-regions.

The multilaterals — the World Bank's International Development Agency (IDA), and the soft loan windows of the regional development banks, and the UN agencies — are the other sources of ODA. The multilaterals account for a third of all ODA (including about a third of total ODA globally to basic social services). Over 1995–6 and 1997–8, on average, about 11 per cent of the IDA's lending went to basic services, registering little difference before and after the IDTs were announced. For IDA and for the regional development banks' soft loan window, total ODA for basic social services was US$ 743 million over 1995–6 (on an average annual basis), and US$ 933 million over 1997–8. Most of the increase was accounted for by basic health and population/reproductive health, while there was a

---

7. Access to safe drinking water is determined by percentage of population using improved water sources. Improved sources are household connection, public standpipe, borehole, protected dug well, protected spring, and rainwater collection. Not improved sources are unprotected well, unprotected spring, river, pond, vendor-provided water, and tanker truck water.

decline in basic education, and water supply remained at roughly the same level.

For aid, an abiding issue has been fungibility; Pronk also raises the issue. The question is whether aid is used for the purposes for which donors provided it. In fact, as McGillivray and Morrissey (2001) argue, fungibility studies have been granted too much attention.[8] It is more important to examine the fiscal response of the aid recipient, to determine the effects of aid on behaviour regarding total spending, tax revenue and borrowing. The evidence, they find, suggests that aid tends to increase total spending by more than the amount of the aid. Hence the risk of fungibility is no argument for not increasing ODA for basic services.

POTENTIAL SOURCES OF ADDITIONAL EXTERNAL RESOURCES FOR BASIC SOCIAL SERVICES

If the unmet needs in terms of access/quality of basic service delivery remain substantial, where are the additional external resources for basic social services going to come from? Several alternative sources can be considered. One source that has been discussed is a tax on foreign exchange purchases and sales (the 'Tobin Tax', proposed by James Tobin in 1972). The end of the 1990s saw a rapid growth of an international movement in support of the tax on excessive speculation in currency and other financial markets. This movement has prompted resolutions in support of such taxes in dozens of cities across the world (including more than fifty in France). Many labour unions throughout the world have also called for such taxes, including the AFL-CIO in the US. Legislation in support of such taxes has been introduced in the French Parliament, the European Parliament, the US Congress, and was approved in 1998 by the Canadian Parliament.

Purchases and sales of foreign exchange amounted to around US$ 1.2 trillion per trading day in 1995–6 (BIS, 1995–6), or US$ 300 trillion in a year. World GDP is about US$ 30 trillion a year (while merchandise exports are about US$ 5 trillion). Hence a 0.1 per cent tax, even if it caused the level of foreign-exchange transactions to halve, would lead to US$ 125 billion being collected, or 2.5 times the current level of ODA to all developing countries. Those who have examined the practicalities of such a 'Tobin tax' argue that it is technically feasible, provided it is adopted uniformly by countries which have all the main foreign exchange markets (eight countries, including Hong Kong, and counting the whole European Union as one). The collection of such a tax would necessarily be through the banks in these industrial-ized countries and therefore the revenue would go to those governments.

8. Pronk (p. 9) agrees: 'on balance and in the long run, catalytic crowding-in effects [of aid] will outweigh fungibility or crowding-out effects'.

However, that does not imply that the governments would retain the revenue: it should be distributed based on some evaluation of global need, perhaps half to the UN and other international organizations, with purposes specified (social and environmental programmes, stabilization), some to collecting governments to give them the incentive to administer it, and the remainder to other national governments based on a fair principle. Such a source of revenue is a source of global public goods (Mahbub-ul-Haq et al., 1996).

A second source could well be a tax on foreign trade transactions. Shorrocks suggests that taxing foreign trade could be done easily within the WTO.[9] Not all countries would immediately participate: an agreement could be reached on the level of the US or the European Union to begin with, to which others could gradually join.

A third source would simply be improved market access to developing country exports — or rather tax income accruing to developing country governments from such increased exports. Recent World Bank research found that tariffs and non-tariff barriers imposed by high-income countries, together with agricultural subsidies, cost developing countries much more in lost export opportunities than the nearly US$ 54 billion that they receive in ODA each year. Industrialized countries often discourage imports of the very products that developing countries can produce most competitively. Industrialized country tariffs on labour-intensive manufactured goods such as textiles, clothing and footwear range from 15 to 30 per cent. Import taxes are higher still on many agricultural products: more than 100 per cent for meat, sugar and dairy products. Fruits and vegetables face even higher tariffs — a US tariff of 121 per cent on groundnuts, Europe's 130 per cent tariff on above-quota bananas, and Japan's 171 per cent tariff on raw cane sugar. In fact, as the Chief Economist of the World Bank suggests, industrialized countries should unilaterally open their markets to duty-free imports from the forty-eight least developed countries. 'Offering poor countries duty-free access for all products will appeal to many people in the rich countries as the fair thing to do. And it would be in keeping with enlightened self-interest. A small number of people in high-income countries would face adjustment costs, but the vast majority would benefit from wider choices and lower prices' (Stern, 2001).[10] However, market access should not be a negotiating ploy. For instance, a small package for tariff-free and quota-free access to developed country markets or debt-relief might be offered as a negotiating incentive for the developing countries to accept a far more damaging link between market access and enforcement of the so-called core labour and environmental standards.

9. Professor A. Shorrocks, Director of WIDER, made the suggestion in an interview with a Finnish weekly, *Suomen Kuvalehti*, 12 January 2001.
10. Pronk (p. 10) agrees: 'aid should be accompanied by policies within donor countries to open their markets for the goods and services produced as a result of aid'.

In other words, ensuring additional resources to achieve the International Development Targets requires much greater consistency in donor policy than has been evident so far. One of the most striking cases of inconsistency in donor policy is that donors have barely increased ODA for basic education. Universalizing access to elementary education and improving its quality is widely recognized as the most effective instrument against child labour. Industrialized countries have repeatedly raised the labour standards and child labour issue in international fora — whether it is in the ILO or the WTO — introducing this as a 'new issue' in multilateral trade negotiations; yet very little assistance is provided to the basic education that can help reduce the incidence of child labour, improve the skill base in developing countries, and enhance productivity (including in the export sector).

Debt relief is also expected to release resources for investment in human capital, according to the Poverty Reduction Strategy Papers. However, there is a structural issue here: the main reason for the crisis of debt facing the HIPCs in particular, given the commodity concentration of their exports, is the long-run secular decline in their net barter terms of trade since the 1970s. The decline in commodity prices has affected not only the HIPCs, but the balance of payments of other developing countries as well. The balance of trade deficit of developing countries was a full 2 per cent higher in the 1990s than it was in the 1970s (UNCTAD, 1999) — partly accounted for by the push for import liberalization ensuing from bank-financed adjustment programmes. Debt relief is not charity: it is merely a means of compensating (only in part) for the net resource flow out of the poorest countries resulting from declining terms of trade. In other words, the cancellation cannot be a substitute for fresh additional ODA. If there is an element of 'moral hazard' in HIPC country debt cancellation, this is no more than the moral hazard inherent in the huge bailout of international banks implicit in the IMF deal in post-crisis East Asia in 1997. But the cancellation of debt alone will not suffice as long as the long-run deterioration in the terms of trade of the least developed countries continues. There is a risk of the current debt trap repeating itself in the future. In fact the World Bank (2000) argues for the provision of such global public goods as global commodity price insurance instruments to address key price volatility problems of developing countries.

At current rates of poverty reduction, the IDT of halving poverty is unlikely to be achieved by 2015. The number of poor (those with below US$ 1 a day) was 1125 million in 1985, and stood at 1214 million in 1998. Addison and Cornia (2001) estimate that with declines of only 2.3 per cent in terms of incidence, and an increase in absolute numbers, the DAC poverty target will not be reached until around 2060, rather than in 2015. A major problem is the increasing within-country inequality in income distribution. If poverty is to be reduced, economic growth would need to be much faster in order to compensate for worsening income distribution. This seriously undermines the donor consensus that income inequality can be largely ignored in the formulation of strategies for economic growth and poverty reduction — another source of inconsistency in donor policies with regard to the IDTs.

CONCLUSIONS

The primary responsibility for the achievement of the International Development Targets lies with developing country governments. However, for over fifty countries in the developing world — not just the least-developed and the HIPCs — the achievement of the IDTs will require international action from bilaterals and multilaterals. If the experience of the 1990s is any indicator, much more additional ODA has to be found. A radical approach is needed in order to increase the overall envelope for ODA. Moreover, ODA for basic services remains seriously deficient in several ways: its level is low; and its composition needs sharp modification in education and water/sanitation, and to a lesser extent, in health.

Finally, there is an urgent need for consistency between aid policy and other policies. Such consistency will vastly improve the chances of developing countries reaching the IDTs.[11] The goal of consistency is not helped by the domestic political weakness of development co-operation agencies, which limits their ability to lobby other domestic ministries, especially trade and finance ministries. However, without ensuring coherence between industrialized country domestic policies and aid policy, poverty reduction and universal access to basic services may remain a mirage.

REFERENCES

Addison, T. and G.A. Cornia (2001) 'Income Distribution Policies for Faster Poverty Reduction'. Discussion Paper No 2001/93. Helsinki: UNU/WIDER.

Beynon, J. (1999) '"Assessing Aid" and the Collier/Dollar Poverty Efficient Aid Allocation: A Critique'. London: Department for International Development. Available at www.dfid.gov.uk/public.

BIS (Bank for International Settlements) (1995–6) *Annual Report 1995–6*. Basle: BIS.

Burnside, C. and D. Dollar (1997) *Aid, Policies and Growth*. Washington, DC: The World Bank.

Hansen, H. and F. Tarp (2000) 'Aid Effectiveness Disputed', in F. Tarp *Foreign Aid and Development*. London: Routledge.

Lensink, R. and H. White (2000) 'Aid Allocation, Poverty Reduction and the "Assessing Aid" Report', *Journal of International Development* 12(3): 299–324.

McGillivray, M. and O. Morrissey (2001) 'Fiscal Effects of Aid'. Discussion Paper No 2001/61. Helsinki: UNU/WIDER.

---

11. In a similar vein, Pronk (p. 10) argues: 'good donor governance should set an example, without which good governance in developing countries has even less chance of sustainability. Good foreign governance may have to precede good domestic governance'.

Mahbub-ul-Haq, I. Kaul and I. Grunberg (eds) (1996) *The Tobin Tax: Coping with Financial Volatility*. Oxford: Oxford University Press.

Mehrotra, S. (2001) 'The Rhetoric of International Development Targets and the Reality of Official Development Assistance'. Innocenti Working Paper 85. Florence: UNICEF IRC.

Mehrotra, S. and E. Delamonica (forthcoming) *Public Spending for the Poor. Basic Services to Enhance Capabilitiies and Promote Growth*. Oxford: Oxford University Press.

OECD (1996) *Shaping the 21st Century: The Contribution of Development Cooperation*. Paris: OECD.

OECD (2001) *The DAC Journal Development Cooperation 2000 Report*. Paris: OECD.

Stern, N. (2001) 'Open the Rich Markets to Poor Countries' Exports', *International Herald Tribune* 25 January.

UNCTAD (1999) *Trade and Development Report*. Geneva: United Nations Conference on Trade and Development.

UNICEF (2001) *Progress since the World Summit for Children. A Statistical Review*. New York: UNICEF.

World Bank (1998) *Assessing Aid. What Works, What Doesn't, and Why?* New York: Oxford University Press for the World Bank.

World Bank (2000) *Attacking Poverty. World Development Report 2000/1*. New York: Oxford University Press for the World Bank.

Chapter 12

Aid Effectiveness and Policy Ownership

Rehman Sobhan

INTRODUCTION

Foreign aid known as official development assistance (ODA) is in a state of crisis. Over the 1990s, ODA has declined in absolute terms, from US$ 44 billion in 1990 to US$ 41 billion in 1999, which means that in real terms it has declined even more sharply (Commission on the Role of the MDBs, 2001). ODA's share of total capital transfers declined in the 1990s so that private capital flows have emerged as the dominant source of capital transfers to the developing countries (DCs). In 1999 Foreign Direct Investment (FDI) accounted for US$ 222 billion of inflows into the DCs which is over five times the inflow of ODA. This has severely aggravated inequities in access among DCs to external resource flows. These inequities in total capital flows are being compounded by the inequities in ODA transfers to the DCs. Instead of ODA playing a compensatory role to correct imbalances in private flows, in 1999 ODA to middle income DCs plus India and China accounted for US$ 25.4 billion compared to US$ 10.6 billion going to the Least Development Countries (LDCs) (UNCTAD, 2000). In the prevailing circumstances aid is losing its capacity to leverage change in the DCs. Today few non-LDC countries look to aid to determine the course of their development whilst LDCs, even those heavily dependent on aid, are hardly receiving enough aid to make a difference to their development capacity.

This paper is designed to review the debate on aid effectiveness within the changing global milieu. I have participated in this debate over the last twenty years (Sobhan, 1982, 1993, 1994, 1995, 1996a, 1996b, 1998, 1999b). Jan Pronk's suggestion that aid should be increasingly used as a catalytic agent for development (this volume, Ch. 1) should be contextualized within this ongoing debate. It is argued here that in an age of declining aid commitments and declining leverage exercised by aid in the DCs even its catalytic role is open to question. What little effectiveness is realized from aid is less determined by its volume or terms, but depends more on the quality of governance in the recipient country. This issue of governance is, however, not limited to the DCs but also extends into the donor aid agencies themselves, particularly the multilateral development agencies (MDAs). It is arguable that due to the growing frustration with the state of aid effectiveness, donors are directing their aid towards hitherto unfamiliar territory such as governance where they have little comparative advantage in influencing effective outcomes.

Confusion of objectives in aid policy is being compounded by contradictory motives where the juxtaposition of political and economic goals in the allocation of aid commitments is compromising its effectiveness. In DCs which have remained heavily dependent on donor advice the continuing attempt by aid donors to influence not just the policy agendas but the political behaviour of the DCs is thus further perpetuating the erosion of ownership over their policy agendas rather than enhancing their commitment and capacity to indigenize policy-making. This loss of ownership has led to the de-accumulation of domestic institutional capacity and eventually the delegitimization of the state in the eyes of their citizens who feel that the DC government is less accountable to democratic opinion at home than to external forces. This has further aggravated the crisis of governance in many DCs and in what are today termed the transitional economies (TEs) of Eastern Europe and the former USSR. Any attempt to improve the effectiveness of aid not only requires a complete rethinking of the policy agendas associated with aid, but also needs to redefine the relationship between donors and aid recipients so as restore domestic policy ownership and accountability.

EVOLVING PERSPECTIVES ON AID

The Philosophy of Aid

Aid commitments were originally designed to fill the resource gaps in a DC's macro-economy. In the post World War II period the rationale for aid, so succinctly cited by Pronk in his essay, was inspired by the theoretical works of the early development economists. In these early writings the need for such aid was always projected as finite. Effective use of aid was designed to bridge the savings/investment gap and the balance of payments gap in the DCs and put them on the path to self-sustaining development. The move to meet the capital deficiency of the DCs was concretized in ODA investment in Project Aid designed to develop the infrastructure of the DCs. Thus, these academically inspired agendas for aid policy found strong support in the business community of the donor countries who were commissioned to implement these largely capital intensive development projects. However, economists and engineers were not enough to build a political constituency for aid in the developed world. Legislators needed to be influenced, in varying degrees, by concerns of *realpolitik,* moral considerations and eventually issues of aid effectiveness. In some countries such as the USA and former USSR, aid was always regarded as an arm of foreign policy and geo-strategy. In other less high profile countries such as the Nordic countries or the Netherlands aid policy derived from strong humanitarian' impulses (as indeed they did in some quarters in the USA).

Given the fact that over a trillion dollars eventually came to be invested in ODA it was hardly surprising that in all donor countries, the issue of aid effectiveness would increasingly come to figure in the concerns of both governments and legislators. The yardstick for assessing aid effectiveness has varied with the era. Whilst economic performance was always seen as an important measure, at all stages donors remained preoccupied with the effectiveness of development assistance in reducing global poverty. The use of the metric of poverty was inspired by the nature of the appeal to those who finance aid — the citizens, largely in the role of taxpayers, in the advanced industrial countries (AICs). Whilst some of the governments of aid giving countries may have once been driven by the *realpolitik* of keeping the Third World safe from communism, the appeal for aid was eventually sustained by the humanitarian concerns of the average taxpayers of the developed world. The exception to this rule appears to have been the Middle East where Israel and Egypt seem to have established themselves, largely for political reasons, as the primary beneficiaries of ODA from the USA.

The Disillusionment with Aid

The contemporary prioritization of poverty in the aid policies of the AICs and multilateral development agencies (MDA) is thus doing no more than giving appropriate recognition to the concerns of those who paid for aid in the first place. By the 1980s there was a legitimate expectation on the part of the taxpayers that substantial numbers of the Third World's poor would no longer be poor and consequently the claims on the taxpayers of the AIC would be correspondingly lowered. AIC citizens were thus quite unprepared to be assailed by TV images of poverty projected from the squalid *favelas* of Rio, the shantytowns of Nairobi and the *bustees* of Calcutta and Dhaka. More to the point they did not appreciate the fact that these *favelas* co-existed with the luxury apartment blocks of Sao Paolo, inhabited by a class who shopped in Paris or New York and even imported their boutiques to Sao Paolo to which they were driven in air-conditioned Mercedes 600 cars. Nor did the AIC taxpayers appreciate the constant stream of media reports about the fortunes accumulated abroad by Third World leaders.

The deep disillusion with three decades of development assistance thus lies both in the persistence of poverty and its juxtaposition with the affluence of the few in many Third World countries. Aid agencies who had to extract dollars from angry legislators to sustain their bilateral aid programmes and replenish the capital base of the World Bank were increasingly hard put to justify this persistence of endemic poverty in many Third World countries. The origins of policy lending and the subsequent rediscovery of governance as the critical component of successful aid programmes, it is argued, originated in the need to justify what was deemed by AIC taxpayers as a massive misuse of their hard-earned money and the apparent deception practised by the aid agencies implicit in the appeals to the conscience of those taxpayers. This demand by citizens of the AICs for visible returns from their aid budgets was itself the by-product of a political climate which was becoming progressively more hostile to increasing taxation and public expenditures. In this changing political environment cuts in the aid budget appeared to serve as politically low cost measures since DC aid recipients do not vote in AIC elections.

The Era of Policy Reforms

This concern with the disillusion of AIC taxpayers was also conditioned by the apparent complicity of the aid agencies of the donors in contributing to the misdirection and misuse of aid, and their collusive role in building up a class of people in the DCs who prospered from aid at the expense of the majority of the DC citizens (Sobhan, 1990). The response of aid agencies in the AICs to this rising sense of outrage in the donor countries was thus driven both by the expectation that this disillusion with aid could be reversed as well as by their compulsions for institutional survival. Aid agencies, seeking to protect their budgets, focused on two themes in seeking to redesign aid strategies: getting policies right; and redirecting aid to the poor.

The second element was, however, largely subordinated to the first because it was believed by the dominant aid donors, led by the MDAs through the decade of the 1980s, that the right policies would stimulate growth which in turn would alleviate poverty. In order to get policies right aid was increasingly offered on conditional terms that policy reforms, on lines suggested by the MDAs, would be put in place in the respective DCs. This agenda for policy reform was, in turn, heavily influenced by the ideological input emanating from the Reagan and Thatcher administrations, which had come to power at the beginning of the 1980s and which politically underwrote the so called 'Washington Consensus'. In country after country, the MDAs, led by the World Bank and IMF, known collectively as the Bretton Woods institutions (BWI), put in place stabilization programmes followed by a package of structural adjustment reforms (SAR) inspired by the Washington Consensus. Up to US$ 75 billion was invested by the World Bank in SAR programmes through the 1980s.

It was, with some distinguished exceptions in the DCs and TEs, the apparent failure of the aid-driven reforms of the 1980s to either promote sustained growth or alleviate poverty which has now inspired a further change of direction in donor aid strategies (Sobhan, 1999a). The sense of frustration amongst the taxpayers of the AICs had by now extended from the political right to the left, led by the NGOs, radical academics and church groups. The critics projected the 1980s as an era of failed reforms: not only had they failed to improve growth, but they had made small factions within these Third World countries very rich, whilst the poor remained poor. The right continued to challenge the very assumptions of aid and remained unimpressed by the decade of reforms initiated in many developing countries under the leadership of the BWI. The strong resistance in the US Congress to the capital replenishment of the World Bank, the regional banks and the IMF, suggests that the reformist zeal of the aid agencies had failed to impress the Jesse Helmses of the US political establishment.

Putting Governance First

To cope with critics from both the left and right, the new focus on aid strategy appears to be directed to *getting governance right* and targeting aid to the poor through meeting what James Wolfensohn, the incumbent President of the World Bank, terms the 'challenge of inclusion'. The literature of the World Bank in the 1990s indicates that it, at least, has recognized that a combination of getting policies and governance right is likely to alleviate poverty. In his essay, Pronk referred to the conclusions of the Bank's empirical work *Assessing Aid* (World Bank, 1998). The Bank's study argues that with *sound country management* (italics mine), 1 per cent of GDP in assistance translates into a 1 per cent decline in poverty. Thus, the Bank study states that a US$ 10 billion increase in aid would lift 25 million people a year out of poverty — *but only if it favours countries with sound economic management* (italics mine). Pronk again refers to this World Bank study on *Assessing Aid,* which further argued that improvements in economic institutions and policies in the developing world are the key to a quantum leap in poverty reduction. Such effective use of aid was also seen to complement private investment (Commission on the Role of MDBs, 2001). Promoting aid effectiveness thus demanded the use of aid in strengthening institutions as well as policies and bringing about an active engagement of civil society in the design and delivery of aid.

Pronk has rightly questioned the universality of the World Bank's development model as well as the attempt to establish a linear relation between good governance and effective aid use. There appear to be a number of serious flaws in the assumptions as well as the design of the analytical model used in the World Bank study, whilst their empirical evidence merits more careful scrutiny. The original definition of 'sound management' incorporates a mix of three policies: *reducing the budget surplus* as well as the *rate of inflation*, and realizing *increased trade openness*. These reforms are packaged with *institutional quality* which is itself defined as an admixture of the *strength of the rule of law, quality of the public bureaucracy* and *pervasiveness of corruption*. It would be necessary to examine the methods for quantifying such abstract concepts as rule of law and bureaucratic quality before assessing the weights assigned to these four variables and three sub-variables defining institutional quality. Such an exercise would demand a fuller appreciation of the empirical work correlating GDP growth with economic policy and institutional quality. It is arguable that the available evidence, at least from the Asian experience, does not conclusively support the conclusions of the World Bank study on the role of governance. The capacity to both design and implement reforms, as well as the entrepreneurial resources to avail of market opportunities do not appear to have been adequately addressed in the analysis of aid effectiveness and governance literature. This limitation in the conceptual base of the work made it difficult for the MDAs to anticipate the Asian financial crisis of 1997 or to design an effective response.

This rethinking of aid policy is not limited to the World Bank. Other aid donors such as the UK, the Nordic countries, Canada and the Netherlands are also seeking to link good governance with aid effectiveness and argue that policy ownership is crucial to the exercise of effective governance over development policy in the developing countries. The recently published *DAC Guidelines on Aid Policy* (OECD, 2000) has built its entire approach towards promoting aid effectiveness around measures to ensure policy ownership within aid recipient countries. All such agendas to promote governance reform focus on the need to prioritize the poor in the donors' allocative regimes. But such poverty alleviating agendas are now increasingly concerned with issues of empowerment of the poor and of women as integral to the process of poverty alleviation. In the remainder of this paper we will attempt to address the impact of this rethinking in the donor community on improving aid effectiveness.

Contradictions in the World Bank's New Aid Strategy

MDA programmes, designed in an era when growth was prioritized over poverty, have not quite worked out how poverty alleviation will be integrated into the earlier generation of SAR programmes. The belief of the 1980s that high growth will reduce poverty may be something of a truism. However, the earlier reforms neither generated growth nor alleviated poverty so that a new development model to reconcile growth with poverty alleviation is still awaited. The current practice of simply adding on poverty related projects to the old adjustment model and building safety nets for the victims of economic reform, appears to be a self-defeating exercise. It is arguable that the original development design failed to address the sources of poverty which originate in the structural injustices which underwrite the political economy of most DCs (Sobhan, 2001). In such an institutional context reform merely served to perpetuate poverty, accentuate inequalities and empower a small elite who have used their wealth to monopolize state power. In such an unjust social order, a few so-called poverty centred projects will not ensure a sustainable assault on poverty or the empowerment of the poor.

Prioritization of poverty in the aid agenda thus demands that the original design of the reform process has to incorporate institutional mechanisms for correcting structural injustice in order to ensure the inclusion of the poor in the development process (Sobhan, 2001). Such a process of inclusion needs to address the design of policies and institutions needed to give the poor more competitive access to the market, moving them up-market in the value addition chain, restructuring resources and institutions to invest the poor with substantive ownership of wealth-creating assets, providing more equitable access to human development opportunities and offering much greater scope for the poor to share political power. Attempts to step up allocations for the poor through targeted aid programmes of micro-credit or allocations for primary education and health care centres are hardly likely to disturb the realities of power in most DCs and TEs.

Serious contradictions also appear to arise between the prioritization of governance in aid agendas and the BWI commitment to policy lending. The distorting impact of policy lending derives from its impact on policy ownership as well as the limited access of the poor to the benefits of such reforms. It has been recognized in the World Bank's World Development Report 2000/2001, as well as in the new DAC guidelines, that reforms without ownership have proved to be unsustainable (World Bank, 2000). Having at least recognized what critics of donor-driven reforms had argued since the mid-1980s, it still appears that the BWI *newthink* on aid has not really resolved the tension between the flawed policy design of the original model and the prevailing commitment of most aid donors to put governance first. The World Bank has in fact not succeeded in developing a coherent model which links such reforms with their original policy design. Nor is there any indication that policy ownership in the DCs is being more actively promoted rather than talked about.

Endogenizing Policy Reforms

Once the MDAs and other donors embrace the proposition that aid effectiveness depends mainly on domestic ownership over policy reforms and the governance of such reforms, which owes to domestic political and social factors, the donors have to come to terms with the limited influence they can exercise over the use of their aid in the DCs. In the wake of this renovation in the donors' approach to policy reforms and aid utilization conditional lending would need to be phased out. The World Bank has again recognized that conditionality is unlikely to bring lasting reform if there is no strong domestic movement for change. Thus, only when domestic constituencies are committed to reform, adjustment loans and foreign aid can help consolidate policy gains. In such a context the central proposition of the DAC policy guidelines that the DCs should get their act together, design their own reforms and commit themselves to the implementation of these reforms, is well taken. However, Pronk's suggestion that aid will be needed to catalyse this indigenous reform process remains more problematic. The rub of the problem lies in deciding what policies would merit donor assistance in the expectation that they catalyse change. At the same time donors will have to come to terms with the prospect that their notions of appropriate policies may not always coincide with those of their aid recipients.

Donors have, for too long, attempted to lead reform and define its goals. This often follows in the wake of slow progress by a country in designing its own policy reforms. Donors tend to lose patience with the tardiness of DAC guidelines particularly amongst LDCs and prefer to call in expatriate consultants, with a façade of local participation added on. This process may not change substantively even in the new age where donors are committed to change their aid priorities and approach to the aid relationship. The institutional compulsions of individual aid agencies make it difficult for them to step aside whilst domestic policy ownership is being registered in DCs which have, for years, remained alienated from the design of domestic policies. Thus, donors also need patience and self-discipline to ensure that they do not rush in to fill the policy vacuum within the DCs. Donors should not make the mistake of *promoting* ownership which would itself be a contradiction in terms. This applies particularly to the latest fad of promoting domestic ownership over *Policy Reduction Strategy Papers (PRSP)* in most DCs.

CONCLUSION: NEW CHALLENGES IN THE AID DISCOURSE

Jan Pronk has challenged development analysts to rethink the role of aid in development. I am not sure if we have adequately risen to the challenge. However, a similar challenge needs to be addressed to Jan Pronk in his role as a political player who has spent over a quarter of a century immersed in the political economy of not just foreign aid but North–South relations. A person with his exposure to the changing *realpolitik* of foreign aid would needed to address questions which have essentially remained concealed in the boardrooms of aid agencies.

We have already observed that today aid is becoming increasingly less relevant to the fortunes of most developing countries. More emphasis is being placed by the DCs on issues of market access, foreign direct investment (FDI), and debt-rescheduling, where aid may serve to play a leveraging rather than a primary role. In this changing environment donors are increasingly reinventing themselves as policy advisers rather than resource providers. In their new role as policy advisers donors have tended to emphasize good governance and greater policy ownership to guide agendas for prioritizing poverty eradication. This contradiction between declining aid leverage and more diversified agendas for policy advice, in fields once alien to the concerns as well as expertise of the aid donors, has yet to be recognized in the donor–recipient discourse. Nor is much attention being given to the increasing emphasis on political considerations governing donor–recipient relations.

Most donors aspire to use aid to promote poverty alleviation, economic reforms and good governance. To press these agendas some donors are more inclined to use aid, along with inducements of market access for DC exports, as strategic resources to influence a recipient country's external political alignments as well as its domestic political orientation. Whilst it may be legitimate to recognize such issues as part of the concerns of bilateral aid donors concerned with threats to national security and mobilizing legislative votes, it is less clear how multilateral development agencies such as the World Bank, IMF or the OECD should lend themselves to promote the strategic and political agendas of particular partner countries, however powerful they may be.

Finally, the aid discourse will need to reconcile the dominant concern of these aid donors to restore ownership over economic policy whilst becoming increasingly assertive in their demands for politically correct behaviour from aid recipients. It is even more problematic if issues of market access to the European market or the North American market are to be made conditional not just on politically correct domestic behaviour but on where a country stands in a particular geopolitical conflict. Indeed it is possible that under particular circumstances strategic considerations may serve as a substitute for politically inappropriate behaviour as well as defective economic policies.

It is therefore time to reopen the discourse on the politics of the prevailing global economic order. We need to address the issue of the use of both aid and trade as instruments of leverage in influencing the political options of developing countries. If such factors are to be incorporated into the new *realpolitik* guiding North–South relations then we need to assess the costs and benefits of such an order. More to the point, we need to understand whether such an order can be sustained through ensuring more transparency and consistency in the application of such political conditionalities. This would encourage the more vulnerable DCs to better educate themselves as to how these new ground rules would apply in determining their access to aid and market opportunities. Failure to address such issues could drive the aid relationship back into the era of the Cold War where donor–recipient relations were driven by an admixture of political expediency and ad hoc humanitarianism.

In such a world it would be extremely difficult for aid and/or trade dependent countries, particularly the LDCs, to develop longer-term plans and policies which seek to restructure their economies and societies in order to eradicate poverty. Nor would governments be encouraged to build domestic political constituencies to support reforms. In such a politicized aid regime, donors stand to compromise the very reforms in aid policy which they have been seeking to put in place in recent years. In such a restructured pattern of aid relationships, aid effectiveness is not likely to be enhanced.

REFERENCES

Commission on the Role of MDBs in Emerging Markets (2001) *Report on the Role of the Multilateral Development Banks in Emerging Market Economies.* Washington, DC.

OECD (2000) *DAC Guidelines on Aid Policy.* Paris: OECD.

Sobhan, Rehman (1982) *The Crisis of External Dependence: The Political Economy of Foreign Aid.* Dhaka: University Press Ltd. (and London: Zed Press, 1984).

Sobhan, Rehman (1990) *From Aid Dependence to Self-Reliance: Development Options for Bangladesh.* Dhaka: University Press Ltd.

Sobhan, Rehman (1993) *Bangladesh: Problems of Governance.* India: Konark Publishers' Pvt. Ltd.

Sobhan, Rehman (1994) 'Aid Versus Markets in the Institutionalization of Consultancy Service: Some Asian Contrasts', *Asia-Pacific Development Journal* 1(1).

Sobhan, Rehman (1995) 'Technical Assistance to Developing Countries: The Failure of Market Forces', *The International Journal of Technical Cooperation* 1(1).

Sobhan, Rehman (1996a) 'Official Development Finance for National Development of the Least Developed Countries', *Journal of International Affairs* (4 July).

Sobhan, Rehman (1996b) *Aid Dependence and Donor Policy: The Case of Tanzania: with Lessons from Bangladesh Experience.* Dhaka: University Press Ltd.

Sobhan, Rehman (1998) *Towards a Theory of Governance and Development: Learning from East Asia.* Dhaka: University Press Ltd.

Sobhan, Rehman (1999a) 'Bangladesh's Experience with Economic Reforms: The Need for a Reappraisal', in Fumiko Oshikawa (ed.) *South Asia under the Economic Reforms.* Osaka: Japan Center for Area Studies.

Sobhan, Rehman (1999b) 'The Future of Development Assistance: An Asian Perspective'. New York: UNDP Office of Policy Studies (mimeo).

Sobhan, Rehman (2001) 'Eradicating Rural Poverty: Moving from a Micro to a Macro Policy Agenda'. Public Lecture. Rome: IFAD/FAO, WFP.

UNCTAD (2000) *The Least Developed Countries 2000 Report.* New York: UNCTAD.

World Bank (1998) *Assessing Aid: What Works, What Doesn't and Why.* New York: Oxford University Press.

World Bank (2000) *World Development Report 2000/2001. Attacking Poverty.* New York: Oxford University Press for the World Bank.

Chapter 13

It is Possible to Just Give Money to the Poor

Joseph Hanlon

INTRODUCTION

'We are giving fifty billion dollars of overseas aid. There are a billion poor people in the world. Why don't we just find the poor and give them one dollar a week and do nothing else. No questions asked. What they do with the money is not our concern. That would probably do more to relieve poverty than anything else', recently argued Meghnad Desai, director of the London School of Economics Centre for the Study of Global Governance (Desai, 2003b).

The debate set off by Jan Pronk has stressed conditionality, targeting, selectivity and various other methods of promoting sustainable development or 'fostering a policy environment conducive to development' (this volume, Ch. 1 and Ch. 14). Pronk and his critics all dream of finding a way of making aid more 'effective' and the result is ever more elaborate and conflicting criteria. 'We impose so many conditions on those countries that receive money: they have to be gender sensitive; poor people must participate directly; they must have sustainability; they must have environmental friendliness; and they must have transparency, accountability, and so on', comments Lord Desai. 'If we think of our own historical development process, or that of any developed country, none of the criteria was fulfilled ... Why, just because we give a pittance to other people, do we expect such bossy behaviour to be received properly? I do not understand why we think that it will be effective in removing poverty, whatever desire we have to show that we are virtuous' (Desai, 2003a).

In his comment on Pronk's essay, Santosh Mehrotra notes that aid is most effective if it is allocated simply according to poverty (this volume, Ch. 11). Pronk himself points to the 'need for a permanent world system of market corrections, income transfers, social securities and public services, just as with individual national economies' (p. 193).

Would it be feasible to simply consider aid as an income transfer to the poorest, and just give one dollar a week to poor people, as Desai proposes? In this article, I will point to recent reports which show that this has been done twice in Mozambique in the past decade, and both times has been efficient and successful. The first example is demobilization payments given to former fighters in Mozambique's civil war, in which nearly 93,000 former soldiers were given roughly US$ 2 a week for two-and-a-half years, at an administrative cost of only 5 per cent (Christie and Barnes, 2001). The second example was a payment of US$ 92 to 106,000 families affected by a flood in 2000 (Miller, 2002). Both used cheques which had to be cashed by named individuals, and had administrative and overhead costs of only 5 per cent.

CASH FOR DEMOBILIZED SOLDIERS

Mozambique's decade-long civil war ended with a peace accord in 1992, a United Nations-monitored two-year peace process, and highly praised multi-party elections in 1994 (see Hanlon, 1996 for more details). A total of 92,881 troops from both sides were demobilized. They were given their salary for two years, the first six months paid by the government and the next eighteen months paid by donors through a US$ 35.5 million trust fund administered by the United Nations Development Programme (UNDP). Payments were made from mid-1994 until mid-1996. Ordinary soldiers constituted 51 per cent of the total demobilized and their salary, 75,000 meticais, was the local currency equivalent of US$ 7 per month in 1995 and 1996. Lower level officers constituted another 35 per cent of the demobilized, with salaries worth US$ 10–24. Because of a falling exchange rate, the trust fund had money left over, and in early 1997 each demobilized soldier was given an extra US$ 52, regardless of rank (Christie and Barnes, 2001).

The United Nations Mission in Mozambique (ONUMOZ) set up a special demobilization Technical Unit, which issued all demobilized soldiers with a photo identity card and set up a database. Soldiers could choose to be demobilized anywhere in Mozambique and were provided with transport as part of the demobilization process. The eighteen months of money from the donor trust fund (plus the unexpected additional money) was to be paid to demobilized soldiers every two months at the branch of the People's Development Bank (BPD, Banco Popular de Desenvolvimento), or at a post office which served as a BPD branch, which was nearest to the place the demobilized soldier chose to go.

Using the Technical Unit database, UNDP printed books of vouchers or cheques for each soldier, which they presented with their identity card at the branch of the bank every two months. Despite the very low level of education (one-third had no schooling and one-third had only primary schooling) the demobilized soldiers had few difficulties handling cheques; in a follow-up survey fewer than 7 per cent of the demobilized soldiers said they had problems in cashing their cheques (Christie and Barnes, 2001).

Perhaps the biggest difficulty was that, at the time, the BPD had branches or post office branches in only 68 out of 128 districts; this meant that one-third spent US$ 2–4 (a significant part of US$ 14) in order to go to the nearest town with a bank to collect payments. The problem would be worse now, because BPD has since been privatized and many of its rural branches closed as unprofitable.

The administration costs were very low — 2.5 per cent to UNDP's reintegration support unit, 0.5 per cent for UNDP headquarters, and 2.5 per cent for BPD (Christie and Barnes, 2001). So of US$ 35.5 million allocated, only US$ 1.8 million was spent on overheads and US$ 33.7 million went directly to beneficiaries — a far higher percentage than with normal aid projects.

What were the development and economic impacts of these cash payments? By the end of the payment period 86 per cent said they were involved in at least some agricultural activities; thus, the money was not their only means of survival, but rather was important as cash on top of their subsistence. The survey showed that the money was largely used locally to help to sustain their extended families and for basic necessities. For the final lump sum, 46 per cent said some would be spent on school fees for children (Barnes, 1997a). The money seems to have been particularly important in restarting economic activity in war-affected areas. One study showed that these cash payments gave 'a new impetus to social life, especially in rural areas' (Lundin et al., 2000).

Most of the money was used for current expenses and only 21 per cent was used for investment in farms or businesses. This leads one study to conclude that 'the money did not contribute significantly to development', perhaps because it 'was not enough to start a sustainable livelihood' (Lundin et al., 2000). But it is useful to note that the amount of money being distributed was far less than the US$ 1 per week suggested by Desai. The average family size for demobilized soldiers was 7.5 people, and ordinary soldiers were only receiving US$ 7 per month, which per person is one quarter that suggested by Desai.

CASH FOR FLOOD VICTIMS

The worst flood in 150 years hit southern Mozambique in early 2000 (see Christie and Hanlon, 2001 for more details). From December 2000 to April 2001 the United States Agency for International Development (USAID) gave cash grants of 1.5 million meticais (about US$ 92) to each of 106,280 flood-affected rural families, in what its own evaluation called a 'unique' project. It had been hoped to distribute the money between August and October 2000, very quickly after the flood, when it would support resettlement. But this was delayed by several factors, including delays by the US Congress in approving funds and a longer than expected time needed to identify beneficiaries and set up the distribution (Miller, 2002). By the time the money was distributed, most people had already rebuilt their houses, for example. But this makes it a much better test of simply handing out money to poor people under something approaching normal conditions.

'Beneficiary identification was a difficult process', notes the USAID evaluation. Initially 219,083 families were identified, and this was reduced to 106,280 by imposing tighter criteria. It was decided that money would be given only to women heads of households for two reasons: polygamy is common and thus a woman and her children were considered to be a family, and 'additionally, the project managers felt that women might be better than men in making spending decisions reflecting family priorities' (Miller, 2002).

After registration, distribution of the money was done at 167 sites covering 730 villages over a period of 94 days. Advance teams informed villages of the distribution dates and village chiefs and village secretaries were asked to organize registered recipients on that date. A local bank working for USAID, Banco Commercial e de Investimento (BCI), organized the delivery of pre-prepared cash packets and provided tellers at distribution sites. A private security firm was present. Chiefs organized recipients in queues. Each eligible recipient was given an identification ticket and a cheque and dipped her index finger in indelible ink (in a system also used in Mozambique to prevent multiple voting during elections). Recipients then went immediately to the bank teller where they cashed their cheques (Miller, 2002).

The implementation cost was small. The grants programme was one-third of a larger post-flood recovery programme, which had a total administrative cost of 10 per cent, which the evaluation notes is much less than the administrative share of other distributions, such as food aid (Miller, 2002). Probably the largest single cost was the identification and registration of flood victims and exclusion of those not eligible. So the actual cost of simply distributing the money was probably only 5 to 10 per cent of the money distributed.

The distribution of funds was intentionally rural and recipients were mainly poor subsistence farmers; 96 per cent of recipients earned their income primarily from agriculture. A subsequent survey found most of the money was spent for basic consumption: 18 per cent of the grants was spent on household goods such as dishes and blankets and on consumer products, 12 per cent on clothes, and 7 per cent on food. But some was for investment, including 14 per cent for livestock, 8 per cent for seeds, 4 per cent for equipment and 9 per cent for construction materials, 'suggesting a long-term development consequence of the programme', according to the evaluation (Miller, 2002).

The use of the money was very diverse. Some was used to repay debts, some to make repairs to equipment and machinery, and one woman used the money to repay her bride price (*lobolo*) in order to divorce her husband.

The female heads of household surveyed estimated that only 1.5 per cent of the money was spend on alcohol (Miller, 2002).

Of the total amount, 55 per cent was spent in the village, 18 per cent in a nearby town and 14 per cent in the district capital, so that 87 per cent remained within the district. Interviews with retailers suggested that as much as half the money was spent on goods produced within Mozambique. Thus the grants seem to have stimulated both the local and national economy (Miller, 2002).

COULD IT BE DONE MORE WIDELY?

These two examples show that it is possible to issue cheques in the range of US$ 15 to US$ 100 to illiterate and poorly educated rural Mozambicans, that the cheques can be cashed and the money used sensibly, and that the administrative cost can be brought down to just 5 per cent. In both projects, selecting beneficiaries and excluding others increased the set-up costs in ways which would not have been the case had it been a universal benefit.

How might one pay Desai's one dollar per person per week? Probably the simplest way would be as a family credit, paid every two months in the same way as the demobilized soldiers were paid. For an average family of seven people that would be US$ 60 every two months. It might not be unreasonable to give preference to naming a woman as head of household, if possible.

To make the system work would require two things — a proper identification system and an adequate banking system. Mozambique already issues photo electoral registration cards for voters and does an annual re-registration exercise for people who have moved, to add those who have reached 18 years old, and delete those who have died. Mozambique also issues identity cards, which most adults carry. Thus it should not be too difficult or costly to upgrade the population register to ensure its accuracy, and to regularly update the family entitlement cards, perhaps annually. Cheques might be issued at the same time. It would not be unreasonable to ask heads of households to obtain confirmation from a village secretary or chief or local teacher or church leader of any changes in family status — births, deaths, children leaving home — and to ask the heads of households to go to the district capital once a year to update their entitlement record. For the electoral system, Mozambique uses mobile registration brigades which go to every village, and such a system could also be used. The budget for updating the electoral register in 2003 was US$ 13 million for nearly 8 million voters (Fauvet, 2003), so one might estimate that the cost of updating entitlement cards and related records and issuing cheques, perhaps on an annual basis, at US$ 1.50 per person per year, 3 per cent of the money being given.

Cheques were cashed and money was distributed in both exercises by a commercial bank, and it would seem sensible to continue such a system. At the very least this would encourage the expansion of the rural banking system; post offices could also be used, and some sort of mobile banks would probably be required, as they were for distribution of the flood money. BPD was paid 2 per cent to dispense the money for demobilized soldiers and to provide proper accounts, and a similar percentage should be sufficient for this exercise. Thus it does seem possible to keep the costs at under 5 per cent of the money given out.

The one remaining issue is that even in the poorest countries, some people already earn more than US$ 1 per day, and should not be eligible. For Mozambique and indeed for most of Africa, the percentage of people over the threshold is small, and it would cost almost as much to exclude them as to pay them. Perhaps the sensible answer is to make the benefit taxable and adjust the tax rates to claw back most of the family benefit given to people already paying tax.

SOUTH AFRICA AND THE BASIC INCOME GRANT

The only place where across-the-board cash payments is being treated as a serious possibility is Mozambique's neighbour, South Africa. A government commission headed by Professor Vivienne Taylor of the University of the Western Cape in 2002 called for a 'basic income grant' of Rand 100 (then about US$ 10, in mid 2003 about US$ 13) per month to be paid to every South African, unconditionally (Taylor, 2002). Although the government says it is 'philosophically opposed' to making payments to 'able-bodied South Africans', the proposal is gaining support from trades unions as well as economists and poverty researchers (Munusamy, 2002). South Africa is very different from the very poor countries where people would receive Desai's US$ 1 a week, but the debate again shows that it is possible. South Africa is a lower-middle income country (DAC, 2003), with only one quarter of its population on an income of less than US$ 1 a day (Thurlow, 2002) but with 45 per cent living below US$ 2 per day (Taylor, 2002). Mozambique uses a different poverty measure, but the only study done so far shows that more than 70 per cent of the population lives on less than US$ 0.70 per day (MPF et al., 1998).

South Africa's basic income grant would not rely on aid, but would be funded by the government itself, in an attempt to redress the heritage of apartheid. A study by the Economic Policy Research Institute in South Africa showed that although the grant would cost Rand 44 billion per year, half of that would go to the better off and would be recouped by a mix of income tax changes and value added tax. The net cost would be Rand 24 billion, about 2 per cent of GDP. It concludes that 'the basic income grant is feasible, affordable, and supportive of poverty reduction, economic growth, and job creation' (Samson et al., 2002). A new identity card system is being introduced and it is expected that by 2005 all South

Africans will have the cards, which would further simplify administration of the grant. A universal basic income grant costs less to administer because it has 'none of the costs associated with a benefit targeted through a means test' and will have a higher takeup rate because it lacks the stigma of a means-tested benefit (Taylor, 2002), while its automatic nature reduces the possibilities for corruption (Samson et al., 2002).

South Africa already operates a state old age pension which is nearly universal, with an 85 per cent take up. Finance Minister Trevor Manual acknowledges the pension as the government's most important poverty alleviation programme. 'The majority of people in poverty who are not white live in three generation households, and the grant is typically turned over for general family use', Manual noted. 'For black South Africans, each pensioner's income helped five other people in the household' (Samson et al., 2002).

Thus South Africa shows it is possible to hand out money to the poor, through a universal benefit to the elderly; a basic income grant for everyone is possible and seems increasingly likely. South Africa can fund such a programme from its own resources, but for poorer countries, there seems no reason not to use donor funds for such a programme.

WHY NOT JUST GIVE MONEY TO THE POOR?

We have shown that it is possible and quite efficient to simply give money to the poor. In the case of Mozambique, the money seems to have been used wisely. Poor people used it mainly to raise their standards of living, but some of the money was spent on productive investment and the money did seem to stimulate the local economy, which suggests it has a developmental impact. The USAID evaluation concluded that 'the fundamental principle of a cash grant program — that without any conditions attached, households would make prudent use of the money — was confirmed' (Miller, 2002).

Meghnad Desai comments that 'I would love to think that if we could give money — perhaps not to governments but directly to the citizens of poor countries — it could somehow enable them to make their own effort to get out of poverty. We are not giving enough attention to how poor people get themselves out of poverty. We always assume that we must do it for them' (Desai, 2003a).

Which leads to the fundamental question that has dogged charity and aid in the West for more than a century: are the poor poor simply because they lack money, or are they poor because of their own stupidity and cupidity? To maintain our own self-respect, we in the North need to believe that we deserve to be rich — that we are rich because we are smarter or harder working or 'better' in some way. Thus we have created an entire 'aid industry' of agencies setting conditions to change behaviour, of development ministries selecting those countries which act as we think they should, of high cost field workers telling peasants how to behave, and so on. We create schools of development studies and journals such as *Development and Change*. But how much development does it accomplish?

We have created an industry with tens of thousands of jobs for people in the North, who receive cash grants not of US$ 1 a week but more than US$ 500 a week. Nor is it just in the North. Aid recipient countries have developed an elite which has become well off through the administration of aid — government officials, consultants, local aid agency staff and workers in non-government organizations which have contracts with international agencies. Jan Pronk notes that despite the best efforts of donors, 'in many instances aid is still serving the interests of a ruling elite rather than those of society as a whole, and particularly the poorest population strata' (p. 195). So there are a great many people in donor and recipient countries who have a vested interest in continuing the present system, and who will argue that if you simply give poor people money, they will waste it. And it is hardly surprising that, as the USAID evaluation notes, the Mozambique experiment was a 'unique' exercise. But it showed that it is not difficult to simply give people US$ 1 a week if we want to do it.

Perhaps we should at least consider the possibility that the main cause of poverty is simply lack of money, and at least run an experiment of giving poor people US$ 1 a week. Lord Desai comments: 'People often say, "These problems are not solved by throwing money at them". I say, "Just try"' (Desai, 2003a).

REFERENCES

Barnes, S. (1997a) 'The Socio-Economic Reintegration of Demobilised Soldiers in Mozambique: The Soldiers' View'. Maputo: United Nations Development Programme.

Barnes, S. (1997b) 'Reintegration Programmes for Demobilised Soldiers in Mozambique'. Maputo: United Nations Development Programme.

Christie, F. and S. Barnes (2001) 'Report of the Reintegration of Demobilised Soldiers in Mozambique 1992–1996'. Maputo: United Nations Development Programme.

Christie, F. and J. Hanlon (2001) *Mozambique and the Great Flood of 2000*. Oxford: James Currey; Bloomington and Indianapolis, IN: Indiana University Press.

DAC (Development Assistance Committee) (2003) 'Development Co-operation 2002 Report', *The DAC Journal* 4(1). Paris: Organization for Economic Co-operation and Development.

Desai, M. (2003a) speaking in the House of Lords, 12 June, House of Lords *Hansard* Column 459, http://www.parliament.the-stationery-office.co.uk/pa/ld199697/ldhansrd/pdvn/lds03/text/30612-30.htm

Desai, M. (2003b) speaking at the Overseas Development Institute, London, 18 June. http://www.odi.org.uk/RAPID/Meetings/Presentation_17/_Desai.html

Fauvet, P. (2003) 'Citizens Urged to Register as Voters'. Maputo: Agência de Informação de Moçambique, 24 June.

Hanlon, J. (1996) *Peace Without Profit: How the IMF Blocks Rebuilding in Mozambique*. Oxford: James Currey; Portsmouth, NH: Heinemann

Lundin, I., M. Chachiua, A. Gaspar, H. Guebuza and G. Mbilana (2000) ' "Reducing Costs Through an Expensive Exercise": The Impact of Demobilisation in Mozambique', in

K. Kingsma (ed.) *Demobilization in Sub-Saharan Africa*, pp 173–212. Basingstoke and London: Macmillan Press; New York, NY: St. Martin's Press.

Miller, J. (2002) 'Mozambique 1999–2000 Floods, Impact Evaluation: Resettlement Grant Activity'. Maputo: United States Agency for International Development.

MPF (Ministry of Planning and Finance, Government of Mozambique), Eduardo Mondlane University, and International Food Policy Research Unit (1998) *Understanding Poverty and Well-Being in Mozambique — The First National Assessment (1996–97)*. Maputo (no publisher cited).

Munusamy, R. (2002) 'Cabinet puts Poverty Grant on Ice', *Sunday Times* Johannesburg, 28 July.

Samson, M., O. Babson, C. Haarmaan, D. Haarmaan, G. Khathi, K. MacQuene and I. van Niekerk (2002) 'Research Review on Social Security Reform and the Basic Income Grant for South Africa'. Cape Town: Economic Policy Research Institute. http://www.epri.org.za/rp31.pdf

Taylor, V. (2002) 'Transforming the Present — Protecting the Future'. Report of the Committee of Inquiry into a Comprehensive System of Social Security for South Africa. Pretoria: Ministry of Social Development. http://www.welfare.gov.za/Documents/2002/2002.htm

Thurlow, J. (2002) 'Can South Africa Afford to Become Africa's First Welfare State?'. IFPRI Trade and Macroeconomics Division Discussion Paper No 101.Washington, DC: International Food Policy Research Institute. http://www.ifpri.org/divs/tmd/dp/papers/tmdp101.pdf

Chapter 14

Aid as a Catalyst: A Rejoinder

Jan P. Pronk

INTRODUCTION

In my original essay, 'Aid as a Catalyst', I distinguished four ways in which development aid could be analysed (Chapter 1 of this volume, and Pronk, 2001). Aid could be seen as a prime mover of development, as a *conditio sine qua non*. Foreign aid could also be perceived as an impediment to the autonomous development of a country. Thirdly, aid could be used to reward a country for a specific development performance, such as stability, growth or 'good governance'. Finally, aid could be conceived as a catalyst, enhancing the workings of other factors which are often more important because they are endogenous to the process of development. I pointed out that analysis shows that aid can help and indeed has helped countries to develop. This finding is an important argument against those who believe that aid does not help at all and should therefore be stopped. This view gained much ground in the 1990s and, in combination with other motives, led to a drastic decrease in foreign assistance. In my view, this cynicism is not founded on evidence and there is every reason to increase rather than to reduce international assistance.

I appreciate the reactions to that article, which were originally published in *Development and Change* and which are collected together here. Some support my line of argument, others are more critical, but all the authors plead in favour of more, not less, aid.

IDEALISM OR POLITICAL REALISM?

James Petras and Henry Veltmeyer are particularly critical of my approach. They place my paper in the tradition of 'idealists' who 'dissociate their discussion of aid from the historical–structural context in which it is embedded and argue in terms of normative values and the degree of compliance with those values by the recipient country' (pp. 64–5). Idealists, they argue, do not analyse the dynamics of foreign aid but focus on policy prescription, disregarding empirical findings as well as the politics of aid.

Against this Petras and Veltmeyer take the position of political 'realists'. In that perspective, aid sets in motion a series of policies that are promoted by, and benefit, the elite. In their view, therefore, my paper 'at best provides a limited and flawed perspective of the dynamics of foreign aid. At worst, it helps obfuscate the real issues involved' (pp. 73–4).

Indeed, I did not elaborate the political setting of aid in my article: I have done that regularly elsewhere (see, for example, Pronk, 2000). The main purpose of my 'Aid as a Catalyst' article was to underline the case for aid as such and to discuss, given the present political situation, some conditions under which aid would function better. I focused on conditions related to development policies, including the governance of these policies. I am aware that such conditions — which I would describe as 'policy conditions' — are strongly related to political conditions, such as the distribution of power within and between countries or geo-political objectives. For analytical purposes, however, I believe it makes sense to make a distinction between policy conditions and political conditions. I wanted to highlight possible positive development effects of foreign aid and the policy conditions that would foster such effects, even when the national or international political environment is not conducive for development. The alternative would be either to wait for a transformation of the political environment or to try using aid to catalyse such a transformation.

AID AS A PRIME MOVER?

I argued that evaluations of foreign assistance show that aid is not a prime mover of development. All authors seem to agree. In his contribution to the debate (Chapter 3), Louis Emmerij presents a lucid review of development theory and thinking of the last sixty years. In that period you might say that thinking has not only progressed, it has gone full circle. At the same time, conflicting theories about development were competing with each other. Emmerij describes how development aid followed the thinking about economic, social and political development, rightly observing that, because aid followed the different trends in thinking, development assistance became dispersed over multiple objectives. In Emmerij's terminology: 'the flight forward had begun ... moving from one priority to the other without solving the preceding one. ... [Hence] development aid ... started losing focus'. I am inclined to appreciate rather than to criticize this. Development aid should follow development theory rather than functioning as a self-willed policy. Moreover, different theories about causes of poverty and mal-development have proved to be valid in different circumstances and countries, while a number of development theories have turned out to be wrong, or applicable only under specific circumstances. If aid is not a prime mover of development but only a catalyst, it is good that development aid has not been used as a uniform panacea. In fact, experiences with aid and consequences of aid have contributed to adjustments in the development thinking, making it less abstract and differentiating it according to different economic, political and cultural circumstances.

Emmerij describes how, according to original thinking (W. Arthur Lewis, Rostow, Chenery and others), development aid was supposed to be temporary, a catalyst of economic growth. Emmerij argues that development aid, through its flight forward, has turned into a permanent feature of international economic and financial relations. I do not agree: in my view it has become a permanent feature not by default, but because of the globalization of these relations. In the context of a world market, a 'world household', there is also a need for a permanent world system of market corrections, income transfers, social securities and public services, just as with individual national economies. In other words: there is a permanent need for some form of international official development assistance. Without that the world household would not be sustainable.

I assume that Joseph Hanlon would agree with this last statement. In his contribution he presents the far-reaching proposal to consider aid as an income transfer to the poorest and give one dollar a week to poor people. This may seem a very old idea: pure, direct and unconditional income redistribution to the benefit of the very poor. Aid practice always was more sophisticated: not direct aid but indirect, through intermediate institutions; not unconditional, but on the condition that development expenditures and policies would be sustained; not consumption but investment oriented. However, Hanlon shows — with the help of some practical experience — that poor people receiving cash grants, without conditions attached, seem to use the money prudently. The money is spent on consumer goods that raise the standard of living and also on productive investment. Such aid stimulates the local economy and has a developmental impact. One could criticize Hanlon's proposal as unworkable and inefficient. However, he shows that cash grants can be made available at low cost. They do benefit the poor and thus are cost efficient. Hanlon, like many other contributors to this book, argues that government-to-government assistance in practice often does not benefit the poor, does not have a developmental impact and can be very costly. Perhaps Hanlon's suggestion is not old-fashioned, but quite modern. Social policies within national welfare states use unconditional direct income subsidies to their poor citizens very often, in conjunction with other policies (such as targeted subsidies, vouchers, tax reductions, tariff differentiation or free provision of basic goods, affirmative action, and so on). In a modern society social welfare payments are a permanent feature, not a charity but a right. Why could such payments to all poor people not be one of the modern policy instruments in a globalized society? It may seem far-fetched, but Hanlon's suggestion is worthy of consideration.

Ajit Singh claims to be perplexed by my remark that in view of all the mistakes made in designing and executing aid programmes, and in view of the unfavourable political environment, it is a 'miracle' that according to some evaluation studies, aid has at times been 'a spectacular success'. In his view the opposite is true: 'In ... circumstances of fast overall economic growth and social improvement in the South, it would be astonishing if the North's public aid agencies would not be highly successful in some developmental sphere or the other' (p. 79). Singh refers to the period between 1950 and 1980 as a period in which developing countries benefited not only from the booming economic conditions in advanced countries for their exports, but also from policy autonomy of a kind which they did not have in the pre-World War II period under colonialism. After that period, Singh writes, the debt crisis and Washington Consensus based conditionalities deprived developing countries of both a positive economic environment and much of their autonomy. Aid, he seems to argue, did not undo these unfavourable conditions: on the contrary, aid itself became subjected to them and started to function as a carrier of intrusive conditionalities, clearly impeding a process of autonomous development.

I wonder whether I can fully agree with this part of the analysis. Singh seems to claim that foreign aid had a different impact before and after 1980: first it seems to have functioned, in his view not surprisingly at all, as a highly successful prime mover, while later on it became an impediment. If this is true, there must have been other factors at play than the two mentioned by Singh. In the 1990s the economies of the industrialized countries were enjoying an even bigger boom than in the 1970s. Why did developing countries benefit less than before? Moreover, did developing countries have much autonomy before 1980? If my politically realist reading of the prevailing conditions during that period is correct, neo-colonial policies of the former colonial powers strongly reduced the autonomy that these countries were aiming to achieve with their independence. The Cold War made the South into a theatre where East and West fought a political battle to strengthen their respective spheres of influence: this had a negative impact on the autonomy of Southern countries in choosing their own development path and their own political and economic governance systems. In such a situation it was not self-evident that aid would work out positively for any country. Or should the analysis be interpreted differently: aid in itself doesn't do the trick; it is the political and economic environment that determines the outcome? But if that is the case, how to justify a plea — Ajit Singh's plea as well — for a substantial increase in aid?

In my view that justification lies in the catalytic effect of aid. It is a modest effect in principle, but that effect can be enhanced by fostering a policy environment conducive to development. Such a fostering may require the setting of specific conditions to the rendering of assistance. In my original paper, I made it clear that I was not referring to the well-known Washington Consensus conditionalities, which still prevail today and which are mainly aimed at the preservation of stability, irrespective of the consequences for poor and underprivileged people. Instead, I referred to a different set of conditionalities, directly aimed at a sustainable improvement in people's lives. Aid can help to bring that about — not only in theory, but also in practice, as shown by many sectoral and thematic evaluation studies. But before elaborating on the positive catalytic effect of aid, it is necessary to comment on possible negative consequences of aid or, in other words, to look at aid as an impediment to development.

AID AS AN IMPEDIMENT?

There is no doubt: aid can impede development. However, this is not inherently so (as I argued in my 'Aid as a Catalyst' article). Most of the negative effects of aid are the result of wrong policies on the part of either the donor or the recipient. Donors often pursue objectives that are not in the interest of developing countries and try to achieve these objectives partly by giving aid: many examples are mentioned in the various reactions to my article. Nor is there any evidence that wrong donor policies are on their way out, despite much discussion in the framework of multilateral organizations within which recipient developing countries have a voice. On the contrary, recent examples — such as tying food aid to the obligation to import genetically modified products, and using aid to ensure the political support of a recipient regime for a geo-political security objective of the donor — show that donors are no less inclined to use aid to serve their own interests than, for instance, in the period investigated by Ohlin (1966). Recipients, too, have used aid for other purposes than to foster sustainable development. It is obvious that, in many instances, aid is still serving the interests of a ruling elite rather than those of society as a whole, and particularly the poorest population strata. Again for analytical purposes, I would like to refer to all this as 'bad aid', 'bad policies' and 'bad governance'. Against this I have tried to describe a general case, in which a donor's only aim is to help reach development targets as defined by a recipient country, and in which the government of that country is supposed to act fully in the interests of the people concerned. Within the framework of such a general case, donors and recipients may have different and conflicting perceptions about what is 'good' for development. What one party perceives as 'good' might be met with disapproval by the other, and might even be labelled as 'wrong': but in the general case, wrong perceptions are not due to wrong intentions.

This is a more explicit and systematic way of 'unpacking' development aid relationships than I attempted in my previous essay. I am using here the terminology introduced by James Boyce, who in his contribution concluded that in order to ensure that aid catalyses broad-based improvements in human well-being rather than deepening inequalities and indebtedness, both sides of the aid relationship must be unpacked. Instead of viewing aid as a relation between 'donor countries' and 'recipient countries', we must ask 'the critical question: aid from whom, aid to whom, and for what ends?' (p. 27).

'Unpacking' aid relationships helps to throw light on political realities. It also helps to achieve a step by step analysis. If we have to take all factors and variables into account at the same time, the picture can become so complicated that we become paralysed about how to act, and conclude that it is better to refrain from any action at all. But the alternative to full realism is the need to make explicit assumptions. I realize that the assumptions made above about the perceptions, intentions and objectives of the different parties in a relationship, as well as those regarding the distinction between policies and politics, are rather heroic. Petras and Veltmeyer may justifiably label them as idealist rather than politically realist. But I hope to have made it clear that it is not naïve idealism which lies at the basis of these assumptions. I consider them useful in an effort to address what I believe to be a central question in the field of international development assistance. That central question is the following: if, firstly, sustainable development would require substantial reforms, while the process of transformation necessary to accomplish these reforms would take much time, and if, secondly, the intentions of donors and recipients would be more or less in accordance with what such a process would require, could aid then function as a catalyst to speed up the transformation, and in the meantime be used to meet some partial development objectives and to help victims of unsustainable development so far? Or would aid always catalyse regression, because it would by its very nature strengthen the already stronger forces which led to unsustainable development?

James Petras and Henry Veltmeyer argue the latter: 'if aid is a catalyst of anything it is not of development but of regression' (p. 64), of reverse flows, designed to benefit the donors themselves. They give many examples of foreign aid, in particular to Latin American countries, which has contributed to what could be termed bad governance: it strengthens authoritarian tendencies in the executive branches of government, helps oil the wheels of corruption, leads to external subordination and to widening social inequalities. In so doing, aid undermines popular support for representative government and thus democracy.

I agree that much aid, too much aid, is having a negative impact. Petras and Veltmeyer seem to imply that this true for all aid, but such a conclusion would be far-fetched. There are good intentions and bad intentions. There is a learning process. Aid has changed. Some donors have realized that the development paradigm that they had advocated was false, that the Washington Consensus, with its over-emphasis on market mechanisms, economic liberalization, adjustment and opening up to global forces, has turned out to be inadequate. An excessive reliance on this leads to ever more social polarzation and poverty. Petras and Veltmeyer recognize that this awareness amongst donor agencies has resulted in changes in aid practice: microprojects, poverty programmes, loans to civil society, self-help community development. However, in their view, this is bound to fail, because such aid tries to address problems that are central to the free market model with marginal means only, leaving the elite class configuration of the state, the monopoly economic organization of the productive system, and the polarized class structure untouched (p. 73).

This is a premature conclusion. Much aid is being given to help developing countries' efforts to transform their societies, to achieve greater equality, better government, more political freedoms, meaningful democracy, improved gender relations, economic empowerment of poor people, and so on. Such transformations occur slowly and should be home-bred. Aid can play a catalytic role in fostering such transformations, maybe not wholesale, but partial, step by step, beginning with social sectors such as health, education, rural development and water, and gradually spreading to hard-core segments of the economy. This goes beyond an approach criticized by Petras and Veltmeyer as 'work within the free market system and provide it a social dimension and a human face' (p. 73). That would be marginal indeed, no more than window dressing. Precisely because such significant transformations take a long time to affect the power base of the elite, however, it is a perfectly acceptable strategy for donors to help advance objectives that are beneficial to poor and marginal people in the meantime. Only in situations where this seems inherently impossible, because the fruits of such efforts would always be reaped by elites, would such a gradualist approach not be appropriate. Then, all aid might be withheld until the necessary transformations have been accomplished. There are situations in which this is the only option, for instance in the case of a fully totalitarian regime which cannot be circumvented. However, I do not think that this is the general case. Neither, it seems, do Petras and Veltmeyer, who end their article by stressing: 'the issue is not aid or no aid, but aid under what conditions and in what socio-historical and political context?' (p. 74). The conditions and the context will have to be carefully studied and society specific. Such an analysis may teach us when and where aid impedes transformation rather than helping it. That again would be bad aid. But Petras and Veltmeyer do not seem to disagree with me that, in principle, good aid is possible, or they would have concluded their article differently.

AID: A CATALYST, NOT A REWARD

If aid is neither a prime mover of development nor an inherent impediment to it, then positive effects from aid — if there are any — result from its functioning as a catalyst. Evaluation studies show that there are indeed positive effects from aid. In my original article, therefore, I highlighted its function as a catalyst. Since a catalyst functions during a process, not at its end, I made a plea that development aid be used as a tool to create conditions for policy improvements that are considered desirable in order to meet development goals. The alternative of using aid as a reward to countries that have already reached such goals does not make sense. The same applies for so-called 'good governance' as a condition. Better governance should be seen not so much as a precondition for development aid, but rather as a development objective in itself. Targeted aid can help foster better governance. To reward good governance with public aid would be a less effective way of spending foreign assistance: the reward already consists of better access to the market.

My argument was based on a critical survey of a number of economic evaluation studies that had been published since the early 1950s, including recent World Bank studies in which a correlation had been found between development variables and good policy indicators. The latter studies had led the authors to the conclusion that aid should be given especially to a selected group of countries that would meet good policy criteria. On the contrary, I argued, aid should be given to countries that were making an effort to enhance their capacity to develop and improve their policy to that end. The aid should not be given unconditionally, but under the condition that the policy intentions between donor and recipient converge. No more, no less: there should be confidence that good governance and sustainable development to the benefit of the people within a developing country — and thus not to the benefit of elitist policy-makers themselves — is the common intention of donor and recipient. Where that basis for confidence is lacking, aid had better be withheld. Where trust exists a catalyst can function.

Of all the participants in the debate which followed my paper, John Degnbol-Martinussen[1] (Chapter 5) is the most explicit in supporting the thesis that aid should not be used as a reward to countries based on what they have already done and achieved, but should be given to assist countries to improve policies and performance. To this he adds two points. First, giving preference to growth-promoting policies and performance implies, at least to a great extent, disregarding other development goals, such as poverty alleviation, human development and democratization. I agree. Such a preference is an example of a uniform approach, not warranted by the complex reality of development that I touched upon above, in relation to Emmerij's contribution. However, in my view the case against aid as a reward for performance is not only valid when performance is measured mainly in macro-economic terms, but also when poverty alleviation, human development and democratization are at stake. Development aid can help to realize these aims; waiting until they have been brought about by other means can put them beyond reach. For that reason I very much agree with the second point made by Degnbol-Martinussen: giving preference to the so-called good performers cannot be justified on a needs assessment. People who are in greatest need of aid often live in failed states, in situations of

---

1. The Editors regret the sad passing away of John Degnbol-Martinussen in 2002.

violence and conflict, in countries characterized by 'half-war, half-peace', in nations with shattered economic and political institutions. In the present context of globalization and increasing world insecurity, such situations are no longer an exception: increasingly they are becoming the rule. This in itself provides another good reason to review both development theory and thinking, and development policy and the aid that assists that policy.

Current practice, however, is quite the opposite. Many donor agencies, both bilateral and multilateral, follow the reward strategy and select recipients on the basis of good behaviour and good performance. In my article, I argued that, for a number of reasons, it is not up to donors alone to decide what is good or bad. Surely it is better to help achieve existing intentions; to use aid to create enabling conditions; to help remove particular obstacles in the development process; to target aid towards specific development goals which can be reached even if the overall policy climate is not yet considered to be ideal; and, last but not least, to avoid counterproductive and negative side effects of aid. In so doing, a differentiating approach is necessary. I agree with Degnbol-Martinussen: what is good policy in one country may not be appropriate in another where conditions, problems and potentials are different.

A number of evaluation studies show that good aid — well focused and attuned to different circumstances — does indeed help, and that concrete development objectives — reduction of child death, enhancement of school enrolment, improvement of policy capacity, recovery after a war, adjustment to an external shock, a higher growth rate, a reduction of absolute poverty, more sustainable food production, improvement in the ecology of a region — can be attributed to factors that were put in place with the help of aid. As I argued in my original article, this is not proof of a direct causal relation between aid and development, but it suggests that giving aid does make sense, because of the catalytic potential of aid.

THE DICHOTOMY OF FOREIGN AID

Can foreign aid catalyse sustainable development if there is an unequal distribution of power not only within recipient countries, but also between donors and recipients? After all, aid — meant to result in a reduction in poverty and thus in inequality — is itself a function of that inequality. It has often been used to manipulate and to sustain the (unequal) status quo. That is the reality of international relations. So, the question is not only how to transform systems in developing countries but also how to transform the international system itself.

That is the dichotomy of aid: how can something which is itself a function of inequality serve to diminish that same inequality? It is clear that Singh and Petras and Veltmeyer have strong doubts as to whether it can. The same is true of Boyce, who explicitly states in his contribution:

Aid is not like rain that falls on whoever happens to be present in a given time and place.
Instead it is more like a set of weights placed on the scale of power at the local, regional and
national levels. Whether by design or by default, aid tilts power balances, strengthening some
individuals, groups and classes relative to others. The distributional outcome of aid often
reinforces existing inequalities of wealth and power. ... The default setting is for aid to flow
to those who wield power. (p. 22).

There is no easy way out, because aid not only strengthens existing
inequalities but, as Gus Edgren argues in his contribution, it also reinforces
itself as an instrument of inequality and dependence. Edgren refers to the
'syndrome of aid dependency that has emerged as a development problem of
its own' (p. 45). He claims that it 'is easy to agree ... that aid is not a
primary agent of development but more like a catalyst' (p. 43), but argues
that unlike in chemistry, where a catalyst is a substance which changes the
velocity of a reaction without being changed itself, the aid relationship does
change while it is functioning. Edgren shows how aid, seen as a catalyst
which results in increased domestic resources mobilization and thus ultimately
reduces the need for foreign resources and the consequent dependency, is
also changing the behaviour of donors and recipients. The incentives in the
relationship are perverse. Giving aid creates a vested interest for donors in
producing results and thus an interest in continuing the aid dependency
relationship. Receiving aid can easily lead to a pattern of behaviour with less
and less room for domestic initiatives, mobilization of own resources and
policy ownership. The result seems to be the reaffirmation of existing inequalities, as well as new and prevailing dependencies. It suggests a negative
answer to the central question posed above: can aid catalyse sustainable
development, despite prevailing inequalities? The answer seems to be no,
because by its very nature aid will catalyse further inequality.

However, if that were the logical conclusion, on the basis of a realistic
analysis of the state of play, it would be quite surprising to find that all the
critical participants to this debate end their contributions with a plea for
more foreign aid. The answer must lie in the conditions under which that
aid should be given. There are two main categories of conditions: those
concerned with the internal situation within recipient developing countries;
and those concerned with the international setting. These two sets of
conditions have a common denominator. For analytical purposes they can
be discussed separately, but it is clear that, to continue the terminology used
above, a 'good' internal situation in a recipient country, set within a 'bad'
international setting — or vice versa — is not conducive to the good functioning of aid as a catalyst for sustainable development. We need a reform
of international relations leading to policy ownership of aid-receiving developing countries themselves, together with reforms within these countries
guaranteeing the access of the poor to the benefits of such reforms. I agree
with Rehman Sobhan that this cannot be accomplished by simply adding on
poverty-related projects to the old adjustment model and building safety
nets for the victims of economic reform. This view is similar to that of Petras

and Veltmeyer, but while the latter do not elaborate a different design — they go no further than claiming the need for 'comprehensive transformations' — Sobhan does sketch the outline of such an alternative:

> Prioritization of poverty in the aid agenda ... demands that the original design of the reform process has to incorporate institutional mechanisms for correcting structural injustice in order to ensure the inclusion of the poor in the development process. Such a process of inclusion needs to address the design of policies and institutions needed to give the poor more competitive access to the market, moving them up-market in the value addition chain, restructuring resources and institutions to invest the poor with substantive ownership of wealth-creating assets, provide more equitable access to human development opportunities and providing much greater scope for the poor to share political power. (p. 177)

As Sobhan emphasizes, reforms without ownership have proved to be unsustainable. What he is suggesting implies a 'triple' domestic ownership: first, domestic ownership over policy reforms; second, domestic ownership over the governance of such reforms; and, third, bottom-up ownership and thus empowerment of the poor. This seems to be a logical conclusion from a compelling analysis. Such a conclusion, strictly applied, would give no room to domestic reforms originating outside the country concerned. As Sobhan argues:

> Donors have, for too long, attempted to lead reform and to define its goals. ... Donors should not make the mistake of promoting ownership which would itself be a contradiction in terms. ... Attempts to step up allocations for the poor through targeted aid programmes of micro-credit or allocations for primary education and health care centres are likely to disturb the realities of power in most [developing countries]. (p. 178)

This would seem to imply that neither targeting of aid to the poor, nor making aid available on the condition that recipients themselves guarantee that the poor will benefit, is an acceptable strategy. It is the conclusion of a purist, following a logical analysis, on the basis of a strict definition of the concept of development as characterized by full autonomy for all participants — those with power as well as those deprived of power. In theory there seems to be no escape from such a conclusion. In practice it would mean that lasting poverty reduction could only be accomplished after a reform brought about entirely through an internal process. This would be ideal; but the more unequal the distribution of power within a country, the more unlikely it is to happen. The distribution of power is not only the most important object of reform, but is at the same time also the overriding constraint to such a reform. There is a relationship between the degree of inequality while a process is taking shape and the time needed to overcome this inequality within the framework of that same process.

Purists may say, 'wait and see; reforms are bound to take place'. That would be ideal, but politically not realistic. I am not trying to reverse Petras and Veltmeyer's analysis for reasons of sophistication. Policy-making goes beyond the application of a seemingly logical analysis in practice. Policy objectives are value-loaded and that means that the time variable is not neutral. Waiting for reforms would be unsatisfactory, if the main objective is to reduce poverty. Waiting for the triple domestic ownership mentioned above might take too long. Poor people will be the victims, and, in the course of waiting, the poverty problem will increase and may become insurmountable.

The reasons for this can be both political and economic. Politically, the accumulation of power may become a major impediment for the change of structural conditions which would be to the benefit of poor people. At a certain moment, when poor people have been deprived of all credible means to press for change, the time for achieving a fully autonomous and more sustainable development path using only internal factors has passed. In a sense, of course, it has never passed definitively, because reforms can be enforced through a revolution. Such a scenario falls outside the scope of this paper. A revolutionary change supported by foreign aid would not be autonomous, and it would be highly uncertain as to whether and how such a change would enhance the chances for sustainable development. The violence and counter-violence which go with it can easily get beyond control.

The economic reasons why continuing and sharpening inequalities may lead to insurmountable degrees of poverty are articulated in the contribution by Santosh Mehrotra. Quoting estimates made by Addison and Cornia (2001), Mehrotra concludes that, given increasing within-country inequality in income distribution, economic growth would need to be much faster in order to compensate for worsening income distribution, if the aim is to reduce not only absolute poverty (the number of people living below a subsistence level of income) but also relative poverty (the proportion of the population below that level). To halve that proportion by 2015 is the official objective agreed to by heads of state and heads of governments at the United Nations World Millennium Summit in 2000. This overall objective has been broken down into a number of specific targets with regard to basic human needs, the so-called Millennium (or International) Development Targets (MDTs or IDTs). The fact that all governments in the world embraced and reconfirmed these targets reinforces Mehrotra's plea for an allocation of development assistance to the provision of basic social services: basic health including reproductive health, basic education and (drinking) water and sanitation. Mehrotra stresses the need to invest in providing access for the poor to these basic services and in improving the quality of the basic service delivery. Like the other authors he pleads in favour of more aid. But he also claims that in order to reduce poverty a sharp modification in the composition of aid is necessary.

This is nothing other than targeting aid. But it goes further than the approach consisting of 'adding on poverty related projects ... and safety nets ... to the old model', which is rightly criticized by Sobhan (p. 176). It is also much more than what Petras and Veltmeyer (p. 73) reject as simply correcting market excesses and providing the free market system with a social dimension and a human face. Mehrotra shows that an effective reallocation of aid requires consistency between aid policies and other policies in the field of international finance, debt relief and trade. In other words: targeting of aid should go hand in hand with some form of transformation of international relations in order to reverse the rising trend in the poverty of nations, which is an essential prerequisite for them to embark upon a path towards more sustainable development. This is what I mentioned in my original essay as 'good donor governance', an element of good international governance which may have to precede good domestic governance (p. 10). It is far from what Petras and Veltmeyer denounce as an approach, 'dubbed "neo-structuralism" ... accepting the basic postulates of the free market economy', choosing 'not to confront ... deep structural conditions' (p. 73). On the contrary, a plea for targeting aid, as advocated by Mehrotra and also by myself in my original article, does confront structural conditions, by linking it to a plea for the reform of international structures and by not taking a wait-and-see attitude towards domestic reforms, but using targeted aid to catalyse these reforms.

AID CONDITIONALITY

Targeting of aid by itself does not do much to promote reform in recipient countries. Targeting of aid is a weak form of aid conditionality: it implies committing aid only if this aid will be spent on specific anti-poverty programmes. Stronger forms of aid conditionality would imply that a donor also requires specific policies to be carried out by the government of the recipient country, in order to make the committed aid available.

There are different policy conditionalities. In my 'Aid as a Catalyst' piece I criticized the so-called Washington Consensus conditionalities, which are aimed at governance in aid-receiving developing countries and oriented in particular to macro-economic stability and economic growth. I explained why, in my view, such a 'good governance conditionality' is missing the point in terms of sustainable development and poverty reduction. I rejected the alternative of making aid available only to those countries which have accomplished so-called good governance — in the eyes of donors, that is, and thus not necessarily in the eyes of their own citizens — on their own, because this would give a reward which would no longer be necessary. Instead, I argued in favour of a different kind of conditionality, oriented towards capacity building, reforms and governance leading towards more sustainable development and poverty reduction.

Singh rejects any conditionality beyond normal technical and administrative conditionality. In his opinion my analysis looks at the question very much from the standpoint of the aid-giver. I regret this, because this is precisely what I wanted to avoid. On the contrary, as I made clear above, I explicitly attacked two presently dominant donor approaches: good governance conditionality and country selectivity. As against this I take a global position — fulfilment of global commitments with regard to the quantity of assistance, as well as sustainable world development, including the reduction of world poverty — and try to look at this from the standpoint of the ultimate agents in a process of sustainable development: not the governments of developing countries, but poor people within these countries. Singh seems to agree with the official position taken by Third World countries, that all conditionality beyond ensuring repayment is 'unacceptable interference ... intrusive ... and ... illegitimate' (p. 85).

Boyce takes a different position. He agrees with me that Washington Consensus conditionality — which he refers to as 'the back-to-basics movement' and as 'the old-time religion' (p. 24) — does not offer a promising recipe for making aid a more effective instrument for the improvement of human well-being. In his view the problem with the back-to-basics approach is not only that it provides a simple, axiomatic answer to the relative importance of different policy objectives, but also that it assumes that the Washington Consensus objectives can be divorced from other issues, such as environmental quality and violent conflict, when in fact they impact mutually upon each other. Boyce postulates that these linkages should not be ignored in aid policy. He emphasizes the need to focus, for instance, on the composition of public spending and on the distributional incidence of taxation and expenditure.

These are examples of policies with consequences for sustainable development. This is what I have in mind when pleading for aid conditionality concerning the governance of sustainable development policies, ensuring the inclusion of the poor, and reforms to that end. Sobhan is very doubtful about such aid conditionality. In his view

> conditionality is unlikely to bring lasting reform if there is no strong domestic movement for change. ... Pronk's suggestion that aid will be needed to catalyse this indigenous reform process remains ... problematic. The rub of the problem lies in deciding what policies would merit donor assistance in the expectation that they catalyse change. At the same time donors will have to come to terms with the prospect that their notions of appropriate policies may not always coincide with those of their aid recipients. (pp. 177–8)

I am aware of these problems with regard to the application of conditionality. There are also other problems, for instance those mentioned by Edgren, who argues that foreign aid is a much too unwieldy instrument for providing sharp and timely incentives to policy reform. The underlying reasons are the mutual vested interest of donors and recipients in the continuation of aid, referred to above, and the fact that in practice donors themselves are not so committed to sustainable development, but have other objectives as well. Boyce also mentions a series of competing interests on the side of the donors.

All the objections put forward by Sobhan, Boyce and Edgren are valid. I myself gave examples of 'bad aid' in my original paper. The present political reality of donor performance does indeed show that there is a wide variety of orientations, interests, preferences and conditions expressed on the part of the donors. The situation has become even more complicated recently, with donors also linking aid to the governance of national and international security. I have argued elsewhere that this is at odds with considerations of sustainability (Pronk, 2003). Not only is aid conditionality *per se* put into an unfavourable light by such a policy; even more worrying is that sustainability itself can be violated by considerations of international security, setting aside values of democracy and human rights. However, all these objections against aid conditionality involve the way in which it is applied, not the concept itself. Unlike the objection made by Singh — that 'conditionality is illegitimate' — those presented by Sobhan, Boyce and Edgren can be overcome through aid policy improvements.

COUNTRY SELECTIVITY

Some of my critics refer to country selectivity as an example of aid policy improvement. I rejected this alternative in my paper, but the question may arise whether, if aid conditionality is meeting so many problems in practice, country selectivity would not qualify as an acceptable second best.

This is the position taken by Geske Dijkstra who, on the basis of a number of international studies, concludes that compliance with the policy conditions set by the Bretton Woods institutions is rather limited. Dijkstra explicitly turns around the adjectives in my original central conclusion by stating: 'Well-focused aid selectivity is better than rigid conditionality' (p. 90). This conclusion is drawn on the basis of three paradoxes. First, why do reforms have to be bought with aid if reforms are good for the country anyway? Second, why take the risk of reducing the incentive of a developing country to carry out reforms by giving aid to that country and thus modifying the urgency for reform? Third, how to overcome the contradiction between the setting of many conditions and the content of one of them, the demands for democratization, accountability and sovereignty?

In my view these questions are only paradoxical if one limits the analysis to macro (that is, Washington Consensus) conditionalities, and if one does not make a distinction between the policy-makers in an aid-receiving country and the people impacted by the policies themselves. This is the case in the simple principal–agent model of donor–recipient relationships, as applied amongst others by Killick (1997). Dijkstra expands this framework by adding some power variables and some explicit assumptions concerning the contents of the policy conditionality. She then uses this in an empirical analysis of the effectiveness of policy conditionality in eight different countries. From this review Dijkstra draws some interesting conclusions about the effectiveness of aid conditionality measured in terms of the degree of implementation of the policy concerned. The most striking of these conclusions is that conditionality is more effective when the policy demands are more specific — 'and thus of less significance' (p. 113). Dijkstra explains this finding by arguing that aid recipients will tend to give in on these, but renege on others. The fact that demands with respect to the political system were not honoured at all, and those concerning corruption only where this was already seen as a domestic issue, adds weight to Dijkstra's overall conclusion that policy conditionality has only a limited effectiveness, although she notes that policies aiming at a reduction of poverty (Dijkstra refers to them as 'pro-poor growth') were not included in the analysis.

Dijkstra adds to this conclusion of limited effectiveness a second argument against aid conditionality: it can be questioned from an ethical point of view, because we cannot be sure that the policy demands or recommendations are correct, or the only way to success. In any case this practice 'denies the country the right to design its own policies and find its own ways' (p. 114). In the case of the eight countries studied, Dijkstra argues that some of the conditions set by donors could be criticized as inadequate, or inconsistent, or as not the only — or even the most appropriate — option for the particular country. This seems to bring the issue of legitimacy together with that of effectiveness into one overall argument against conditionality. Thus Dijkstra, following some of the authors that I criticized in my original article, concludes that it would be preferable to reward good performance *ex post* rather than buying reform *ex ante*.

I am not convinced by this, for two reasons. First, while I am tempted to leave the terminology aside and concentrate on Dijkstra's line of argument, it should be noted that 'buying reform' again suggests a principal–agent relationship. In such a relation a donor 'buys' something in his own interest. In an expanded framework, however, there are other parties as well, for instance people affected by policies, in whose interest donors might take not the position of a buyer, but that of a broker. In that case there is much less against conditionality than Dijkstra claims. As I have postulated above, discussing the issue of autonomy posed by Sobhan, sustainable reforms to bring about human development require not a double but a triple domestic ownership.

Second, I agree with Dijkstra that the application of conditions can be criticized in practice on grounds of inconsistency and inappropriateness for the country concerned. However, that could be just as forceful an argument against criteria for the selection of countries that would be eligible to receive aid. Wil Hout also shows that for a donor which officially claims to apply good governance criteria it is difficult to be consistent: the choice made by policy-makers simply may not correspond with the criteria that they themselves wish to apply. Other allocation criteria — need, donor interests, conventional Washington Consensus wisdom — also play a role in practical policy-making, and they may sometimes run counter to governance criteria. They may in particular become dominant when non-fulfilment of governance criteria would call for an end to the aid relationship; this is also argued by Dijkstra and, as we saw above, by Edgren. Taking the case of the

Netherlands as a donor, Hout argues that aid money is spent on countries which, according to the intended governance criteria, do not deserve it, while deserving counties are excluded.

So, leaving legitimacy aside, there is no reason why, on the basis of effectiveness, country selectivity would do any better as a policy than aid conditionality. In principle the governance criteria would have to be the same. The only, but overriding difference between the two consists in their application *ex ante* or *ex post*. As I argued in my original article: not only can the application *ex ante* be seen as a paradox (like those postulated by Dijkstra), but the application of these criteria *ex post* can also be considered paradoxical. Why reward a country with aid when it is no longer necessary, because the effect of policy reform — access to financial and trade markets — has been achieved already? Why should donors waste scarce resources by spending aid less effectively, at the same time setting a bad example to aid-receiving countries that are asked to carry out economic policies which can stand an efficiency test? Mehrotra reports that the same model which convinced donors that reallocation of aid to countries with efficient policies would give better results than increasing their aid budgets, also produced the argument that reallocation according to poverty criteria would produce even bigger benefits than reallocating on the basis of policy indicators. While the first conclusion has quickly been put into practice, the second has easily been neglected.

I do not want to overstate my case. After all, aid policy-making in practice shows many nuances. Good governance criteria are used not only to choose partner countries *ex ante* or *ex post*, but also to determine volumes of aid, sectoral or thematic allocations as well as partners within an aid-receiving country (for example, not just the government as a whole, but specific departments and, in addition to this, civil society groups or private business). These three types of decisions might reveal an aid allocation pattern that shows a more reasonable association with both need and poverty variables as well as governance variables than the pattern of recipient countries alone.

One could argue that such an association would throw light on the consistency of a conditionality rather than a selectivity approach. In practice, the degree to which criteria such as governance are met is used by donors as a motive to change the volume and/or the direction of aid. The relation between donors and recipients changes during the aid process, as was argued by Edgren. The parties continuously respond to each other in an ongoing relationship. This makes the distinction between selectivity (*ex post*) and conditionality (*ex ante*) a little theoretical. I wrote that selectivity means that a country has to perform first and will then qualify for aid as a reward, while conditionality means helping countries to perform and to meet certain criteria. In an ongoing aid relationship such a sharp distinction cannot be made. However, my intention was not to analyse aid policies in practice, but to argue against recent rigid recommendations made by World Bank related authors, which seem to lead to less rather than more aid, while opportunities are clearly missed to use aid as a catalyst to raise other resources and to start reforms to address the most important problem of our time — the ongoing exclusion of more than a billion people from the ever increasing wealth of nations, which is not ethical and which carries great risks for the sustainability of global relations.

Aid can help to counter this exclusion: but not all aid and not under all circumstances. In my original article I presented a critical review of the international debate on the usefulness of aid. I tried to outline conditions under which aid can play its catalytic role. I appreciate the comments from the other participants in this aid debate. Many of them have nuanced or strengthened these conditions and added some others. Having done this three steps are necessary: first, to draw lessons from experience, such as those presented by Emmerij; second, to increase international assistance flows and to tap new sources of aid, as proposed, amongst others, by Mehrotra, Singh and Boyce; third, to improve international governance, in order not to undermine the possible effects of aid through an international policy that is stifling developing countries and jeopardizing world sustainability.

REFERENCES

Addison, T. and G. A. Cornia (2001) 'Income Distribution Policiesfor Faster Poverty Reduction'. Discussion Paper No 2001/93. Helsinki: UNU/WIDER.
Killick, Tony (1997) 'Principals and Agents and the Failings of Conditionality', *Journal of International Development* 9(4): 483–96.
Ohlin, Goran (1966) 'Foreign Aid Policies Reconsidered'. Paris: OECD Development Centre.
Pronk, Jan P. (2000) 'Globalization: A Developmental Approach', in Jan Nederveen Pieterse (ed.) *Global Futures: Shaping Globalization*, pp. 40–52. London, New York: Zed Books.
Pronk, Jan P. (2001) 'Aid as a Catalyst', *Development and Change* 32(4): 611–29.
Pronk, Jan P. (2003) 'Security and Sustainability', in Paul van Seters, Bas de Gaay Fortman and Arie de Ruyter (eds) *Globalisation and its New Divides: Malcontents, Recipes and Reform*, pp. 25–34. Amsterdam: Dutch University Press.

Index

Abrahamsen, R. 135
Addison, T. 168
advanced industrial countries (AICs) 173–4
Africa 79, 81, 119
aid, according to needs 60, 85; analysis
  of 5; availability of 102–3; background/
  development 1–3; better policies for
  15–18; as catalyst 7–10, 58, 77, 83–5, 119,
  171, 191, 197–9; categories of 3–4;
  challenges to 2; charitable objective 3,
  22; conditions of 74, 203–5; data on 5;
  decline in 118–19; dependency 45–8,
  119; description of 21; dichotomy of
  199–203; economic objective 3, 22;
  as empowerment of civil society
  organization 55; as enhancing state
  capacity 55; foreign aid concept 63,
  64–5; and good governance 10–12, 191;
  historical-structural context 65–6; impact
  of 5–7, 51–2; as impediment 7–10,
  195–7; as income transfer 181–2; micro-
  macro paradox 11–12; mistakes in 43;
  one-sided nature of 127; as pillage/
  exploitation 65, 68; political objective 3,
  23; position paper on 4; as prime
  mover 3, 192–5; private finance 119;
  and productive capacities 85; quality
  of 10; and recipient country policies 12;
  as reward 13, 191, 197–9; selectivity/
  allocation of 13, 205–8; as strengthening
  state-society/institutions-procedures 55;
  substitution effect 9; as success 79; total
  amount/allocation 85–6; as useless/
  harmful 43; value of 4–5; well-
  focused 16, see also aid effectiveness;
  Official Development Assistance (ODA)
aid effectiveness 4, 13, 14–15, 77, 119, 181;
  challenges for 178–9; disillusionment
  with 173–4; endogenizing policy
  reforms 177–8; evolving perspectives
  on 172–8; measurement of 4–5; and
  New Aid Strategy 176–7; new
  challenges 178–9; philosophy of 172–3;
  policy reforms 174–5; putting governance
  first 175–6, see also aid; Official
  Development Assistance (ODA)
Amsden, A.H. 135
Asian financial crisis 82–3

Assessing Aid (1998) 175
Asylum and Immigration Act (UK, 1999)
  138
augmented principal-agent 94; and
  probability of implementation 94,
  98–103; and threat of aid suspension
  94–5, 103–9

Bangladesh 22, 95–111
basic social services, additional external
  resources for 166–9; and debt relief 168;
  education 163–4, 168; health 164;
  improved market access 167; ODA
  for 162–6; population/reproductive
  health 164–5; and taxation 166–7;
  water/sanitation 165
Bauer, P.T. 2
Beynon, J. 161
Boone, P. 12, 14, 45
Boyce, J.K. 26
Brand, W. 1
Bretton Woods institutions (BWI) 174, 175,
  177
Burnside, C. 12, 13, 14, 161

capacity building 58–60
Cape Verde 95, 96, 109
capital markets 9, 26
Carter, N.G. 7, 8
Cassen, R. 119
Centres of Excellence 38, 39
Chenery, H.B. 6–8
China 80, 135
Clifford, J.M. 6
Cold War 23, 44, 79, 117, 118
Collier, P. 13
colonialism 65–6, 79
Commonwealth 124, 135
conditionality 16, 23–5, 55–6, 59, 71, 81–2,
  144, 177, 181, 203–5; analytical
  consideration 82–3; as buying of
  reform 112; and compliance 92, 95–7;
  definition 90; developing countries
  perspective 85; domestic factors 111–12;
  and donor/recipient credibility 112–13;
  effectiveness of 89–90, 92–5, 109–11,
  113–14; experiences of 95–111; increase
  in 81–2; international perspective 83–6;

Printed and bound by CPI Group (UK) Ltd, Croydon, CR0 4YY

09/06/2025

14686107-0001